Naked
in the
Marketplace

ALSO BY BENITA EISLER

Chopin's Funeral

Byron: Child of Passion, Fool of Fame

O'Keeffe and Stieglitz: An American Romance

Naked in the Marketplace

THE LIVES *of* GEORGE SAND

BENITA EISLER

COUNTERPOINT
A Member of the Perseus Books Group
New York

Published by Counterpoint Press
A Member of the Perseus Books Group

Counterpoint books are available at special discounts for bulk purchases in the United States by corporations, institutions, and other organizations. For more information, please contact the Special Markets Department at the Perseus Books Group, 11 Cambridge Center, Cambridge MA 02142, or call (617) 252–5298 or (800) 255–1514, or e-mail special.markets@perseusbooks.com.

DESIGN BY JANE RAESE
Text set in 13-point Bulmer

Cataloging-in-Publication Data is available from the Library of Congress.
ISBN-10: 1-58243-349-6
ISBN-13: 978-1-58243-349-3

06 07 08 09 / 10 9 8 7 6 5 4 3 2 1

Irreplaceable Friend

CELIA ROSE EISENBERG

1925–2004

Heroic Editor

ELIZABETH MAGUIRE

1958–2006

Contents

"... for the genius on both sides happened to be
the genius of eloquence. It is all rapture
and all rage and all literature.
... The lovers are naked in the market-place
and perform for the benefit of society."

HENRY JAMES

on George Sand and Alfred de Musset
Notes on Novelists with Some Other Notes, 1897

Naked
in the
Marketplace

1

A Voyage

IT WAS JUST BEFORE NOON on a May morning in 1845 when George Sand finished her packing. Then, gathering her family together, she prepared to set sail on a long sea voyage to foreign parts.

In reality, the voyage was only a day trip and the family consisted of her son, Maurice, twenty-three, an art student. The schooner waiting to transport them to distant isles turned out to be a humble *sapin*—"pine box" in local slang, the hired horse-drawn cab that carried Parisians from one part of the expanding city to the other.

Her journey across Paris today, with its "tease" of an opening—the conceit of a sea voyage to distant climes—is a classic journalists' ploy, intended to hook the reader by throwing her off guard. (Is this a parody of travel writing or the real thing?) The article in question was commissioned by the publisher of a deluxe album to be called *Le Diable à Paris* (The Devil Visits Paris). Contributions by famous writers and artists, Sand and Balzac among them, depicted Parisian life in its picturesque reality: courtesans and roués, beggars and con artists, the weird and exotic—like the "wild Indians" in their midst.

Sand was traveling light, but the contents of her single bag—glass beads and other cheap jewelry wrapped in a length of red cloth—hinted at her destination. From her apartment on the rue Saint-Lazare the cab threaded through busy Right Bank traffic, stopping at the Salle Valentino on the rue du Faubourg Saint-Honoré. Over the years, the cavernous colonnaded galleries have housed tenants of every type, animal and human: an exclusive men's riding club, a visiting circus, an all-night dance hall.

For the last months, the Valentino has served as theatre, art gallery, and hostel for a troupe of Native Americans, of the Ioway tribe of Plains Indians, brought from London to Paris by the American painter George Catlin. From the walls, chiefs and young warriors, along with their wives and children stared down, unsmiling, a fraction of the hundreds more Catlin portraits of Plains Indians in tribal settlements the length of the Missouri and Mississippi rivers. The remaining wall space was hung with ceremonial artifacts: feathered headdresses, beadwork, rattles, and tomahawks.

In her article "An Account of a Journey to the Savages of Paris," Sand invites readers to shudder in horror with her as she points out bits of human scalp, strands of hair still attached and clinging to the hatchets' gleaming blades.

Before daring to enter, visitors peered warily through the flap of a teepee made of painted animal skins that rose at one end of the long central space. Portraits, artifacts, teepee—these exhibits were a prelude to the main event, the attraction that for weeks now had lured Parisians to pay an unheard-of six francs a ticket: Twice a day, fourteen Ioway warriors reenacted ceremonial dances, miming buffalo hunts and battle scenes (including scalpings). Then, the galleries echoed with the sounds of drumming, chants, and war cries.

George Sand had seen the performance several times; on each occasion, she had brought friends, among them Chopin and Delacroix. Each visit left her more ecstatic. But this was her first appointment backstage. Armed with a long list of questions, she came as both guest and reporter. Earlier, Monsieur Catlin had advised her what to bring, and she now presented the gifts sure to please her hosts: the red cloth they prized above all other white man's manufacture, the glittering beads, and the bright trinkets.

White Cloud, the star performer, was also prepared. He had been told that Madame Sand was no ordinary journalist, but a famous writer and the most celebrated woman in Europe.

Like her fellow Parisians flocking to see the "live savages" (the spectators included King Louis-Philippe, who invited the troupe to perform at his castle in Saint-Cloud), George Sand was fascinated by America, especially its native people. As a girl, she had wept over the poignant love story of the doomed Indian maiden in *Atala,* by René de Chateaubriand, and had devoured the "Leatherstocking" novels of James Fenimore Cooper, probably in the original language. Alone among her literary contemporaries, she read and spoke English—the legacy of two years in a convent school run by an Anglo-Irish order of Augustinian nuns.

A keen student of history and politics, Sand had done her homework. Before her first sight of the Ioways, she had read widely on the vexed question of Indian relations with the white man's government in Washington, their lands taken by his broken treaties, their ancient tribal wars made deadlier by his gunpowder, their settlements decimated by his diseases: typhoid and smallpox.

It had been fifteen years since George Sand's first published piece—an unsigned newspaper column—appeared in *Le Figaro.* Since then, she had mined her every interest, observation, passion for her writing. Theatre, music, politics, poetry, Paris, her native province of Berry, her friends and lovers (barely disguised by the fig leaf of fiction), all found their way into topical articles, literary criticism, political commentary, memoirs, stories, and novels. The last category of works, numbering almost ninety by the time she stopped writing and published in eagerly awaited installments, had made her a best-selling author and a rich woman. Still, she always needed money. With two establishments, Paris and Nohant, in rural Berry, many "causes," eleven dependents, she always spent more than she earned, and never turned down an assignment.

An incurable romantic about men, George Sand always loved a hero, and White Cloud, the star of the Ioway troupe, was the hero of her piece. His bronze torso, bared for the performance, linked him to warriors from classical antiquity, she noted, but unlike his man-made image, White Cloud was all movement, an embodiment of the power and grace but also the ferocity of his people.

His life story, inseparable from the story of his tribe, was the stuff of novels, and Sand the novelist delighted in every chapter.

Following a narrow escape after his father's overthrow and murder, White Cloud, renouncing vengeance and burying the tomahawk, was elected chief of the tribe. No sooner was the young leader pledged to a new era of peace than he was captured in a raid by the Sauk, the tribe's sworn enemy. While a prisoner, he fell in love with a Sauk maiden, abducting her in the course of a daring getaway. O-Kee-Wee-Mee became his third wife, but her husband was exceptional among his people. His bride, Sand tells us, was the "exclusive object of his love." Meanwhile, as chief of the Ioways, White Cloud's official visits to Washington convinced him that the Native Americans must adopt the ways of the white man or perish. This message caused dissent within the tribe. In view of enhancing his prestige, he decided to study white civilization across "the great salt pond." Accompanied by his family and other tribal worthies, he left for Europe. Either before their departure or soon after their arrival, White Cloud and his wife were converted to Catholicism. Like the recusants of old, however, they had to practice their religion in secret.

At least, this is the version of their story that White Cloud (through an interpreter) related to Sand in the course of several "intimate conversations." She accepted his account as consistent with her own mythologies. A "modern Jason," she christened him. White Cloud was an emissary of all that is beautiful and majestic in his culture: The white man's prejudices about display meant nothing to him. "Robed in his most splendid costume, his face gleaming with precious vermillion paint, he sits, like the prince he is, among his proud acolytes, solemnly smoking his pipe. He gives thanks to the Great Spirit for having led him safely to these white peoples whom he esteems and admires, commending them and his own to heaven." Following this "affectionate and noble discourse," he ordered, first, a war dance, then a gentler one of the peace pipe. He seized a tambourine or a rattle and, "in tones both sweet and guttural, joined his own voice to the chant of his comrades. The fearsome warriors, graceful children, grave and chaste women, leapt and ran in a circle around him; occasionally, he succumbed to their transports, and remembering his home, the glory of his ancestors, and his love for his native land, he rose and joined the dance."

Sand, too, was transported; she recalled nothing less than a mystical experience in which both performers and spectators were joined in a state of sublime understanding and love: When the dancing stopped, the audience—"moved from fear to sympathy"—mingled with the performers. Artists were the first to draw closer, Sand reported, "to admire the beauty of the dancers' bodies and nobility of their faces, while the more generous spectators jostle one another to offer little gifts, both from a wish to pay their respects, and to give pleasure to those poor exiles, offerings accepted with dignity; more rounds of tumultuous applause—the universal language understood by all peoples—follow; then the same hands reach out to greet and touch the visitors from far away."

Even as Sand put forward this stirring account of the Ioway's performance as a kind of love-in, she noted dissenting views among her fellow Parisians. There were stories of the troupe's exploitation for the profit of a mysterious "middle man" and by Catlin himself; their ignorance of what it meant to be "exhibited" for six francs a show—like wild animals or displays in a waxworks museum. Indeed, no one really knew how a tribal chief had been persuaded to perform in what was the first Wild West Show.

For White Cloud and his family, the journey was cursed by tragedy. Before leaving America, he had suffered the deaths of two of his children with O-Kee-Wee-Mee. Then, months after their tour of Britain began, their third and youngest child, a three-year-old boy, had sickened and died in the north of England. The father, Sand tells us, proved no less heroic in tragedy than he had been in battle or captivity. With each loss, which was "felt bitterly as with all Indians," he made a deep incision in the flesh of one thigh to appease the wrath of Manitou, the Great Spirit, and to bear witness to his love for the three dear creatures who left them. On the death of their last little boy, he had held the small body in his arms for forty-eight hours. He had heard that the white man treated his dead without respect, and the thought of his beloved son falling into the hands of a medical student was unbearable. Finally, he allowed the child's lifeless form to be embalmed and placed in a cedar coffin, which he entrusted to a Quaker gentleman bound for America. The sympathetic stranger promised to return the remains to the tribe to rest among the bones of their ancestors.

O-Kee-Wee-Mee, the young mother, would not be consoled. She wept without stopping, refusing food and water. Her kinsmen despaired of her life. When Sand first saw her, she lay on a pallet on the floor, her head pillowed by her long, coiled braids. Her face was still lovely, Sand wrote, "but the tawny complexion has taken on the grey-green pallor of death. Her husband never moved from her side except when he must perform. He stroked her head as a father would his child's showing her the gifts he has received, happy when he can make her smile."

George Sand returned once more to the Salle Valentino. This time she went straight to the empty room where O-Kee-Wee-Mee lay. Kneeling on the floor, Sand placed a white cyclamen in the still hands that tried to close over the stem. The dying woman seemed to rally; she told her visitor of vast meadows near the Missouri River where the cyclamens grow wild. A man can walk for several days and nights through the flowering plants, which grow to the height of his knees. Sand's offering had come from a Paris hothouse. But suddenly, the writer was carried back to the one time when she, too, saw cyclamens growing wild in an Alpine meadow; she was so ravished by the sight, she dreamed about the flowers for nights thereafter. But to O-Kee-Wee-Mee, with the petals lifted to her face, Sand had brought the perfume of home.

In reporting on her visits to the Salle Valentino, George Sand, the woman and the writer, bursts upon us like a bareback circus rider bounding through a hoop of flame, a figure in perpetual motion. How did she stay still long enough for Nadar to fix the famous image on his glass plate?

She was never a mere observer, describing people and events. One of the first reporters to interview her subjects, Sand engaged with her contemporaries in a spirit more attuned to our own times than to her own, each encounter an exchange: Curiosity, energy, imagination—her qualities as a writer are inseparable from the woman. She took it for granted that through human sympathy, strangers recognize each other. She *became* the men and women—fictional or living—who enthralled thousands of readers. In the process, she discovered, and recovered, her own feelings as a child, lover, wife, parent. Talking with the Ioway visitors, as they huddled together in exile and mourning between performances, she revisited her own early memories of separation: from beloved faces and surroundings, grief made worse by the need to hide it. In her adult life, those who touched her heart did more than trigger ghost pains of loss. Moved by need, by affliction, by powerlessness, by talent crushed in poverty, she reached out to inform the world, but also to encourage, to console, or to help, or simply to make a fellow creature feel less alone.

2

War Zones

HER BIRTHRIGHT was the clash of opposites, at least in Sand's later telling of her life. On her father's side, a line of bastard aristocrats led back to Augustus II, king of Poland, and earlier elector of Saxony. His affair with a beautiful, black-eyed Swedish noblewoman, Aurore de Koenigsmark, the first Aurore in the writer's family, produced in 1696 an illustrious son, Maurice de Koenigsmark, who later became the Maréchal de Saxe, Napoleon's most brilliant field marshal and George Sand's great-grandfather. The Maréchal, hero of boudoir and battlefield, fell in love with a bewitching courtesan of lowly origins, Marie Rinteau, who had rechristened herself Mademoiselle de Verrières de Furcy. Their daughter, Marie-Aurore de Saxe, Sand's grandmother, made a brilliant second marriage to Maurice Dupin de Franceuil, a royal tax collector. Thirty-three years older than his wife, Maurice, on his death, left her a large fortune and a young son. With her husband's gold salted away with the family silver, Marie-Aurore managed to escape the Terror, buying the property of Nohant in Berry, the remote center of France.

Antoinette-Sophie-Victoire Delaborde, Sand's mother, was a pure-blooded daughter of the proletariat. She came from that race of Parisians too humble for genealogy and whose names emerge briefly from the anthills of poor neighborhoods to register, erratically, an apprenticeship, a marriage, a birth, a baptism, but most reliably, a death. Her father, Antoine Delaborde, Sand's maternal grandfather, had first tried tavern keeping; then, moving outdoors, he sold canaries, golden finches, and other songbirds on the quays of the Seine. Neither work raised him or his family from poverty. But his stubborn insistence on self-employment and his trade (unlike that of butcher or fishmonger) suggest a love of nature and its creatures and the same mix of poetry and grit notable in his famous granddaughter. The elder of his two daughters was born in 1773 with the ambition lacking in her parents. Alluring and clever, Antoinette-Sophie-Victoire's hard little face, in her one surviving likeness, also announced a determination to rise in the world through the only means available to a poor girl: men.

In George Sand's thousands of pages of autobiographical writings, no subject seethes with the contradictions and inconsistencies, with shifting versions of fact, as do her mother's early years. No relationship caused such bruising pain—on both sides. For all her notorious affairs with men, Sand's passionate and unrequited attachment to her mother is the real love story of her life.

In all her accounts of Sophie Delaborde (early on, Sand's mother dropped the other two names), accusation and defense collide. For her "little Mama," the adult Sand claimed both respectability and heroic outlaw status, along with pity, censure, and admiration for this parent, who was both victim and tormentor.

When her mother was barely a teenager, Sand tells us, she was cast out into the world, to become "the lowest kind of actress" in a theatre that was little more than a brothel; its stage served to display the sexual charms of child performers to potential "protectors." At this same time, Sand claimed, Sophie married and gave birth to a son. Records of the father's name survive, but there is no evidence of any legal union with the mother, and the child—like so many other unwanted infants—simply disappears from the record. Then five years before Sand was born, Sophie gave birth to a daughter, Caroline, of father unknown.

At this point, the pretty young mother's alternatives seem to have narrowed. Putting her infant daughter out to board, she left Paris for Boulogne, a staging area for Napoleon's peninsular army. There she rose from the ranks of anonymous camp followers, becoming mistress to a succession of officers. When Maurice Dupin, the aristocratic young aide-de-camp, met Sophie, she was in Milan, where her charms had led to a recent promotion: From the household of a quartermaster, she was now companion to a much older adjutant general—on whose staff was Corporal Maurice Dupin. Instantly smitten, the besotted Maurice lost no time in carrying off his prize.

Maurice and Sophie returned to Paris in early June 1804, she very pregnant and determined that her baby should be born on

French soil. On June 5, a month before the birth of Aurore-Lucile-Amandine Dupin, the future George Sand, her parents married.

For officers to form liaisons with women who followed the army was commonplace; a few men might even acknowledge and provide for children born of these unions. What is extraordinary is that Sand's father, at twenty-six a handsome young man of rank, distinguished family, and promising future, married a thirty-year-old working-class woman who had drifted upward through prostitution. At the least, this act, in defiance of class and convention, confirms that Sophie was no ordinary creature. Driving a lustrous sexuality was a commanding—even terrifying—force of will.

Sophie Delaborde wasn't the only powerful woman in Maurice Dupin's life. He was so frightened of his mother, Marie-Aurore de Saxe de Franceuil Dupin, that he failed to inform her of his marriage for two years. In the course of several visits, and in the many adoring letters he dispatched to this grand lady in Paris or Nohant, he mentioned his love for the poor but worthy young woman, and even their baby daughter, Aurore, strategically named for her grandmother. But faced with the outpourings of his widowed mother, her jealousy and feelings of betrayal, to confess to this mismatch, shattering her hopes for a glittering alliance, proved more than her son could bear. He was also dependent upon mama to provide the ample allowance required to outfit a general's aide-de-camp: the uniforms, horses, servants, and spending money. His fear was not misplaced. When Marie-Aurore learned of the deed, she sweetly professed acceptance of the union, while seeking the advice of both a prelate and the mayor of Paris's fifth *arrondissement* as to how the marriage could be dissolved.

Despite making off with the mistress of his commanding officer, Maurice, too, was promoted: He returned to the peninsula a major and an aide to Joachim Murat, marshal of the empire and imperial lieutenant for Spain. Maurice shared the commander's headquarters at the Palace of the Prince of Asturias in Madrid. Meanwhile, in Paris, his wife and little daughter were squeezed into a garret where a restless Sophie obsessed about the beautiful Spanish women swarming about her vulnerable husband.

George Sand's first memories summon an unsafe world. She recalled being dropped by a maid, and as she fell, her forehead was gashed by a corner of the mantelpiece. With eerie precision, Sand remembered the liver-colored marble, the flowing blood, and her swollen flesh. The slatternly caretaker was replaced by an adoring "uncle," Monsieur Pierret, a strapping neighbor whose constant presence cheered her mother; she stopped scolding and slapping the child. Instead, Sophie contrived a makeshift playpen, in which Aurore, seated on an unlit brazier and safely fenced in by a couple of rush-bottomed chairs, looked at picture books. Her mother, Sand relates, could barely read or write, but she was a thrilling storyteller and possessed of a sweet, clear voice. She sang popular songs and recited fairy tales and Bible stories. Devout in her primitive, unwavering faith, she taught Aurore her prayers and daily took her to Mass.

Then, seven months pregnant, Sophie packed up her belongings and, with Aurore, headed for Madrid. Space was scarce in the carriage Aurore and her mother shared with another army wife. Forbidden to take her only doll with her, the three-year-old left Paris in a rage of tears. Rattling south, they crossed the Pyrenees, descending into the valley of Asturias, baking under a July sun. The first villages reminded them that Spain was ravaged by war. Emaciated peasants announced that soldiers had requisitioned everything; food was limited to whatever could be shot or trapped. At a primitive inn, the winning black-eyed child was given a white dove as a pet; wandering into the kitchen, she saw its fellow birds' necks being wrung and feathers plucked in readiness for dinner. When she offered her own to the cook, her mother punished her for being a perverse, unfeeling child. Never having owned a pet, Aurore was merely acting as the grown-ups did. Not for the last time, she was mystified by her mother's anger.

Their arrival in Madrid made a dazzling contrast to the journey. Swept up in her father's arms, Aurore was overpowered by the scale of her new surroundings: the massive gilt and brocade furnishings, the profusion of silver and servants, the fantastic toys abandoned by the infanta when the royal family fled. To the delight of Marshal Murat, her father presented Aurore dressed in a miniature aide-de-camp's uniform, complete with gold epaulets and a shako.

A few days later, she was banished for hours, locked out of the family's apartments onto a sun-baked balcony. When she was finally allowed indoors, Aurore was startled to see her mother lying, pale and silent, on a chaise longue, holding her infant brother. (Sophie had not uttered a sound during labor, her daughter noted proudly.) But the baby was frail, and there were whispers about the strange, milky color of his eyes. Then, two weeks after the birth, the army received orders to leave Spain. Carlos IV had abdicated in favor of Napoleon's older brother Joseph. Murat, the emperor's brother-in-law, was rewarded with the throne of Naples, where Maurice would join him, following a few weeks of home leave in France.

If the trip to Spain left Aurore with a confusion of memories, the journey home would remain with her in images evoking Goya's *Disasters of War:* a lawless, raped country, rife with violence and death. While the dashing Maurice pranced at the head of the troops on his new charger, the "ungovernable" Fernando VII, his family rumbled along at the rear in the miserable carriage he was lucky to find for them. The wheels shuddered through a nightmare landscape: gutted houses, smoking ruins, a ragged, starving populace. Sophie tried to pull the inquisitive three-year-old away from the carriage windows and the sight of roadsides strewn with the rotting corpses of soldiers circled by vultures, the ruts and potholes puddled with blood. But she could do nothing about the stench or the crunch of wagon wheels over human bones. Food was so scarce that at most stops, raw onions were the only choice. Sophie refused; Aurore munched away. At one shelter, soldiers offered to share their mess kit with the hungry little girl. When her mother came to inspect the contents of the bowl, she found that the soup had been made of the melted ends of burnt-down candles. Feverish and constantly thirsty, Aurore's face and body were now blistered with scabies; soon mother and son were infected. This time, when they crossed the Pyrenees into France, they were greeted by fresh food and water—baths and sulfur powder for Aurore.

Despite the relief from the maddening itch, she recalled more vividly her shame at the dreadful smell.

Sophie could bear no more overland travel. She prevailed on Maurice to rent a sloop for the coastal journey to Bordeaux and home. But nearing shore, the boat started sinking. Only her father's courage and ingenuity saved them, along with the essential carriage. Finally, on July 21, 1808, they turned off the main road and, at the end of an allée of poplars, crossed a tiny village square and entered the gates of Nohant.

Aurore had never seen anyone like the tiny woman who now greeted them. Dressed in the faded elegance of the past century, her silvery wig crowned by a silk cap with lace cockade, Marie-Aurore de Saxe Dupin de Franceuil clasped her son in her arms, politely dispatching her daughter-in-law and baby to the care of servants. But it was her granddaughter, still feverish and covered with an angry rash, whom she took to her heart. She gave up her own bed—a canopied feather-stuffed cocoon, curtained in silk-lined brocade—to the sick child. Now four years old, Aurore was welcomed to another world, the world to which, as her grandmother would often remind her, she now belonged.

Thanks to the care she received, Aurore recovered in days. Her infant brother, Louis, was not as lucky. Although his rash disappeared, the fever persisted, and less than a week after the family's arrival, he died in his mother's arms. Even had he lived, the local doctor confirmed, he would have been incurably blind. In her grief, Sophie showed signs of the paranoia that more and more would come to shadow her behavior. She insisted that the newborn had been blinded intentionally by the surgeon who delivered him: "Here's one who will never see the Spanish sun," she claimed she had heard him say. Now, convinced that her baby had been buried alive, she demanded that her husband exhume the tiny corpse under cover of darkness. Hysterically, she tried to revive him.

Maurice had to get away. A week after his son's death, and overriding the pleas of his wife, he rode off to nearby La Châtre to visit friends. Returning late at night, his Spanish stallion stumbled on a pile of stones. Rearing suddenly, the horse threw its master to the ground. His neck broken in the fall, Maurice died by the side of the road.

Minutes after her baby brother's death, Aurore had been whisked off to play. Now, she remained by her mother's side. In the depths of her grief, Sophie was sensitive to a child's perplexity. "When Daddy's finished being dead, will he come back to see us?" Aurore asked. Her nonbelieving grandmother saw this as the moment to explain the stark material facts of death. Her pious mother would not hear of it. The possibility of her father's return was left open.

In the devastated household, there was no further need to maintain an appearance of warmth between the two women. Proud and prickly, Sophie felt the constant snubs beneath the proprieties of mourning. She was still more sensitive to the grandmother's seduction of her daughter. She wanted nothing more than to get away, taking Aurore with her.

Already, the world of Nohant had begun to transform the little Parisian. Her grandmother worked on her speech and deportment and taught her music. Her father's tutor, Monsieur Deschartres, now promoted to estate manager, gave her lessons in reading and penmanship; with the aid of wooden braces, he tried curbing an unruly, childish hand into aristocratic cursives. He was even less successful with her illegitimate half brother, the wild Hippolyte, aged nine. Maurice's son by a local servant girl, the boy, called 'Polite, was as mad for horses as his father had been. When 'Polite and Aurore were sprung from the classroom, he taught his fearless little sister to ride and jump. Here the sensible tutor intervened: If Aurore were going to ride like a boy, she should wear boy's clothing. This was Aurore's introduction—officially sanctioned—to the freedom of masculine dress.

Then, a fateful visitor appeared: her grandmother's half brother and Aurore's great uncle, Charles-Godefroid-Marie de Beaumont de Bouillon. A secularized abbot, Beaumont was aristocratic, cultivated, and a man of compelling wit and charm. Now, he distracted the family from grief with games and amateur theatricals. He devoted himself to Sophie, and winning the suspicious woman's trust, he persuaded her to accept an allowance from her mother-in-law in exchange for signing away the rights of guardianship of her daughter.

Sophie needed money. With Napoleon's defeat, she had lost a promised annual pension of fifteen hundred francs from rents assigned to officers from conquered Prussian property. Madame Dupin de Franceuil now offered to replace the vanished income, plus a handsome supplement of one thousand francs. Although the agreement was disguised at first by an uneasy arrangement of visitation rights, the stricken child would soon realize that she had been sold by her mother.

For the next seven years, Aurore lived with her grandmother. They spent the winter months in Paris, staying in Madame

Dupin de Franceuil's grand apartment on the rue Neuve-des-Mathurins where the rooms were furnished with pieces salvaged from the ancien régime and the walls hung with blue silk damask. From here, her mother was allowed to take her on excursions to their favorite places, like the Chinese baths. These outings were followed by dinner at home with Sophie and Caroline, in the familiar, cramped attic rooms, now smaller and shabbier than Aurore had remembered. Her stepsister was not welcome to return the visit. When Caroline appeared one day, the maid, on instructions from Madame, slammed the door in the face of the weeping twelve-year-old. This was Aurore's first experience of the brutalities of class—and of her own complicity. She wept and vomited the entire night, she later said.

When Aurore and her grandmother returned to Nohant in the warmer weather, Sophie was invited—without Caroline—to stay as long as she liked. For the next few years, she might be in residence for several weeks or several months at a time. The unpredictability of her comings and goings added to the child's anxiety. More and more, Aurore's upbringing became a battleground, pitting Sophie—semiliterate, intuitive, emotionally explosive—against her mother-in-law, class-bound, rigid, and repressed. Fantasy and superstition battled rationality and discipline.

Her mother, Sand later recalled, "had the most profound respect for childhood and its needs." Aurore was given to spells: Sitting on a stool at her mother's feet, eyes staring vacantly, mouth half-open, arms hanging limply at her sides, the six-year-old "looked like an idiot," her grandparent worried. Nonsense,

Sophie replied. She had simply retreated to her private thoughts. Ruminating had always been her way.

At the same time, every exchange between mother and daughter was pitched at the extremes of emotion. Screams and blows ended with tears and kisses—like lovers' quarrels. Immune to passion herself, the elder Madame Dupin had a particular horror of flesh on flesh. When her spying maid, Julie, reported that, late at night, Aurore crept into her mother's bed, where she had seen their two bodies entwined, her mistress was horrified: Such behavior was not only "unclean, but unchaste."

Feeling her influence wane, Sophie punished Aurore. She saw her younger child co-opted by her grand relatives and, anticipating rejection, retreated to her own kind, to Caroline, her other daughter, and to Pierret, her neighbor and, probably, lover. Aurore responded by clinging ever more desperately to her mercurial mother. Partings became dramas of screams and sobs.

The sale of her child was a mutual wound that would not be healed. In her guilt, Sophie now repeated her earlier betrayal. To end one harrowing scene, she held out to Aurore the promise of paradise restored. Together, mother and both daughters would open a hat shop in Orléans. (Sophie was a skilled seamstress, and millinery her specialty.) Distrust had made Aurore legalistic: In a signed contract, her mother had given her up. Now she wanted her parent's promise in writing. The night before Sophie was to leave for Paris, Aurore left her mother a note, directing Sophie to place behind a portrait of Aurore's grandfather a letter spelling out the plan to reclaim her child. She awoke to find that her mother had gone without a word.

A terrible truth emerged from this bitter dawn: Sophie had sold her, then disappeared, abandoning her in a smoke screen of lies. Of her "two rival mothers," it was the grandmother—cool, critical, and undemonstrative—who was the reliable parent. Aurore accepted this fact. But her heart was broken and her innocence gone.

3

Liberations

AURORE, the obstreperous tomboy, turned subdued—even submissive. Deferring to her frail, demanding grandmother, she tried to obey her ironclad rules of decorum. The girl was to make a little curtsy before addressing an adult of her own class; no speaking the Berrichon dialect like a peasant, no hanging around the kitchen with the servants, with whom she was never to engage in personal conversation. In return, her grandparent, Sand recalled, "recognized my superior intelligence" and set out to cultivate the child's quick and curious mind. It was never too early to develop a taste for the best writers; together they read and discussed classics of French style. Aurore soon shared her freethinking grandmother's love for Voltaire. Studious by day, the girl now fell into a lifelong habit of reading or writing through the night. But it was as a music teacher that Marie-Aurore would be most gratefully remembered by her granddaughter. Accompanying herself on a small harpsichord, "Grandmama" painlessly imparted the principles of harmony and theory, with examples from her favorite composers, Haydn and Mozart, while her namesake lay curled up on a corner of the carpet with "Brilliant," Madame Dupin's favorite dog. What musical sensibilities would she now possess, Sand later mourned, if this tutor had not been replaced by teachers who came close to killing her love of music?

And still, the seven-year-old never stopped missing her mother. Her grandmother tried to make it up to her and took over her daily lessons. In contrast to Sophie's carping and violent outbursts, the older woman offered praise, sweets for work well done—even hugs. But Aurore withdrew, cold and angry, at the slightest gesture of affection. Tenderness reminded her of the absent mother, and she had to fight the urge to cry. On her infrequent visits, Sophie herself scolded the child for her distant manner toward her grandmother. Too proud to notice this rejection herself, Marie-Aurore would have her revenge.

Earthly loyalties weren't the only battleground. Religion unleashed further hostilities. Her mother's unthinking faith and her grandmother's defiant rationalism ended in a spiritual stalemate for Aurore. Here she was, being prepared for her First Communion and "understanding nothing in the catechism," she recalled. "When I wept over the sacred drama of the life and death of Christ, I hid my tears; I was afraid my grandmother would make fun of me." Indeed, when forced to deal with Scripture, Marie-Aurore referred to Jesus only as an "estimable person." Sophie, on the other hand, could explain nothing, but believed everything. Aurore's favorite readings were Homer's stories of the gods and goddesses made human. Then, to confuse matters further, her friends among the local farmers' children summoned supernatural beings—werewolves, witches, animals, and people possessed by demons—with far more familiarity than they did the saints or seraphim. Among the Berrichon peasantry, Christianity was for special occasions. The powers that aroused fear and trembling took pagan form. Aurore responded by inventing her own deity: "I only did what mankind had done before me. I sought a mediator, an intercessor, a man God, a divine friend of our accursed race."

Christened Corambé, the deity was without gender or even form. The name, Sand later said, came to her in a dream—meaningless syllables that might serve "both as the title of a novel and the god of my private religion." Her composite deity was "as charitable and pure as Jesus, as shining and beautiful as the angel Gabriel; but I also conferred upon him the grace of the nymphs and the poetry of Orpheus. Less austere than the Christian God, he would have more soul than the Homeric ones." Most significant, however, was Corambé's final attribute: He would be dressed as a woman, because, Sand explained, until that point, "what I had loved best and understood best was one woman—my mother." Physically, Corambé was defined by place—for Aurore, the most reliable attachment. In a thickly wooded part of Nohant's garden, hidden by a wall of tangled leafy brambles, was a small clearing, a "green room." Here, at the foot of a maple tree, Aurore placed the temple consecrated to her god(dess); under garlands of flowers, she raised an altar decorated with shells, polished stones, and the freshest moss, along with seasonal offerings of leaves and flowers. Daily, she brought visitors—birds and insects—to set them free again, in tribute to the spirit of liberty and protection promised by the deity. Then, when one of the local children discovered her temple, its mystery and charm evaporated. Corambé, the cult, and the shrine now seemed childish make-believe. Aurore dismantled the altar, burying the garlands, stones, and shells beneath the funerary mound.

In the house, meanwhile, another war raged. Madame had never cared to adjudicate the servants' quarrels. Now, as symptoms of weakness and age took hold, she seemed to abandon all authority, leaving battles below stairs to erupt unchecked. Rose, the reigning tyrant, harbored a special hatred for Deschartres, the elderly estate manager and Aurore's tutor; she took to beating him with a broomstick or attacking him with kicks and punches. But Rose and the cook were also at each others' throats; plates hurled to the floor, accompanied by shouts and screams. Valets came and went, their lives made a misery by the maids. Aurore fled. She spent as much time as she could outdoors, where the order of nature, the stoic industry of the farm families, gave refuge from the anarchy ruling the Nohant domestics.

Soon enough, she was swept up in the violence that the powerless inflict on one another. Rose took every excuse to beat her, too. She could have told her grandmother, and the maid would have been punished—or even dismissed. Aurore feared that possibility more than any other. Rose was the only member of the household who adored Sophie, and Aurore loved the maid, clinging to her as a maternal substitute whose sudden rages and harsh punishments, followed by tender embraces, recalled her mother's volatile moods.

Another maid, Julie, was the real enemy. Fanatically devoted to the elder Madame Dupin, she detested the interlopers Sophie and Aurore. She goaded Aurore into admitting that she would prefer a life of poverty with her mother than all the advantages of Nohant. Then, Julie rushed to report the thankless child's words to her grandmother. Stricken, the old woman barred the door of her rooms to her grandchild. Now that the girl had fallen from favor, the servants no longer spoke to her; she ate alone in the kitchen.

Three days later, she was summoned to the darkened bedroom. Kneeling by her grandmother's bed, she lifted a frail hand to kiss as a prelude to begging forgiveness, when the sick woman coldly cut her off.

"Listen carefully," her guardian said, "because I will never say these words again." And in an icy, bitter tone that Sand would never forget, she recounted her own life and that of Aurore's father. "Then came my mother—at least, what she knew and understood of her history. But she knew and understood nothing," George Sand later said. She told the thirteen-year-old that her mother was a whore—"a fallen woman"—and that, far from repenting her past, Sophie had brazenly returned to her old amoral life. Should Aurore choose to live with her mother, she would forfeit any hope of a place in her grandmother's world—a place that she had done everything in her power to secure for her namesake. But what she had to say next was so painful, if less explicit, that it would haunt the young girl throughout her long life as George Sand. Leaving the question unanswered, Madame Dupin raised the possibility that her son might not, after all, have been Aurore's father.

In her autobiographical writings, Sand anxiously skirts the issue of her paternity. She circles the question with a strategy of advance and retreat, by hinting at doubts, only to dispel them. During the period when she had to have been conceived, she tells us gratuitously, her parents were never apart. But in fact, for the next thirty-five years after her grandmother's revelation, Sand would worry the truth of this assertion. Finally, in early 1848, she took advantage of a friend in the war ministry and the memories of her father's Villeneuve cousins, his closest relations, seeking hard evidence of Maurice's whereabouts during his military service. What Sand herself discovered was all but conclusive: Maurice Dupin could not possibly have been her biological father. Given legitimacy by her parents' marriage a month after her birth, she nevertheless remained "of father unknown."

In view of Sand's insistence on her "dual heritage" and dramatic "choice" between conflicting class loyalties, her own research and the subsequent concealment of the findings reveal the most profound conflict of her life. She had constructed an identity turned self-mythology on the basis of her "mixed blood." The core of her personal narrative, as the supposed child of a working-class mother and an aristocratic father, was the decision to define herself as a "daughter of the people" and, later, the belief that her mixed heritage gave her, along with unique insight, an emblematic role as "Representative Woman" of her time. Her discovery robbed her of a father, his legacy, and its renunciation.

As to the primal interview with her grandmother, how should we understand such cruelty? Only that it bears the stamp of love betrayed. Aurore had wounded her grandparent mortally (a wound flayed by the venomous Julie), and the older woman now lashed out, tearing down her rival and shaming the thirteen-year-old Aurore in her purest feelings: her love for her mother. The effect was the reverse: Hearing her "little mama" vilified, she loved Sophie more: more protectively, more tenderly—more romantically, even. Her head now filled with fantasies in which she heroically rescued the martyred Sophie, providing her mother with a life of comfort and ease.

As an adult and politically engaged writer, Sand would place her grandmother's denunciations in a larger context: In condemning Sophie, the older woman had shown "neither intelligence nor pity, because . . . the lives of the poor are swept along by forces, sorrows and fatalities that the rich will never understand, and which they judge as a blind man judges colors. She had no notion of the inevitability that a poor girl, orphaned at 14, would be exploited by men."

Madame Dupin had not finished her counterattack. Shortly after the scene at her bedside, she announced to Aurore that she could no longer live at Nohant; the girl had become too wild and ungovernable. Having made progress toward becoming a young lady, she had regressed into a willful, lazy, slovenly child. It was all arranged. She had enrolled Aurore in a convent boarding school in Paris, a closed order with no visitors (except for strictly rationed outings with family members) and no other contact with the outside world.

But Aurore heard only the word *Paris.* "Then, I can see my mother!" she burst out. She had had her revenge.

In fact, she believed that Sophie would intervene. Her mother would never countenance a child of hers being shut in a convent in order to ape the speech and manners of aristocratic young ladies. This act would galvanize her parent to challenge Marie-Aurore's guardianship, as Sophie had often sworn to do "since no law can supercede a mother's natural rights to her child," she had said.

To Aurore's shock, Sophie was in complete accord with her mother-in-law's decision. It was high time that her daughter, allowed to run wild for too long, learned to take her place in society. There was no question of challenging Madame Dupin's rights as the designated parent; Sophie did not even care to be inscribed as a close relative who would be allowed to take the boarder for holiday outings. Aurore's mother had returned to her own life, where there was no place for her younger daughter.

On January 12, 1818, Madame Dupin de Franceuil brought the fourteen-year-old Aurore to the convent of the English Augustine Ladies Order, a vast, walled establishment enclosing a space the size of several city blocks and separated from the world by a door with a small grill looking on to the rue des Fosses-Saint-Victor.

When the time came to say good-bye, Madame Dupin took her granddaughter in her arms and began to weep. But Aurore, dry-eyed, merely kissed her guardian politely. Stung, her grandmother thrust her away, saying, "'Heartless child! You haven't a single regret in leaving me.' And the old woman rushed from the parlor, covering her tear-streaked face with her hands."

Looking back, Sand would insist that she was astounded by her grandmother's outburst. With her sermons on stoicism and self-mastery, Marie-Aurore should have been pleased by the girl's display of courage and resignation. But, in fact, this would always be Aurore's preferred weapon—in fact or fantasy. Whether beaten by Rose or her mother, or humiliated by Julie, Monsieur Deschartres, or her grandmother, the prisoner would never show weakness.

Once inside the convent, Aurore's behavior amazed the nuns: She skipped off to join her new classmates, the Mother Superior wrote to Madame Dupin. It was recreation period, and they were choosing up teams for tag in the garden.

The new pupil did everything in her power to insure that role-play became reality. To wean herself from the bonds of family, she refused, for the duration of her first cloistered year, even such excursions as were permitted. She did not want to be taken out for the day by anyone—neither grandmother, Villeneuve cousins, not even her mother: "I rejoiced in the convent," she later tells us. "I felt an overwhelming need for respite from all these inner conflicts. I was tired of being the apple of discord between two beings, both of whom I cherished. I almost wished they would both forget me. Thus, I accepted the convent—and so readily, that I was happier than I had ever been in my whole life. I think I was the only happy child there."

It was a real little pagan whom the freethinking Madame Dupin had left in the sisters' charge. Aurore had no idea how to make the sign of the cross and, as Mother Alippe discovered to her horror, was ignorant of the most basic elements of catechism. Stymied by the question "Where do unbaptized infants go when they die?" Aurore seraphically replied, "To the bosom of God." And when a helpful classmate hissed the right answer, "To limbo" (in French, *aux Limbes*), in her ear, the new pupil heard "Olympus," correcting herself, to the mirth of all.

Traditionally, the girls naturally fell into three cliques: Devils, Idiots, and Goody-goods. No need to wonder which group proudly boasted Aurore as its ringleader. As God most loves the sinners, the sisters, all well-born British ladies, adored the wild and wayward child. They recognized an exceptional intelligence, were awed by her wide reading, and sensed the yearning for affection that took the form of outrageous bids for attention. In turn, Aurore soon directed all the intensity and idealism of the teenager into love for one of the nuns. Sister Marie-Alicia.

"I had experienced only one passion in my life—love for my mother," Sand recalled. In "adopting" the vulnerable student, the plump, innocent-hearted nun allowed this love to continue, with herself—the "idealized, holy 'mother of choice'"—its object. "My real mother was unpredictable in her response to me: sometimes she showed me too much love, at others, too little." In Sister Marie-Alicia, the young girl could act out the dream of maternal love as refuge—the antithesis of the jealous passions generated by the rival mother and grandmother. This happy transference, "free of emotional blackmail and fear," Sand said, "promised to restore me to myself."

By the end of her first year, the troublemaker had become the school leader. The youngest in the advanced class, she was loved, admired, and trusted by the sisters and surrounded by adoring friends. Then, in the middle of her second year in the convent, Madame Dupin decided to spend several months in Paris. She lost no time in making known her unhappiness with the girl's progress; Aurore still carried herself badly, curtsied awkwardly, had no reserve of lighthearted, flirtatious banter to draw on: "There was something in my simplicity and unfortunate absence of coquetry that she simply couldn't accept," Sand recalled, "something distasteful that she couldn't overlook, perhaps something akin to original sin, or—despite her efforts to eradicate it—a lingering trace of the proletarian."

Her grandmother's visit and disappointment underlined the purpose of Aurore's Parisian exile. In failing health, Marie-Aurore's principal concern before she died was to see her granddaughter—and heir—safely married and free, once and for all, of her mother's plebeian influence. To this end, during each of Aurore's half dozen visits to her grandmother that winter, a parade of eligible young nobles filed through the elegant salon. When she wasn't faced by this dispiriting survey of her future, she was yawning through teas with Madame Dupin's circle of "old countesses" or dinner with the now-ancient Uncle Beaumont. She looked forward to returning to the "calm and gaiety" of the convent, and all the more so, as she was now rewarded by the ultimate expression of confidence, "a cell of my own."

Then, what Sand called a revolution took place: "Like a passion which ignites in a soul ignorant of its own power," faith inflamed her. While she sat alone in chapel, a ray of light illuminated a mediocre painting, *Christ on the Mount of Olives.* She had looked at the picture a hundred times before, but now she saw Jesus as if for the first time, and she wept.

Her grandmother had defended her against the temptations of religion. To counter Sophie's primitive belief in miracles, Madame Dupin had cited the most mocking ripostes of Voltaire. But "from this day on," Sand recalled, all struggle ended. "The heart once conquered, all reason was thrown away with a will, with a kind of fanatical joy. I accepted everything, I believed in everything, without struggle, suffering, regret or shame. To blush for what one adores? To need others' approval to give myself to what I knew to be perfect and worthy of being cherished above all things? Impossible!"

Another painting sealed her conversion. It portrayed the moment when Augustine—patron saint of the order, hears a child's voice speaking from a fig tree. The voice commands the young dilettante, "Pick up and read" ("*Tolle legge*"). Directed to the apostles' witness of Christ, the future saint is led to believe and to write himself into history. More than the short-lived religious fervor of the adolescent, the voice seems to prophesy Aurore's vocation of writer, if not of saint. Gladdened as they were by the rebel's new cause, the nuns had seen enough of adolescent girls' intense fervor directed to God to reserve judgment on Aurore's miracle. The pupils' confessor, Father Prémord, was still more cautionary: She was to make no vows—neither to herself nor to the sisters. Nor should she ever speak of the wish to become a nun to her family, which, like that of all other pupils' families, would be already pursuing a suitable marriage for her. If, however, at the end of two or three years of leaving the convent, she was still unmarried and was convinced that the life of a wife and mother was not for her—if she had remained firm in her vocation—then they would explore the possibility again.

Without a word from Aurore, Madame Dupin learned the terrible news. Much as the child might have succumbed to typhoid or cholera in the convent, her granddaughter had caught religion. Instead of learning the airs and graces of an aristocrat, she was making professions of faith and even, the grandmother had heard, claiming a religious vocation. Aurore must be removed immediately and prepared to take her place in the world.

4

Knights Errant

THRUST FROM THE SAFETY of the convent, Aurore, at seventeen, faced the world's expectations of a young and propertied woman. Her grandmother's decline, signaled by a series of strokes, prompted the entire Nohant community—tenant farmers, household servants, gardeners, and stable boys—to look to their young mistress for day-to-day decisions, as well as for the seasonal planning crucial to the management of a large and self-sustaining agricultural property.

She took on this powerful new role, first with trepidation, then with pride. But still, she was stalked by pain and fear. Parentless, she had no one to turn to or to trust. Letters to her mother pleading for a visit, or just a reassuring word, went unanswered. Then, weeks later, Aurore would receive from Sophie a vague reply that she couldn't leave Caroline, now twenty-one, alone in Paris unchaperoned. Looking back, the adult George

Sand recognized that early—even premature—responsibility and self-reliance had also been a gift: "If fate had thrust me immediately from the domination of my grandmother, to that of a husband or of the convent, it's possible that, used to submission to established authority I would never have become myself. But chance also determined that by the age of 17, there would be a suspension of outside influences, that I would be left entirely on my own for almost an entire year, to become, for good or ill, who I would be for the rest of my life."

Intellectual isolation nurtured the freethinker—encouraging, as her grandmother had done, a skeptical cast of mind, symptoms of which had already begun to worry the Augustine sisters and their father confessor. They were right: Aurore now began a slow, if never complete, break with the Catholic Church. Her doubts took root on political ground, stirred by the siren song of Jean-Jacques Rousseau. She had long put off reading him as a deferred pleasure. Now the subversive *Confessions* and *Social Contract* fell into her hands at a decisive moment. Rousseau's self-invented morality (which included justifying theft and the abandonment of his five children) addressed Aurore's own disenchantment with the established order, she recalled, widening a rift already begun.

Revolution, Sand reminds us, was a historical fact. In Europe, the nations of Italy and Greece had fought for independence and a democratic government. The church, in unholy alliance with the monarchy, rose up against "these generous initiatives, even to the point of supporting the Ottoman empire against the Eastern Church! This monstrous frivolity, the sacrifice of religious to political interests, repelled me," she recalled. "In contrast, the liberal spirit became for me synonymous with religious belief. I can never forget—I will never forget—how the Christian impulse swept me, unhesitatingly, from the first, into the progressive camp where I remain to this day."

Still, humanitarian sympathies and alertness to social injustice provided no structure to replace the church that had failed her. Overwhelmed by this absence, by the daily evidence of her grandmother's inexorable slide into death, Aurore succumbed to melancholy. Her mind turned so often to thoughts of suicide that she was afraid to go near her favorite places on the River Creuse lest she throw herself into the rushing waters.

VISITORS, HOWEVER WELCOME, left her more bereft than before. Pauline de Pontcarré, a convent friend, came, accompanied by her mother. But excursions with Madame de Pontcarré and her daughter reminded Aurore of her own mother's defection. Sophie had announced that she would not set foot in Nohant "until the old lady was good and dead!" Aurore's brother, Hippolyte, arrived, on leave from his Hussar regiment. From teaching riding to the cadets at Saumur, he now drilled the fearless Aurore in the most basic equestrian skill: "No matter what anyone tells you, the only rule is not to fall off the horse." And he helped her train her spirited mare, "Colette," the preferred companion of future outings.

Throughout Aurore's adolescence, Hippolyte had been the light of her life. His uncomplicated love of the country—*their* country—and his sensual, instinctive pleasure in food, wine, animals, and games opened her to feelings she had learned to suppress. Then, 'Polite returned to his regiment, found a bride, and resigned his commission. A wife and child proved no deterrent to his drinking. Before long, his fondness for the strong local red, right out of the barrel, left him in a nightly stupor, while his sister's anger and contempt widened the rift between them.

Not for the first time, Aurore became the subject of village gossip. For some years, her old tutor, Monsieur Deschartres, had functioned as physician for the entire dependent population of Nohant, both tenants and servants. He could treat simple, work-related injuries and he now hoped that Aurore, gentle and dexterous, could help him set the bones of the farm laborers. In view of extending her knowledge beyond his own, he hired a young local savant to instruct his apt former pupil in anatomy.

Stéphane d'Ajasson de Grandsagne was the youngest of ten sons born to an impoverished aristocratic family of La Châtre. He had wanted to train as a physician, but poverty forced him to become a self-taught amateur scientist instead. Two years older than Aurore, handsome, and brilliant, he proved irresistible to the romantic adolescent. It was inevitable that the anatomy lessons using the female skeleton he provided would give way to more carnal knowledge. Beginning in 1820, when Aurore was sixteen or seventeen, Stéphane and Aurore became inseparable, first as friends, then lovers—on and off—for the next eight years. Seeing them together unchaperoned, neighbors whispered, but the source of the gossip proved to be someone close to the Nohant household itself. This same year, Madame Dupin suffered a series of strokes that left her comatose. Aurore, used to the adult companionship of an equal, became understandably more dependent on her mentor and lover. While Stéphane was in Paris attempting to educate himself in the natural sciences, he dispatched to Nohant dozens of volumes that Aurore requested; the young lovers then eagerly discussed the books by maîl, until he returned. Sadly, their correspondence, consisting of almost 125 letters and last seen by Stéphane's son in the early twentieth century, has disappeared. But a single quote by Stéphane from one of these letters reveals a young man who both loved and understood—perhaps all too well—who Aurore was and what she would become: "True philosophic soul, you are right, but yours is the truth that kills."

On the day after Christmas 1821, Marie-Aurore de Saxe Dupin de Franceuil died. One of her last acts was to secure her granddaughter's consent to have her guardianship legally transferred to their Villeneuve cousins. The young woman must never again be returned to her mother's custody. The guilt Aurore might have felt was muted by fresh evidence of Sophie's indifference: When her mother finally did write, it was to relay gossip about Aurore's scandalous behavior (receiving a young man in her room!) and to demand, in the tone of a Mother Superior, an accounting. Aurore's reply, a model of respect and dignity—if not honesty—appears only to have further enraged her mother.

When the day came for the reading of the will, Sophie made a dramatic appearance in Nohant, supported by her tiny, birdlike younger sister and her brother-in-law. On learning, first, that her allowance had ended with her mother-in-law's death (leaving her annual income of fifteen hundred francs reduced by one-third) and, second, that guardianship of Aurore had passed to the Villeneuve family, Sophie went berserk. She screamed obscenities about the dead woman, reviled her daughter's disloyalty and betrayal, and denounced the girl's promiscuous behavior, condoned, of course, by the deceased. Never would any member of this dissolute family be allowed to take her child from her. She had only begun to fight!

René de Villeneuve, Aurore's cousin and newly appointed guardian, was witness to these scenes. On an earlier visit, which had been shrewdly arranged by Madame Dupin, the cultivated, charming forty-two-year-old had won the girl's trust and affection, feelings Aurore soon extended to his charming wife and daughters. She looked to him now for rescue, for the moment when he would assert his legal rights and sweep her off to his family, awaiting their arrival at the ravishing château of Chenonceaux. Horrified by this display of gutter vulgarity and hysteria and frightened by the force of Sophie's fury, René fled Nohant—alone. Within days, Aurore received a chilly note from her cousin, saying that he was prepared to carry out the terms of his guardianship *only* if Aurore swore never to see or communicate with her mother again. As he explained, she could never be married to anyone "of good family" were she even to be seen on the streets of Paris with such *canaille.*

For Aurore, this was an impossible choice. She would not be the one to sever relations with her mother. Further, her own pride was affronted on hearing Sophie and her aunt dismissed as trash. Writing thirty years later, George Sand insisted that her class loyalties were already established; she would never deny her "plebeian" blood, the source, she always insisted, of her strength. By that date, however, she would have known that there was no aristocratic side of her heritage, no blue blood to counter the red. She had decided to allow the world's perception of her "choice" to remain unrevised.

The faithful daughter was ill rewarded. A gloating and triumphant Sophie asserted her new power; with the grandmother gone, Aurore became the target of the mother's revenge, the victim of all of Sophie's accumulated rage. The little chatelaine of Nohant, the pet of snooty English nuns, would no longer be allowed to do as she pleased, Sophie sneered. As relics of her former life, Aurore could take with her to Paris her maid, her dog, and one or two books. Lack of space was not the issue; mother and daughter now moved into the late Madame Dupin's grand apartment on the rue Neuve-des-Mathurins, the rooms' furnishings a constant reminder of ancien régime privilege. Once in Paris, Sophie's spite and venom knew no bounds. Threatening constantly to crush Aurore, she tore books from her hands, screaming that the lies they contained encouraged the girl's "perversity" and "viciousness." She sent Aurore's maid packing and destroyed her dog. Incidents of physical violence in Sophie's behavior suggest that earlier descriptions such as *bizarre* and *eccentric* were euphemistic or that her condition had deteriorated. She now appeared deranged, with full-blown symptoms of paranoia. After the death of her mother-in-law, she fixed on her daughter as the enemy and agent of her persecution.

When Aurore entered the convent, Sophie had seemingly lost all interest in her younger child. Now that her older daughter, Caroline, had recently married, the mother had reportedly reverted to her former anarchic life. As the prime irritant to Sophie's state of constant rage, Aurore assumed that her mother would be relieved to be rid of her. The girl broached a plan to return to the convent as one of a few graduate boarders, to live and study there until she reached her majority in three years. But Sophie needed a victim and, for herself, the power of inquisitor and jailer. Declaring the convent, which had given the girl exalted ideas of her intelligence and social station, enemy territory, she now read aloud letters from Nohant. From this correspondence, to which she had only alluded earlier, she read accounts detailing all of Aurore's local trysts, adding tidbits of slander (including orgies and black masses), reports now certified as coming from her grandmother's physician and friend, Dr. Descerfzs.

There was one happy if unintended consequence of her mother's mental illness and to her own otherwise "intolerable life," Sand recalled. In sinking to the bottom of society, beyond the pale of respectability, a great weight was lifted from her; she was relieved of the burden of making a "good marriage."

When Sophie was not seized by one of her fits of rage, there were tender moments between mother and daughter. Then, Aurore was reminded of the protective, loving parent whom she had adored when she was a young child. In these brief periods of calm, the angry woman seemed to enter a state of remission; the sufferer then recognized her transports as a sickness, sorrowfully acknowledging the violent injustice she had visited on her daughter, but against which she was powerless to resist. And indeed, looking back, George Sand blamed her mother's brutal early life and lack of education for failing to give her any rational tools to battle the irrational furies that beset her. Sophie did, however, manage one objective conclusion about her periodic breakdowns: They were seasonal, she noted, and they started coming on toward spring.

This may have been one explanation for Sophie's impulsive decision, at the end of March 1822, to accept an invitation from a family she had met only three weeks earlier to visit them at their country property in Melun, near Paris. A retired captain in the king's musketeers, Jacques "James" Roëttiers du Plessis and his wife, Angèle, Sand recalled, seemed as much in love as when they had married twenty years earlier. Moreover, their household, consisting of five daughters, various pets, and constant visitors (including many eligible young officers) welcomed Sophie and eighteen-year-old Aurore as part of the family. On their arrival, Sophie told her hosts that her daughter, pale and run-down, needed a good dose of country air. Then, restless as always, Sophie left after one night. Promising to return and collect Aurore the following week, she disappeared for five months.

During that time, the Roëttiers du Plessis happily assumed the role of foster parents, beginning with the purchase of a new wardrobe to replace Aurore's single shabby dress and pair of worn shoes. In the company of her adoptive sisters and astride her own horse provided by her hosts, she blossomed again, roaming the gardens, meadows, and woods of the large property. With sensitivity and tact, both Angèle and James made it clear that they were aware of her mother's troubled state of mind and that she was welcome to stay as long as she liked. As father to a family of girls, James reminded Aurore that she was of marriageable age, and he offered to vet any of the young men who frequented the house and who might appeal to her as a likely husband. But when Aurore expressed her horror at the thought of marrying, Jacques assured her that the subject would never be raised again by him.

As it happened, her hosts had no need to play matchmaker. Even after she returned to living with her mother, Aurore continued to spend much of the time with her adoptive family. On one visit, after an evening at the theatre in Paris, they all repaired for ices at the fashionable Café Tortoni on the Boulevard des Italiens. From an adjoining table, a slender, young cavalry officer had been staring at the dark-eyed, vivacious Aurore. Baron Casimir Dudevant had known James slightly during the latter's military service and could now present his respects to the older man, along with requesting an introduction to the charming young woman in his party.

The illegitimate son, but recognized heir, of a minor Gascon noble and a maidservant, Casimir now became one of the uniformed regulars hovering around the du Plessis house and its six pretty girls. He differed from the others—or appeared to—according to Sand's later recollections, in neither flirting nor making more overt sexual overtures to her. Careful chaperoning was not her hosts' style. And while grateful for the affection and generosity of the family, Sand later concluded that the free and easy atmosphere of the household encouraged seduction, leaving her feeling vulnerable and afraid. For many months, Casimir's visits were companionable and even brotherly. Trust turned to love. But Aurore also faced a stark reality: She could not continue the nightmare of life with her mother, but with the du Plessis daughters now marrying, she could not live indefinitely on the hospitality of her friends. Furthermore, as heir presumptive to family property and a modest paternal title, Casimir appeared to be neither a fortune hunter nor a blueblood willing to "forgive" her dubious heritage. And, most important, he seemed to share her dream of a warm and intimate family life, lived productively on the land. Swiftly approved by the Roëttiers du Plessis, Casimir's ardent proposal of marriage was accepted by Aurore.

Initially, Sophie opposed the match, claiming that the prospective bridegroom was not handsome enough; she would only be seen on the arm of a good-looking son-in-law, she said. She then gave her consent before changing her mind again. The price of her final agreement, however, was the renegotiation of the complicated marriage contract. Thus, to her unreliable mother, Aurore owed the right to retain (but not manage) the principle of her 500,000-franc dowry, with a 3,000-franc allowance from the interest, to be paid her annually by her husband. From being her jailer, Sophie became the agent of her daughter's freedom.

5

True Confessions

George Sand's *Story of My Life* was begun on January 15, 1847, when the author was forty-three. Seven years later, in early October 1854, the first installment was published in the newspaper *La Presse.* A first volume appeared a month later, and by Christmas, all four volumes were for sale in bookstores. The memoir's French title, *Histoire de ma vie,* sets an agenda of ambiguity. The word *histoire* means either "story" or "history," and Sand the novelist took full advantage of the space between the two meanings to arrange, improve, embroider, invent, and omit in her self-portrait. Then, too, the edited life conspires with the blurring effects of time and memory. Chronology gets chancy. Invention steps in to fill in the blanks. The shared pain of an unhappy couple becomes the martyrdom of the partner who owns the narrative. In Sand's retrospective view of herself, unruly sex disappears offstage. By the time she tells her story, the private Aurore Dupin Dudevant had become the public figure George Sand. Beloved in old age as "the Good Lady of Nohant," she had begun to sanitize the past; episodes of passionate abandon, followed by notoriety and scandal, were transformed into platonic or maternal relationships. One of her lovers, Alfred de Musset, published his own version of their wild affair. But who believes a mad poet? George Sand always had the last word.

On this one chapter of her life, everyone—from the newlyweds themselves to friends, family, lovers, and servants—agreed. From the start, the Dudevant marriage was a disaster.

Weeks after the wedding, Aurore found that she was pregnant. After spending their first winter in Nohant, they decided that its rural isolation increased the dangers of a first childbirth for both mother and baby. Instead, they found a furnished apartment in Paris in the Hôtel de Florence, on the rue Neuve-des-Mathurins, the same street where her grandmother had lived. There, in a pavilion at the back of the garden, Maurice Dudevant was born on June 30, 1823, to the joy of his mother, whose prayers for a son had been answered.

Paris was too expensive for the young family. But that still left the problem of where to live. They begged the question by a year of wandering. The irony was not lost on Aurore: Now that she had a family, she was homeless. "We both loved the country," she recalled, "but we were afraid of Nohant; what we really feared was being alone together." They moved into and out of a series of smaller, cheaper apartments in Paris and then, weary and discouraged, made an extended visit to Aurore's surrogate family, the Roëttiers du Plessis near Melun. Here, while Maurice was spoiled by servants and family, his mother happily reverted to schoolgirl antics as leader of the pack of mischievous young people. On one occasion, while Casimir and his hosts were taking coffee on the terrace, Aurore, playing below with her friends, tossed sand at their table. When a request to aim in another direction was ignored, Casimir strode down the steps and slapped his wife's face. More than the sting of the blow, the humiliation was the beginning of the end of their marriage.

Shame cut short their stay. They left Melun for a small, rented pavilion in Ormesson, a suburb of Paris near Lake Enghien. Aurore loved the house's English gardens and the water, inviting a succession of friends to visit. Casimir was away most of the time; he often went to Paris for the day, ostensibly on business, or he spent weeks at a time in Nohant, familiarizing himself with the property and its management.

They had run out of alternatives. Returning to Nohant, Aurore felt like a stranger. Casimir had "improved" the property so that she barely recognized her childhood home: Old servants had been dismissed; aged dogs and horses put down; even the elderly peacock that had tottered about the garden, greeting visitors by fanning his few remaining tail feathers, had been destroyed. Everywhere she looked, she was overcome by feelings of desolation. As always, her misery assumed symptoms of illness: strep throat, stomach pain, migraine attacks, insomnia.

They tried another visit to Paris, where Aurore, accompanied by Maurice, decided to make a retreat to her old convent. (Indifferent to religion himself, Casimir approved of piety in women.) She hoped that the example of the nuns' lives of simplicity and purpose would cure her spiritual emptiness. But she was also nostalgic for the privileged state of favorite pupil. Instead, the nuns gently reminded her that she had outgrown their sheltered existence. Her life must now be dedicated to her "charming child," was Sister Marie-Alicia's admonition.

Then, like many unhappy couples, the Dudevants resorted to travel, hoping that the bustle of journeys, new places, and new people would ease quarrels, resentment, and boredom. In July 1825, with Aurore's improved health in view and accompanied by Maurice and a nursemaid, the pair set out for Cauterets, a stylish spa in the Pyrénées.

Wild and dramatic scenery would always delight her. In a letter to her mother, Aurore wrote that the trip, via Bordeaux and through perilous mountain passes with their jagged peaks looming above, reminded her of the journey she and her mother made to Spain over these same mountains twenty years before.

On arriving, she found, to her distaste, that their hotel was full of fashionables taking the cure. She also discovered that Casimir's professed love of the country was based on opportunities for killing the local wildlife. Every day before dawn, he was off with guns and dogs.

"Monsieur hunts with passion," Madame noted coldly. "He kills chamois and eagles. He rises at two o'clock in the morning and returns at night. His wife complains. But he doesn't foresee that the day will come when she will rejoice in his absence."

In fact, the day had already arrived. Among their fellow guests was a young magistrate from Bordeaux, Aurélien de Sèze. The young man was accompanied by his fiancée, her family, and another unmarried young woman, Zoë Leroy. With Casimir gone every day, the trio—Aurore, Aurélien, and Zoë, Aurélien's spirited childhood friend—became inseparable. While a complicated friendship instantly united the two women, Aurore and Aurélien fell in love. As Zoë tactfully withdrew to the role of go-between, confidante, and witness, the unhappy young wife and the reluctant fiancé were drawn together by passion made the more intense as its consummation was long deferred.

Scion of a prominent Bordeaux dynasty of jurists, Aurélien was a rising legal star in his own right. Following his father and grandfather, he was also a fervent monarchist and an Ultramontanist, the most conservative of Catholics who believed in the absolute authority of the pope. Inevitably, this most proper young man would be drawn to the rebellious young wife, who was already spouting radical heresies—political, social, and sexual. With his social and intellectual distinction and a mind trained in Jesuitical argument, Aurélien can also be seen as the antithesis of Sophie—the anti-mother. Indeed, Aurore would always be torn between these two male polarities, as represented by the marginal idealist and atheist Stéphane de Grandsagne and the rising young pillar of the establishment Aurélien de Sèze.

Soon, the pair, sighted together, became the talk of the gossipy resort. Once, they took a little skiff out on a nearby lake, carving the identical first three letters of both their names, A-U-R, into the wooden prow. But in fact, they had few occasions to be alone. And soon, Aurélien had to return to Bordeaux, leaving the desolate Aurore with those most dangerous of companions: pen and paper. From October 19 to November 14, 1825, she kept a journal in the form of letters to Aurélien. Evidently, these were not mailed to the addressee, but, kept together in bundles, Aurore sent them to Zoë, who delivered them to the beloved. In between these dispatches, however, Casimir found a stack of the damning pages (or perhaps copies), as he was no doubt meant to do.

Typically, Casimir would have preferred to overlook the evidence of his wife's infatuation. But Aurore would have none of this civilized behavior: She would always demand authenticity (or drama) in her relationships, at least when she was the transgressor. Now, she provoked Casimir into confrontation: "Admit it! You're jealous," she goaded him. In fact, Casimir's strongest emotion seems to have been dread of public embarassment. What could he do, but halfheartedly provide the scene demanded by his wife?

From the written evidence, moreover, Aurore's so-called romantic friendship—the rapture of mutual understanding, the adoration, and the need expressed in her letters to Aurélien—would have been more damaging to any man's ego than mere adultery. This time, Casimir decided to rise to his wife's challenge: He would behave in a way worthy of the lovers, nobly and forgivingly. In return, Aurore promised to earn his trust; there would be no further exchanges between Bordeaux and Nohant that he wasn't welcome to read! As she wrote to Aurélien, "Together, we'll restore his confidence and peace of mind. He's shown us so much kindness and generosity that we can't fail to convey to his soul the noble certainty of ours." Poor Casimir!

For her part, Aurore was neither hypocritical nor disingenuous. Love as the ultimate virtue would become the guiding principle of her life—and the principal theme of her novels. And if the sexual would not always be as sublimated as she claimed of her friendship with Aurélien, it was never as important to Aurore as were other bonds. Some critics insist that her impulse to elevate the erotic to the platonic—what D. H. Lawrence would mock a century later as "sex-in-the-head"—was a cover for frigidity. In Aurélien, she was sure that she had found the ideal partner in sinless passion: Idealizing the beloved, she exalted his soul "so vast and splendid . . . your mind so powerful and keen. In my eyes, you're a man superior to the point of infallibility. Compared to you, I'm nothing!"

Initially, the young magistrate thrilled to this celebration of shared virtue and sacrifice—not to speak of the worship that he inspired. His code, moreover, required that a woman be pure; virginal if unmarried, to be sure, but also, superior to lust if she was already a wife and mother. Together, he and Aurore lofted a veritable duet of romantic denial: "Resist me," he commanded.

Barely had the drama of the discovered journal-letters died down than Casimir, anxious to prove worthy of Aurore's faith in his nobility of character and generosity of spirit, agreed on a family visit to Bordeaux. Once installed, as a further measure of his trust, Casimir reverted to his routine of daily hunting, leaving his wife and young son behind. One day, returning early, he burst into the salon, to find Aurore seated with her head resting on Aurélien's shoulder. Dreadful scenes followed. Now it was Casimir's turn to receive from his wife pages of self-justification, in the form of a famous "Confession Letter."

For Aurore as for the later George Sand, *confession* should not be confused with the religious act, with its acknowledgment of sin, acceptance of guilt, plea for forgiveness, vow of repentance, and promise to sin no more. In contrast, her model was Jean-Jacques Rousseau: confession as a form of autobiography, whose redeeming value lies in the writer's "sincerity" and self-knowledge. More Freud than Jesus. Truthfulness implied absolution and, better yet, the liberation of both the sinner and sinned-against.

Not that she or Aurélien had been guilty of any real sin: "Tempted as we were, neither of us could have contemplated doing such a thing! If nothing else, the thought of the damage to your honor would have stopped me," she wrote. Reassuring perhaps, but hardly flattering. Nor is the following proposal: that her husband assume a paternal role in this triangulated friendship. "Casimir, my friend, my indulgent judge, stop being my husband and master. Be my father, let me open my heart to you, let my tears of repentance flow over your breast. Forget your silly prejudices, your false sense of honor that so often turns a husband into a hated tyrant. Be generous to the ultimate degree, so that my sincerity will be proof of my contrition."

He should be aware, moreover, that he bore some of the blame for his wife's having "strayed." He had failed to share her passions. He fell asleep over his book after dinner; he left the room when she played the piano. Other than killing its wildlife, he didn't even like the country! Preoccupied by the obstacles placed in the way of their marriage—obstacles that had united them against the world—both of them were blind to a complete absence of common interests. As to the sexual, his respect for her purity before the wedding left her unprepared for the violation that was a husband's right. At the least, she seems to have encountered an insensitive, if not brutal, lover.

All was not lost—yet. *If* Casimir could meet the challenge, she assured him, he would be reinstated in her affections: "It's by proving yourself to be as large-spirited and generous as you've been until now, that will you re-conquer the rights to my heart." This new understanding, however, required Casimir to become her confidant. He was asked to hear out all her troubles with Aurélien, in particular, how love had become obsession.

Before Casimir had a chance to react, the family's visit to Bordeaux was cut short by his father's death from a stroke on February 20, 1826. The young Dudevants rushed to Gascony to mourn with the widow. An added cause of mourning was the will: The deceased's only son was left a token bequest and the modest title of Baron. The entire estate had been left to Casimir's stepmother, who saw no reason to share her unexpected good fortune. Her stepson was left ever more dependent on his wife's property and income.

On returning to Nohant, their entente proved short-lived. More vulnerable now to quick-money schemes and with no head for business, Casimir invested thirty thousand francs of Aurore's marriage settlement in a merchant ship that turned out not to exist. Outraged, she now demanded a larger voice in the management of Nohant—a role she had largely ceded to him at the time of their marriage. Shamed, and with too much time on his hands, Casimir began to spend his days drinking with Hippolyte, who now joined cause with his brother-in-law against his sister. Sharing a love of drink, the two became accomplices in debauch. Casimir began an open dalliance with Aurore's Spanish maid, Pepita. When she was fired, he took up with Claire, her counterpart in Hippolyte's household nearby. As if matters weren't bleak enough within her marriage, Aurore's romance with Aurélien showed signs of cooling. Letters from Bordeaux were more polite than passionate. Aurore suspected that her "God" had found a flesh-and-blood liaison close to home.

She now began to suffer every symptom of ill health: violent headaches, palpitations, and burning chest pains. In early December 1827, she went to Paris without Casimir, escorted by Jules de Grandsagne, Stéphane's brother. The ostensible purpose of the visit was to seek medical advice, and Aurore apparently did consult several specialists. None of them found anything definitive. As it happened, Stéphane was also in Paris. She had kept up with his activities through Hippolyte himself, who rented a pied-à-terre on the rue de Seine, spending considerable time in the capital. Her brother had reported that the ambitious young scientist was "working himself to death" on a projected People's Library, which was eventually to consist of two hundred small volumes on every subject needed for a working man's or working woman's self-education. Together, Aurore and Stéphane visited the Jardin des Plantes, famed for its library and lectures and now school to the self-taught scientist. They slipped into their old intimacy. She kept putting off her return to Nohant, arriving home finally on December 21.

Nine months later, on September 13, 1828, Aurore gave birth to a daughter, Solange, named for the patron saint of Berry. The birth certificate was signed by the father and Aurélien de Sèze, visiting as a friend of the family. Aurore claimed that the baby was born before term. The child was given the name Dudevant, but as would become clear from Casimir's deposition during the couple's separation proceedings, he was aware from the beginning that his wife had gone to Paris to meet Stéphane, the probable father of Solange.

Solange's cradle proved the grave of her parents' marriage. In the next months, Madame Dudevant found reasons to spend more time in Paris—alone. When she took Maurice, he was parked with friends, while his mother skipped off to Bordeaux to renew her friendship—no longer platonic—with Aurélien de Sèze.

Then, one day in December 1830, Aurore was looking for something in her husband's desk when she found a packet of papers addressed to her. Ignoring the injunction that it was not to be opened until after Casimir's death, she was horrified by what she read: With his fear of confrontation, the aggrieved husband used this "testament" to enumerate every instance of his wife's "perversity" toward him, along with his own reactions of rage, not omitting "feelings of contempt for my character," Aurore recalled.

"To live with a man who neither respects nor trusts his wife is a living death" she wrote to Jules Boucoiran, Maurice's tutor and her new confidant. She had made up her mind "swiftly and irrevocably." She was moving to Paris. The children would remain at Nohant. And she wanted her allowance sent to her. This first round of demands was purely a negotiating strategy: She had no intention of leaving the children or Nohant. And it worked. Terrified, Casimir agreed to her real plan: Aurore would alternate three months in Paris—without the children—with three months in Nohant. She would continue to receive from him three thousand francs annually in allowance. The door had opened halfway. Aurore could leave without stepping into the void.

6

Rebel into Writer

When Aurore arrived in Paris on January 6, 1831, she was no longer a schoolgirl, a visitor, or an overwhelmed young wife and mother. She came as an independent woman, on her own and with a small income to spend as she liked.

Independent, did not, however, mean alone. Six months before, during the first anxious days of the July Revolution, a group of Aurore's Berrichon friends, all men and all younger than she, congregated at Nohant, sharing the news that trickled south, in bits and pieces, from Paris.

It was a strange revolution taking place in the capital—more like a series of neighborhood uprisings, guerrilla actions carried out by home-grown insurgents aided by civilian sympathizers. Their weapons of choice—paving stones torn from the streets to make missiles and barricades—would become synonymous with radical Paris for the next 150 years. The rebels themselves were skilled laborers, factory workers, and students. But their hatred for Charles X and the Bourbon Restoration that had ruled France since the last of Napoleon's Hundred Days in 1815 was shared by the middle classes and, most importantly, by the press. "Charles the Simple," as he was dubbed by a reporter, had amply earned the hostility of every class—from bankers to vagrants. The king's first attempt to divert the nation from his own growing unpopularity and France's lost European empire was to attack Algiers—a colonial legacy that still haunts his country. In the next months, this adventure would also drain the regime of troops needed to defend itself. Then, sweeping aside the charter negotiated earlier between representatives of the people and the returning Bourbons, he decided to rule by *ordonnances,* or royal decree. Suspending freedom of the press, he dissolved the newly elected Chamber of Deputies, excluding the commercial bourgeoisie from future elections.

Meanwhile, the economy had sunk to its lowest point in a decade; wages had fallen as prices and unemployment soared. One-third of the population qualified for bread vouchers. Then, on Monday, July 26, 1830, a heat wave enveloped Paris. Factories shut down, freeing workers to take to the streets. This was one revolution, a historian recently noted, that was legitimized in newspaper offices, where forty-three journalists, representing eleven newspapers, signed protests. The next seventy-two hours, mythologized by writers as "the Three Glorious Days," saw six hundred dead and two hundred wounded among civilians, four times the number of royal military casualties. Charles X abdicated the following month, and the House of Orléans, in the person of Louis-Philippe, "the Citizen-King," and his furled umbrella, returned from exile in London.

Communications were so slow between Paris and rural France that anxiety continued well after the fighting was over. For weeks, Aurore had had no word of her mother or other relatives and friends. Thus, she and Casimir had come to depend on the visits of her acolytes, who were in closer touch with the capital. A few of these young men were childhood friends, sons of families that had known her grandmother and father. Hovering in that limbo between student life and careers, they were united, first, by their adoration of Aurore, but also by republican sympathies and artistic ambitions.

A new addition to their ranks, Jules Sandeau, eighteen years old, was a recent law graduate with literary dreams. He and Madame Dudevant, eight years his senior, lost no time in becoming lovers. When Jules returned to Paris, he had Aurore's promise that she would join him.

Where to live posed the immediate problem, with respectability and economy being the main requirements. Hippolyte offered Aurore his pied-à-terre on the rue de Seine as temporary quarters, but relations between the two remained troubled. Her half brother openly sided with her husband, considering Casimir the wronged spouse. At the same time, Hippolyte was honest enough to feel shamed by Aurore's sisterly loyalty to him and by her generosity to his own family. During Hippolyte's frequent trips to Paris, Aurore had taken in his wife, Emilie—so depressed she rarely left her bed—and mothered Léontine, their needy little girl. So Hippolyte had finally offered his "willful" sister a free roof and, more important, a cover address until the end of March. But this came with a price. In early March, two months after her arrival in Paris, Aurore received a letter from 'Polite, twisting the knife of maternal guilt: "The best thing you've ever created is your son; he loves you more than anyone in the world. Watch out, or his tender feelings for you will wither."

Most probably, 31 rue de Seine served only as a mail drop. From the start, Aurore and Jules lived together in a series of furnished rooms until February, when they settled into what was officially Aurore's establishment at 25 Quai des Grands-Augustins, enjoying spectacular views of the Seine and the facade of Notre-Dame.

"I'M EMBARKING on the stormy sea of literature; I have to earn a living" Aurore wrote to a friend.

In fact, her embarkation, with compass needle pointed firmly toward "professional," had been delayed, deferred, and all but suppressed. Her early need to write, later recalled by Sand as a "torment," had become another weapon in the war between her "rival mothers," a conflict so bruising that for most of Aurore's adolescence, a torrent of tales, stories, and even novels was confined to her head.

When she was twelve, her grandmother was so proud of the child's compositions that she had sent the pages to Sophie in Paris, as proof of Aurore's growing mastery—of subject, style, and an ability to reason. But the mother made fun of the girl's literary efforts: Aurore's facility with words and her wide reading were deemed an affront, a display of class superiority, and one more sign that she had gone over to the enemy: "Your pretty little sentences made me laugh out loud," Sophie wrote to her daughter. But there was no mistaking the note of threat under the laughter: "You had better not start talking that way!"

Denying the burden of shame imposed by her mother's mockery, Sand internalized Sophie's judgment, insisting—even thirty years later, "I was not in the least bit mortified by the reception given my poetic effusions. I thought she was absolutely right. . . . I thereafter stopped *writing*, but I never stopped making up stories in my head."

Four years after her mother's dismissal of her writing, distanced from Sophie by the convent walls and safely supported by the Augustinian sisters, she ventured a self-described "novel" in the form of a fairy tale. Then in the late 1820s, Aurore began to write prolifically.* She eased into fiction with the species of hybrid favored by romantic writers and especially by those practitioners of the Gothic style: travel pieces with elements of fantasy ("The Journey of M. Blaise," "The Tale of a Dreamer"). The premise is the traveler who, losing his way, falls into a twilight zone between dream and reality, one peopled with imaginary creatures. But she was also honing the skills that would later serve both her journalism and her fiction. Personal writing, in the form of letters and journals, including actual travel pieces, sharpened her powers of observation and expression, along with her ability to analyze both individual psychology and social structures: marriage, family, community.

---

*Unpublished until recently, most of these early texts, often unfinished sketches, are difficult to date precisely.

She had brought with her to Paris the manuscript of her first novel, *Aimée,* but well before leaving Nohant, she alerted her Paris contacts. Introducing herself in a letter to Felix Pyat, an influential editor and a friend of Jules Sandeau, she described the novel, closing with the coy request that he provide the beginning and end to her neophyte's effort. Then, less than a week after she arrived in the capital, Aurore called on yet another Berrichon literary connection, now firmly established as the cultural czar of Paris.

Louis-Hyacinthe de Latouche, known as Henri, was founding editor of *Le Figaro,* not the present-day newspaper of that name, but a literary journal of satiric bent, whose cachet was due to the taste, skill, and, not least, the industry of its fierce editor. A man of parts, Latouche churned out novels and poetry, forgettable and forgotten. But as he himself recognized, not without bitterness, his real gifts lay in spotting, polishing, and promoting the talent of others. His great discovery was the young Balzac, whose brilliance the editor had recognized from the early chapters of his first novel, *Les Chouans.*

After Aurore's introductory visit, Latouche agreed to hear her read from her fledgling fiction, *Aimée,* at their next meeting, advising her in advance that he intended to be "severe." Forewarned, she was not quite as devastated by his dismissal of the work as "deplorable," since he had also tossed her a few crumbs of encouragement *if* she were willing to work like a dog on her writing. Assuring him fervently of her dedication, Aurore also pressed the feminine advantage. Although she and Sandeau were collaborating on articles for other publications under Jules's name, she decided that she would get much farther with Latouche if she presented herself as a young woman striking out on her own in pursuit of a literary career and who had borrowed a male friend's name out of feminine modesty. Latouche, she observed shrewdly, would be unlikely to help a couple. Indeed, in response to Aurore's immediate needs, he offered her a job; she would be the only woman on the staff of *Le Figaro.*

More adroit still, she managed to solicit help from another Berry literary connection, Latouche's archrival, A.-H. Kératry, while keeping both prima donnas from discovering that she had sought to become the protégée of the other. She described to a friend how she had told Kératry of weeping buckets over his recent potboiler, explaining, "I want his help in selling my little novel."

She was in a period of transition, not even sure at this point what pen name she was using. Informing Jules Boucoiran, Maurice's tutor, that she had had an article accepted by *La Revue de Paris* (probably a story called "La Prima Donna"), she announced this coup as "a huge step forward—the only way to get my new name known, which I can't tell you yet since I don't know what it is myself." Seated at a little desk by the fire—the most coveted spot in Latouche's living room, which also housed his journal and its staff—Aurore churned out short pieces of fiction, bits of reportage, and those fillers, still called *fait divers* in French newspapers, of the man-bites-dog genre. As a recent critic noted, "her apprenticeship was served under the aegis of journalism and the market for fiction, while her beginnings as a writer fell under the sign of production." This rough-and-tumble introduction to the writer's life, what her contemporaries across the Channel would call Grub Street, was grounded in the practical and commercial. She grew up literally taking for granted the worth of words—their equivalent in cash, fees, contracts, royalties—at the farthest remove from the idea of art for art's sake, or making one's mark, or joining the immortals.

Along with exploiting all her connections who could help launch her career, Aurore started feeling her way around the politics of the capital, which was still in postrevolutionary turmoil. Word of a new movement called Saint-Simonianism had intrigued her from afar. The founder was Claude de Saint-Simon, a descendant of the famed Duc de Saint-Simon, the memoirist attached to the court of Louis XIV. One of the Utopian sects, Saint-Simonianism had its roots in revolution—the successive upheavals beginning in 1789 and continuing with the promises and betrayals of the July Revolution of 1830. As set down by Saint-Simon and propagated by his leading disciple, Eugène-Prosper Fromentin ("the Pope"), the protosocialist ideology proposed an end to inherited wealth, encouraged the common ownership of goods, and called for the complete enfranchisement of women, who were seen as men's equal in every sphere. Even God was given a new, androgynous gender. Shared property, along with free love, was integral to the adherents' experiment in communal living in the suburb of Menilmontant.* Meanwhile, Aurore mentioned attending some classes, as well their regular meetings. Her tone was lightly mocking ("I heard the Saint-Simonians, alas!"). For Aurore, distrust of movements and ideology always trumped an attraction to the ideas themselves.

*Reports of orgies led to the society's suppression by the government in 1832.

At this point, dipping a toe into Saint-Simonian waters was simply part of Aurore's determination to see and experience everything the capital had to offer, especially the remnants of revolution. In February, after witnessing the sack of the archiepiscopal palace of Saint-Germain l'Auxerre by a mob, she wrote excitedly: "I don't have to tell you that I went everywhere and saw everything with my own eyes. I love the noise, the storm, even the danger and if I were selfish, I'd hope to watch a revolution every morning, it's so much fun! Moreover, as I haven't got a penny, I've nothing to lose but my life." From there, she rushed off to the Chamber of Deputies: "You've never seen anything as ridiculous or absurd as their goings on." The irrelevance of the latter, she was quick to observe, was hardly unrelated to the constant unrest that just as often erupted into riots.

"Revolution is as permanent here as the Chamber itself," she reported. "And we're just as light-hearted, encircled by bayonets, riots and ruins—as if we were in the midst of peace." On another level, though, she realized that her larky view of working-class violence was restricted to the privileged, those who, like herself, had no direct experience of privation or of being silenced by power. Now, like all sheltered young radicals, she tried to lose her innocence. When *Le Figaro* was seized by the king for "seditious tendencies," she lofted the hope that her mocking articles on street fighting, which revealed how outbreaks were incited by the national guard, would land her in jail. Primed for prison, she was disappointed when the government dropped the case. Already, Aurore had acquired a sophisticated view of the value of serving time, and she had coolly appraised the boost a stay in prison could have given her career. "What a shame! A political condemnation would have made my fame and fortune!" she complained. Barely two months after her arrival in the capital, she was poised to drive a brand-new engine of literary success: publicity.

As eagerly as she embraced progress in her political and social ideas and in her emerging sense of herself as a free woman, where her writing was concerned, she clung to a safely traditional past. Already, she had pieces rejected as too sugary and sentimental. Tastes were changing. But Aurore's idealized view of what art ought to show would never really change. Sneering at Balzac, who was forcing his contemporaries to look at themselves and their society as it was, she dismissed his realism as sensationalism, as pandering to readers who "craved novelty . . . to make sure it's new, it has to be ugly. Balzac is all the rage for painting a soldier's passion for a tiger and that of an artist for a castrato. Good God, what's this all about?" Still, she wanted a taste of his success badly enough that she would try to depict her world à la Balzac. "So monsters are the fashion. Fine, let's do monsters!"

Aurore's own passion for her "little Jules," her lover and now collaborator, was everything the romantic Madame Dudevant had fantasized about in her Nohant isolation. Although Madame Bovary had yet to be created, Aurore was an Emma Bovary whose dreams had come true. In Paris, she and Jules were the only couple in their rowdy circle of single young men; followed by the envious glances of their companions, they would dash away from group outings, rushing up the stairs to their garret rooms to make love. Letters exchanged by the pair have been lost, but long, intimate pages scrawled by Aurore during the periods she spent with her family in Nohant, to Émile Renault, a young medical student and Sandeau's best friend, reveal worries about Jules. He was misunderstood by those who lacked his finer qualities, she fretted. Many found him cold, arrogant even, when he was really hypersensitive and self-protective. Worse, she wrote, Jules's spells of self-doubt and depression, leaving him unable to work, made him appear lazy. This being the gossip, their collaborative writing was already assumed to be largely the work of his nameless but more productive lover.

According to her arrangement with Casimir, Aurore's three months of freedom in Paris were to be followed by equal time in Nohant. As always, the mother and free spirit were in conflict. She missed the children, and her constant injunctions to their tutor, Jules Boucoiran, that he should speak to them often of their mother reflect her fears that she would be forgotten. Her letters to Maurice, with their pleas to write more, invariably close with the promise of alluring gifts, like a hussar's uniform, bribes that reveal the guilt of the prodigal parent. How could she know, moreover, what their father was telling them in reply to questions about her absence?

Returning to Nohant early in April, Aurore's first days of reunion with Maurice, eight, and Solange, a plump three year old, were a feast of love. With constant hugs and kisses, they expressed their delight in having her home, while she felt raptures of joy mingled with relief. In a few weeks, however, the drama of mommy's reappearance had yielded to children's normal reaction of taking parental presence for granted. Now, Aurore needed reassurance from Paris. Writing to Jules's friends, she begged them to confirm that he was well, eating properly, and not too depressed by her absence, but also that all her worshippers missed her as much as she did them. She had no one to talk to; she felt bored and unappreciated. At the same time, she bristled at their suggestions that she simply move up the date of her return to Paris: Didn't they understand how torn she felt? Couldn't they sympathize with her constant effort to balance her own needs against the claims of family? Had they forgotten the irreplaceable role of a mother in her children's lives?

Today, this conflict is all too familiar, but Aurore's tone—high-flown, melodramatic, self-righteous—discourages sympathy. Still, no one can question the authenticity of her feelings. She was then, and would remain, roiled by warring claims, her own and those of others. Her newfound passion for writing, her ambitions to succeed in the great world, her love for Jules, and her pleasure in the carefree, masculine world of student bohemia—theatre parties, music, dinners, politics, and, not least, the sexual freedom—acted on her like a drug. She could be anyone—or no one. She now wore the latest style in male student attire: long, gray fitted coat with matching waistcoat and trousers. And her favorite possession of all, a pair of hobnailed boots, enabled her to fly around Paris in all weather and, best of all, unnoticed in her disguise.

At the same time, she loved and missed the children. For Aurore, the image of herself as the perfect mother would always be crucial to her identity. She was proud that she had sewn the layettes, pureed the baby food, administered the enemas and medicines, taught her children their letters—herself. Then there was Nohant: both sanctuary and prison. She resented the place for forcing on her the constraints and obligations that, limiting her freedom, made her want to flee, yet it was also her only home, cherished for its reassuring continuity. The house, the land, the servants, the neighbors—these surroundings offered all that was familiar, secure, and beloved from her childhood.

In Nohant, now, she longed for Paris. Impatiently, she deputized the reliable Regnault to find a real apartment—as opposed to furnished rooms—for her and Jules. The essential requirement was a back room, preferably with a separate entrance, from which her lover could make a hasty escape or at least be safely hidden should Casimir appear unannounced. The apartment their friend found on Quai Saint-Michel, a corner building with a balcony overlooking the river, met all their needs but one: economy. Its bare rooms needed furnishing. Everything—curtains, carpets, mantelpiece, kitchen equipment—had to be purchased. Jules didn't have a sou, and Aurore's allowance barely covered everyday expenses. Having bought everything on credit, she now begged both Casimir and Hippolyte to obtain a loan for her—no matter how—to cover her debts. When neither took any action, she became increasingly desperate—and angry. According to her brother, he received a letter from Aurore threatening that if he and Casimir continued conspiring to make her miserable, to deprive her of her children, to keep her in perpetual poverty, she would drown herself. She told him to warn Casimir, lest he, too, have her death on his conscience. Her tone was so hysterical, her brother told Casimir, he was afraid she meant it.

Finally, Aurore managed to borrow five hundred francs from her friend and Berry deputy, François Duris-Dufresne. (This fair-minded man probably saw the loan as repayment for help the Dudevants had given in getting him elected.) Borrowing another two hundred from her editor Latouche, she would just make it through the summer. She informed Casimir that she had signed for the loans herself on the assumption that he would cover both debts (the larger falling due in six months) since, according to their agreement, the new Parisian pied-á-terre would be used by him when Aurore was in Nohant. Their informal arrangement reflected Aurore's hope that one parent would always be at home, while the couple would spend as little time as possible under the same roof.

In September, when husband and wife were both obliged to be in residence in Nohant, Aurore took the occasion to make flagrant assertion of her sexual freedom. Leaving her friend and neighbor Gustave Papet to stand sentry, or rather to lie down, since he was assigned to a ditch in the garden, Aurore received Jules in her bedroom. There, with the added excitement of Casimir "sleeping like a pig in his room nearby," the lovers fell on each other in a "rage of pleasure; nothing could have torn us apart. Even in the midst of our wildest transports," she assured Gustave, they blessed their friend, who far below, risked getting shot or, at the very least, suffering a severe attack of rheumatism. Smugly, Aurore enumerated the physical evidence of her lovemaking: "I must be insane," she crowed to Regnault, her confidant in their group. "I'm covered with bites and bruises; so weak I can hardly stand I'm in such a frenzy of joy." In a burst of polymorphous lust, she added, "If you were only here, I'd bite you too until blood flowed, just so you could share a little of our savage raptures."

In a state of sexual delirium, in a torment of impatience for more, and wracked by throbbing palpitations, she still managed to keep her work schedule. This same night, she told Regnault, she had found time to make major changes in the manuscript of their first full-length novel, the collaborative *Rose and Blanche.* Nothing would ever stop Aurore from writing.

7

"Madame Dudevant Has Died in Paris . . ."

"IDEAS POUR OUT OF YOU in a torrential rush, wide as a river," Sand's great friend Flaubert told her in 1866, at the end of her career and when his was just beginning. The younger writer's remarks were no valedictory; with her first novels—five alone published between 1832 and 1835—George Sand burst into unstoppable storytelling.

Flaubert had gone straight to the beating heart of Sand's endless invention of plot and character: Ideas propelled her fictions, driving her characters—men, but especially women—to feel and to act.

Indiana, the first novel she wrote without Jules Sandeau, tracks the careening slide of a miserable marriage. Sold to her elderly husband, Colonel Delamare, a retired Napoleonic officer turned businessman, Indiana, an orphaned Creole, is banished from her tropical Eden, the Ile d'Orléans (now La Réunion). Arriving in France with her mulatto maid, Noun, the exiled Indiana begins her legal imprisonment as the wife of a coarse and brutal profiteer. Her only relief from the pain of a loveless union is the occasional visit from her English cousin Sir Ralph Brown. Then, passion enters her life in the form of a handsome, brilliant, and predatory neighbor, Ramon de Ramière. First seducing Noun (in Indiana's bed) and promising to marry her, Ramon decides that the mistress is bigger game than the maid and lays siege to the lonely wife. Abandoned, Noun drowns herself. Her tragedy is only the beginning. Ramon, soon tiring of his latest conquest and seeking an advantageous marriage to further his political ambitions, abandons Indiana. When the colonel's business ventures fail, the Delamares leave France and the reconciled pair tries to begin a new life in her tropical childhood home. But Delamare's sudden death renews false promises from her old lover. Indiana is lured back to Paris, where she is dismissed again by Ramon. Destitute and ill, she moves from sordid boardinghouse to charity hospital.

These are but a few of the narrative twists in the novel—one of Sand's shortest—until the happy ending: Indiana is rescued by her rich, adoring cousin, Sir Ralph, who was waiting in the wings with silent passion. Fleeing the corruption of the Old World, the couple settles in Ile d'Orléans. But a sense of sin haunts them. Atop a waterfall, they pledge their love with a suicide pact. Then, in a change of heart, they renounce death, deciding instead to dedicate their lives and wealth to the native population.

A postcolonial soap opera, *Indiana* is both daringly modern and maddeningly dated—a conflict that would color all its author's future fiction. Male readers and reviewers especially were shattered by Sand's dissection of marriage as a prison for both spouses. Deconstructing the contractual unions as market-based mergers that turned women into "domestic animals," she shows that men, too, are victims of these unholy alliances. Colonel Delamare's death is caused in no small degree by the hatred, fear, and contempt he inspires in his captive wife.

As an engaged journalist-turned-novelist, Sand unveiled a larger political agenda. Indiana's perfidious lover Ramon is also a careerist job seeker who stops at nothing to obtain patronage from the new Restoration government, while Colonel Delamare's ruin is tied to the rampant speculation encouraged by the July Monarchy. Of Ramon's two credulous victims, the white woman must share the burden of her servant's suicide—possibly the first depiction of racial guilt in a novel.

After her frontal assault on marriage, this most sacred of Christian institutions, the fledging novelist pulled back on issues of sex. Her heroine is not technically an adulteress until her husband is safely dead. Even then, both she and her cousin, Sir Ralph, are racked by guilt—the basis of their suicidal plan. Scenes of unnerving realism: Indiana, delirious, wandering the slums of Paris in the rain, look ahead to Emma Bovary, Anna Karenina, even Jean Rhys. Unlike these heroines, Indiana never pays the ultimate price for choosing passion over duty, for demanding sexual fulfillment over a loveless marriage: Her knight stands, literally, at the ready, offering love with security. Her sins—if such they be—have been washed away, and her sufferings redeemed by the return to an Eden, lost and found.

With her first novel, the neophyte had discovered a new formula that all but guaranteed critical and commercial success: a skillful mix of controversy and convention, romance and rebellion. Mr. Right isn't dead; he's the strong, silent cousin next door. Unlike the other later heroines, Indiana's (read Aurore's) revolt against a sterile marriage will be rewarded. Her dreams of a perfect union—sexual, spiritual, companionable—will not destroy her; instead, they will be realized within a larger Utopian contract: service to humanity in a primitive paradise.

Before she could speak in her own voice, Aurore needed a name of her own. And while *Indiana* was in the press, she sought advice on how to launch the "new" author. Neither of her family names would do: Her mother, Sophie, was as horrified by the prospect of a Dupin woman's name on a book cover as was Aurore's mother-in-law, Baroness Dudevant. With no role in the writing of Aurore's first novel, Jules Sandeau wanted no credit, not even the vestigial initial "J." But their literary godfather, Latouche, pointed out that "Sand" already enjoyed recognition and success. He advised Aurore to keep the one-syllable half, and choose another initial or first name.

Sand would later claim that she fixed on "George" in tribute to her own roots in Berry and to the most famous classical writer's homage to his rural source, Virgil's *Georgics.* This suggests a lofty, after-the-fact, literary imprimatur. Aurore's own English connections seem more plausible, starting with her passion for the poetry of another poet, George Gordon, Lord Byron, along with the two years she had spent in the convent of the English Augustinian Ladies—the "happiest of my life." Here, she had acquired her knowledge of the language, but more important, this bastion of Britishness, in providing a refuge from her warring mother and grandmother, had allowed the adolescent to become herself. Thus, with her first full-length work of fiction, she was reborn. The poetic, romantic Aurore (a name that means "dawn" and that, coincidentally, was the name of Byron's illegitimate daughter) became matey, hands-in-the-pocket "George," spelled not in the French style, but in the English, without the *s*. What better tribute to her first experience of freedom than to choose, in inventing a new self, a name that invoked England's patron saint and its most infamous poet?

WITH THE PUBLICATION OF *Indiana,* George Sand, like Lord Byron, awoke to find herself famous. The novel appeared in bookstores at the end of April 1832, in the worst days of the cholera epidemic and, perhaps helped by all the bad news, garnered immediate notice. Reviews sprouted everywhere, outdoing one another in superlatives; the only exception was the Olympian whose godlike status was apparently challenged. Displaying his envy like stigmata, Victor Hugo demanded, "If *Indiana* is the 'masterpiece of the century'; what does that make *Notre Dame de Paris,* a whore?"

Readers and critics alike—the latter all male—joined in the belief that the novel held a dark mirror up to contemporary life and revealed where foundations of the past were crumbling; some focused on the author's exposure of the unbridgeable chasm between men and women. In writing the "story of modern passion," one writer noted, Sand had also told, for the first time, "the true story of women's hearts, hearts which alone have retained their primitive passions while men have lost theirs. . . ." The most acute reviewers caught the androgynous element of both style and content. Both husband and lover are, in their own ways, villains; they define the masculine as bullying and obtuse or predatory and duplicitous. Sir Ralph, on the other hand, if not feminized, is neutered. As a blood relation, he plays a role that remains fraternal and protective; the pair returns to the island of their birth as brother and sister, a disabused version of the beloved eighteenth-century French idyll *Paul et Virginie.*

Besides *Indiana*'s complicated gendering of passion and innocence, of both marriage and adultery as the grave of love, critics noted stylistic disjunctions in the writing, a "delicate," feminine sensibility with assertive—even harsh—passages that revealed a masculine mind at work. Thus, George Sand's first independent work was read as yet another collaboration.

Virtually all commentary seized on the word *modern* both to describe the triangulated sexual relations in the novel and to find a synonym for the moral upheavals of the characters' troubled times. The newly christened George Sand was compared to Balzac in "his" unblinking exposure of "lost illusions."

Exalted to sudden fame spiced with notoriety, and facing reporters, editors, and fans literally lined up at her door, Aurore felt only distress, she claimed. Reasonably enough, she counted on being able to continue writing with the freedom from expectation conferred by obscurity. Discreet—except when she chose not to be—she felt trapped in the glare of sudden celebrity. Intensely personal, *Indiana,* like its author's life, was a work in progress, and the author was alarmed to see the novel depersonalized, cast as both autopsy, which lay bare the pathology of the age, and cure, one radical enough to raise the corpse.

In Paris, suddenly, there was no place to hide. Aurore had become George Sand to thousands of readers; from now on, friends, lovers, and soon even her children would call her "George." When she left Paris with Solange on July 30, 1832, she returned to Nohant another woman. This new self was born of success: She was independent now in the most basic economic meaning of the word. *Indiana* quickly sold out three printings, earning an unheard-of twenty-four hundred francs for its author. Although she hesitated before the demands of journalistic deadlines, she signed a contract with a new publisher, François Buloz, to produce thirty-two pages every six weeks for his *Revue des Deux Mondes.* She could now count on a guaranteed income of four thousand francs a year, over and above what fiction she might sell. With so many ideas in her head, George had barely unpacked at Nohant when she began work on her next novel.

Valentine launched the fifty-five works of fiction that would be set in Sand country, the land around Nohant, which the author renamed the Black Valley. Her pages evoking its gentle, "intimate" landscape, the narrow paths arched with flowering branches, the streams trickling by the side of roads whose steep embankments "could only be climbed by a small child or donkey," count among the loveliest Sand would ever write. This first story takes on the issue of social class from several points of view. Principally, *Valentine* hinges on the drama of an aristocratic young woman in love with a youth of peasant origins. Along the way, the author elaborates a slashing satire of nouveau riche farmers whose aspirations to gentility result in caricatures of consumption and bad taste. Their worst sin, though, consists in raising their children to ape the leisure classes: indulging a spoiled daughter and an adopted son—the latter overeducated in Paris to become a useless aesthete (a phenomenon the author had clearly observed firsthand among her transplanted Berrichon acolytes). If Sand also exposes her own ingrained snobbery—peasants should know their place—her comic gifts are revealed as acute and, in terms of her vast future production, sadly underutilized.

More than momentum lashed George to her grandmother's desk—actually a chest of drawers, with a drop leaf that served as a writing surface. Buoyed by the success of *Indiana,* she had returned to Nohant armed with a contract from her new publisher for the novel in progress: The freshly baptized George Sand now emerged fully formed as a tough negotiator; she had sold *Valentine* for three thousand francs—double the money she had received for *Indiana*. This, together with her four-thousand-franc contract with Buloz for journalistic commentary, meant that she would no longer need to beg Casimir for advances on her allowance or plead with Hippolyte to guarantee her loans. In terms of earned income alone, George was now a rich woman.

Two contracts, double commitments, and impressive earnings further justified her frenzied work schedule. Her nocturnal habits also provided Casimir with an ego-saving cover for their now officially separate sleeping quarters. George's small study-bedroom was so crowded with writing materials, art supplies for her watercolors and drawings, and her collections of minerals and plants, there was no room for a bed; its human inhabitant slept in a hammock above the disorder below. George's pet cricket was not so lucky. Invisible in a room whose every surface was covered, he was crushed by a maid closing the window, but his remains joined the dried flowers and fossils collected by his mourning mistress.

If conjugal relations with Casimir were not missed, neither was Jules's presence in her bed; the days of wild, clandestine passion, with their friend on guard below, were over. There had been stormy scenes in Paris: George's sudden celebrity had reduced Jules from the lethargic to the catatonic. Their friends blamed her for his decline. Now, to George's relief, he was visiting his family in Parthenay in the Deux-Sèvres department. The decks were cleared; George was free to work, an occupation that usually produced her happiest state of mind. Instead, by late summer, she was paralyzed by her own crisis of discouragement and suffered from "spleen," a miasma of boredom and melancholy to which romantic artists were especially prone. Whether through inexperience or the high of success, she seems to have underestimated the burden of new writing commitments—and their deadlines. Claims of the Nohant household proved more of a drain on time and energy than did the single life in Paris. She was wracked by mysterious money worries. George would always spend more than she earned, and on the basis of contracts just signed, future as well as current income seems to have already been spent.

News of Jules's desolation was not long in reaching Nohant. How he longed for her return, when she would make "autumn pudding" for him in their cozy garret rooms! Guilt-stricken, she made a flying trip to Paris. Once she arrived, their troubles melted away; everything was glorious—even better than before, George proclaimed. But not for long. Dropping by unexpectedly at the rue de l'Université *garçonnière* she had earlier rented for Jules as a retreat from the relentless scratching of her quill, George allegedly found the inconsolable lover in bed with his laundress. Although George and Jules continued to see each other for the next six months, they were no longer a couple. In late October, Sand gave up the Quai Saint-Michel aerie for more spacious quarters with fewer stairs, taking over the lease for nearby 19 Quai Malaquais from their friend Latouche. Not as sunny as the old rooms, the "Blue Mansard," as George baptized it, barely reached above the taller trees in the gardens of the École des Beaux-Arts below. But she reveled in its greatest attraction: Except when she chose to receive visitors, it was hers alone.

On December 1, 1832, George, accompanied by Solange, left Nohant for Paris, where they would remain until the following August. Nine days after their departure, her novella *La Marquise* was published in the *Revue de Paris.* A first-person narrative in the form of confession, the heroine is another aristocratic young woman, sold into marriage at age sixteen. Her elderly husband, a cynical noble of great wealth, has the grace to die soon thereafter, leaving his beautiful young widow faced with the expectation that she will remarry suitably or enjoy a series of lovers—or, ideally, do both. Brutalized by her husband's cold sensuality, the marquise feels only revulsion—physical and moral—toward all men, she tells her male listener and narrator, allowing that the "fault" may be her own. Then, for the first time in her life, the marquise falls in love, "losing her head completely" and at first sight. The object of her passion, she notes coyly, "is neither the King of France, nor the Dauphin [the future Louis XVI], but an actor!"

One fateful evening at the theatre, Lélio, a young Italian performer, appears onstage, and the marquise is instantly besotted. Confiding her passion to her female companion, the lovelorn aristocrat is warned against ever speaking of the player in such tones to anyone else. "For a well-born woman," the friend says, "an actor is not a man."

Even playing a man, Lélio is a failure. Small and frail, he is deemed too feminine to fill the heroic roles of Racine and Corneille. Worse, his voice, the actor's most important instrument, is "high and piercing" rather than deep and masculine, his interpretations "too restrained" (ladylike?) to meet the larger-than-life expectations of the classical stage.

To avoid attracting attention, the marquise (like her creator) disguises herself as a man and, yielding to her obsession, shows up every night at the theatre, where she watches her beloved from a special hiding place. Inevitably, Lélio becomes aware of her hungry gaze and magnetic presence; he recognizes the lover he has been waiting to meet. Their first encounter is disappointing. Instead of a twin soul, the marquise finds a coarse, uneducated actor. But soon, her passion for the genius transforms the man: The negligible, effeminate player fulfills his latent (male) greatness and heroic possibility—in life as in art. He grows to fill the hero's role. Now, he implores the marquise for another rendezvous—their last. She agrees, still reminding him that their love is impossible, but not because of his lowly rank and her exalted status. She renounces Lélio because *she* is unworthy of *him;* she has been defiled by the sexual possession of another, lesser man, her late husband.

A month after the publication of *La Marquise,* Sand met and fell instantly in love with the sensation of the romantic theatre, Marie Dorval. The two women became inseparable, upstaging all other Parisian gossip. They were seen everywhere together. During the day, George was instantly recognizable in her long, gray coat, matching waistcoat and trousers, stovepipe hat, as she strolled arm in arm with the tiny, fair-haired Marie, wasp-waisted, bonneted, and crinolined. At night at the theatre, George, lounging in the box reserved for friends and distinguished guests, sported evening dress, a new black cutaway, and dazzling shirtfront: "white tie and tails."

"Madame Dudevant just died in Paris," she crowed to a Berry friend, "but George Sand is famous as a dashing man about town."

8

"Lélia"

IT BEGAN WITH A FAN LETTER. Like all her contemporaries, George was addicted to the theatre. Under the July Monarchy, the stage was at the center of Paris cultural life, delivering excitement and novelty and, above all, talent. Victor Hugo, Alexandre Dumas, Alfred de Vigny, Alfred de Musset—all set their sights on writing successful plays and, not incidentally, on making real money. With her first incandescent performances, Marie Dorval became their muse and the incarnation of the romantic heroine: beautiful, fragile, suffering.

She burst into Sand's life with the same meteoric grace. Flinging open the door of the garret apartment on 19 Quai Malaquais, Marie swooped inside and, throwing her arms around a startled George, who was sitting over bowls of breakfast coffee with Jules, declared, "It's me! Here I am!"

Her appearance was unannounced, but not unexpected.

Mesmerized by the artist on stage, George had written to Madame Dorval to say how much the actor's genius meant to her as a writer. Would she call on her one day? And here she was! Jules was just as enchanted by Marie, and he compared her slender, supple form to the swaying plume on her hat. "You could comb the universe without finding a feather as light and graceful as the one she discovered. It must have descended towards her through the law of affinities, falling from the wing of a fairy in flight." But Jules was only one of many who, trying to summon the spell of Marie's charm, fell into bad poetry.

Born out of wedlock in 1798, Marie Thomase-Amélie-Delauney, the child of strolling players, was pushed out of a theatrical trunk onto makeshift stages as soon as she could talk. At fifteen, she married a fellow actor, a Monsieur Allan, known as Dorval, and when he died a few years later, she was left with only his name and three little daughters. She remarried a Monsieur Merle, playwright, journalist, and, most important, a husband who, in exchange for being supported by his wife, looked the other way in matters other than money.

Dorval's acting style, characterized by simplicity and pathos, launched her as the darling of the boulevard, shorthand for the popular theatre whose headquarters was the Saint-Martin. Located in a working-class district, the theatre was traditionally associated with melodramas featuring scenery-chewing emotional displays or broad comedy. Marie's most famous lover, the aristocratic poet Alfred de Vigny, probably helped transform her career; when she and Sand met, Marie had just been anointed the new star in that firmament of talent devoted to classical and contemporary literary repertoire, the state-supported Comédie

Française. Here, her only rival was the aging tragedienne, Mademoiselle Mars, whose declamatory style harkened back to another era. When both performers costarred in Beaumarchais's *Marriage of Figaro,* Sand had written a review contrasting Mars's mannered artifice with Marie's naturalness and grace.

Dorval's specialty became the hugely popular historical plays by Hugo and Alexandre Dumas. Her most famous vehicle was Victor Hugo's drama *Marion de Lorme.* Based on the life of the seventeenth-century courtesan, Hugo's play, in turn, had been adopted from the historical novel *Cinq-Mars,* written by Alfred de Vigny, Dorval's lover. The Paris theatre was a small, if not to say incestuous, place.

A long-running argument among Sand scholars concerns the relationship between the gender-bending novella, *La Marquise,* and George's passionate involvement with Marie Dorval. Those who maintain that similarities between Sand's art—in this instance, her tale of a noblewoman who falls in love with an actor seen only on the stage—and her life are coincidence point out that the fiction was published in December 1832, a month before Sand and Dorval met in mid-January 1833. But Sand herself recalled that she had first seen Dorval in *Marion de Lorme* (the performance that prompted her letter to the actress). Hugo's weepie premiered in 1831, when Sand, like her heroine, could have been smitten by Marie on stage and before the actress's famous visit to the writer. We can only imagine the effect on George—as on the rest of the audience—when Marie/Marion, the courtesan who counted Cardinal Richelieu among her protectors, now enamored of a peasant lad, proclaims, "Love has given me a new virginity."

Among their contemporaries, no one doubted that George and Marie were lovers; each woman's friends warned her against the sapphic reputation of the other. Sand's notoriety stemmed from her cross-dressing and cigar-smoking; Marie was known to have been involved with younger actresses. After Marie's death in 1849, her daughter destroyed whatever letters from Sand to her mother she could get her hands on. And since George was by far the most voluble of the pair, Dorval's legacy of letters written by Sand to the actress was by far the larger portion of their correspondence. Sand seems to have written to her friend daily over the next year. What does survive—thirty-two letters from each woman—offers glimpses, rather than certainties, about the nature of their relations. Among the papers that escaped the flames are brief notes that, before the age of the telephone, served only to arrange the time and place of meetings. Still, even from these few scrawled lines, it's clear that George was the supplicant, pleading for attention and begging to see Marie, offering to visit the actress at her apartment at rue Meslay (a few doors down the same street where Aurore Dupin had been born twenty-nine years earlier), or merely to sit with her in her dressing room before a performance. Other notes, promising privacy with no interruptions, urge Marie to stay the night at Quai Malaquais.

Even allowing for the actor's fixed commitments—rehearsals, performances, and tours, which left little free time—Dorval seems to have been a dodgy lover. One of Sand's few long letters to have survived is a cry of despair. Marie had taken off without giving George any notice that she was leaving Paris and with no word of her whereabouts or date of her return. "Where are you?

What's happened to you? I've searched every newspaper but haven't seen a single notice of any appearances. . . . I know that wherever you are, my beautiful angelic one, you're being admired and adored by all, but I don't know where that is. . . . Why were you so cruel, leaving without saying good-bye to me, without telling me where you were going so that I can run after you? Leaving without a single word hurt me terribly. I was in the lowest imaginable state, I could only conclude that you didn't love me any more and I've been bawling like a donkey. Since you left, I can't even count the friends who've tried to persuade me that you're not worth loving. Can you believe it! People I hardly know and who've never even met you have said—and even written to me—that you've betrayed me! . . . But their idiocies brought me to my senses," George insisted.

"I keep telling myself that you couldn't have forgotten me, that you just didn't have the time to see me, and that I should have come by to see you. What kind of friendship is it that fears being indiscreet, that stands on ceremony or keeps score of who visits whom. I'm just an idiot. Please forgive me . . . Now, I want to join you for a few days. But where are you? Where should I go? Will I be a nuisance? Well, I don't care! I'll try to be less moody than usual. If you're sad, I'll be sad. If you're happy, here's to joy! One line from you and I'm off. If you're otherwise engaged, or if I'm de trop for whatever reason, just send me to work in another room. Let's not listen to anyone who tells us not to trust each other. . . . Nothing can stop me from being with you—not even cholera—or another lover!"

George's anguish over Marie's unannounced departure was no act. Frantic, she now swallowed her humiliation and wrote to

Vigny, asking for Marie's whereabouts. Sand must have been aware that the poet, archconservative and jealous lover that he was, loathed George. But she could not have been prepared for his arrogant "incivility" (as she reported to Dorval). Refusing to address her personally, Vigny sent an icy message through their mutual friend, the critic Gustave Planche, noting that Marie's theatrical itinerary had been published in the Parisian entertainment broadsheet *Le VertVert,* which, had Sand troubled to read it, could have told her that Marie was now performing in Laon, with future engagements in Sens, Caen, and Soissons.

At some point, Vigny also read Sand's letter to Marie. (Perhaps that seductive charmer, playing one lover against the other, showed or gave it to him.) In the margin, next to the date and George's distinctive signature, Vigny scrawled in pencil: "Forbade Marie to reply to this Sapho [sic] who is harassing her!"

It's been said that the crucial question to be asked about sexual obsession is the degree to which its object summons an elusive parent. Seen in this light, there are arresting similarities between Dorval and Sophie Dupin, the unreliable mother who had also aspired—if unsuccessfully—to a theatrical career. With her small, heart-shaped face fringed by ringlets, Marie bore a striking resemblance to the mercurial Sophie. A creature of instinct, the barely literate Dorval shared a primitive religiosity with the mother and, as it turned out, with the daughter as well. Surrounded by freethinking rationalists, Marie's and George's faith was their dirty secret and one of their deepest bonds. Confirming her maternal role, Dorval, six years older than George, also served as confidante about her younger friend's relations with the men in her life. And we have no reason to assume that

Dorval ever took any vows to forsake all others—of either gender, as witness her ongoing, operatically tumultuous affair with the married Vigny.

Sand's swaggering self-portrait as a "dashing man about town" says as much about her provocative new image as it does about any fixed sexual preferences. In her relations with Marie Dorval, George also displays for the first time a new self-consciousness. She revels in her role as a public person, a celebrity whose private life is fodder for general dissection, or at the least, talk within the confines of that large, contentious family that was Paris bohemia. In the same imploring letter to Marie, abject and self-abasing as it is, George nonetheless makes a bow to an unseen audience—her readers. If Marie quickly answers "Come," it will not only be to George directly that she replies, but to "all of literature."

George's passion for Marie Dorval ran its course. (It's not clear that Sand's feelings were ever shared by the performer.) What ended their intimacy was Marie's compulsive indiscretion. George had succumbed to the persistent attentions of Prosper Mérimée, piqued perhaps by the reputation of the writer, whose sword was said to be mightier than his pen. But Sand's one-night stand with Mérimée had proved a disaster: The "weapon" in question, George confided to Marie, was "a little thing," after all. Dorval couldn't resist passing on this news to her next-door neighbor in rue Lazare, Alexandre Dumas. It might as well have been the next morning's newspaper headline. Stricken, Marie confessed.

George's response was forgiving, but chilly. She wanted Dorval to know that she, George, would be incapable of retelling *her* secrets. Still, their friendship would survive Marie's one little betrayal, Sand assured her. But in truth, it was over.

George had killed off Madame Dudevant; in these same months, she would rid herself—not without pain on both sides—of Jules Sandeau. Her still more public passion for Marie Dorval had also flamed out. Unlucky in love, she now refocused her energies on her career. She successfully negotiated and renegotiated two contracts with separate publishers. Acting as her own literary representative, she had no hesitation in talking tough to publishers, all too accustomed to calling the shots with authors who—unlike Sand, with her independent means—were entirely at their mercy.

When Depuy, the publisher of *Valentine,* managed to lose the entire concluding paragraph (less a single line) of one chapter in the press, he wrote, with barely an apology, asking whether Sand did not want to supply the missing lines for the next edition. "Add whatever you want, my dear publisher," she replied, "and go screw yourself."

She was already on to the next—and far more important—novel.

FROM THE DAY OF ITS PUBLICATION, *Lélia* has been more identified with its author than have any of Sand's other eighty-eight works of fiction. Her first popular twentieth-century biographer, André Maurois, titled his best-selling life of Sand *Lélia* (1953), after his subject's own best-seller. The prolific Maurois has since stood accused of overidentifying the author with her best-known fictional creation, but he was simply following Sand herself, who went even further, pedantically providing "readers' keys" to the principal characters—who all turned out to be George herself, at various stages of her life so far.

Indiana is the novel as Romantic grand opera; its exotic locale, an island in the middle of the Indian Ocean, provides the occasion for love scenes atop a waterfall and wanderings through an inland desert, à la *Manon Lescaut.* When the scene shifts to Paris, Indiana moves from sumptuous ball to sordid boarding-house, foreshadowing Balzac's dramatic polarities of splendor and poverty, but also the stage worlds of *La Traviata* and *La Bohême.*

In contrast, *Lélia* is a cantata. With the barest of settings or costumes, its principal characters are clothed and identifiable largely through their ideas. In place of their musical antecedents whose texts are based on the Old and New Testaments, Sand's principals argue the conflicting gospels—and heresies of her own day.

She was now a seasoned and successful enough author to cannibalize her earlier work. Names and nationalities are recycled: Borrowing from *The Marquise,* Sand refeminizes its hero, Lélio (whom love had earlier promoted to heroic masculine roles), here reborn as Lélia. But readers would also have recognized Byron's Leila, the faithful-unto-death harem slave. Then, reaching back to her first collaborative novel, *Rose and Blanche,* Sand again pairs two sisters: Lélia, her new heroine, is cast as a figurehead of independence who seeks a way to be in the world as a woman refusing the protection of men. After years of separation, she encounters her sister, Pulcherie. Sensual and pleasure-loving, Pulcherie, an actress, needs the applause of an audience to exist, but in her hunger for luxury, she has become a courtesan for sale to the highest bidder. (Was this Sand's revenge on the self-adoring and extravagant Dorval?) In homage to the most famous and popular literary hoax of all time, *The Songs of Ossian* (1762), two of *Lélia*'s male characters are Anglo-Irish: Trenmore (whose name was to have been the novel's original title and who along with Sténio, the teenaged poet, lays claim to Lélia's love), and Magnus, the murderous Celtic priest.

Narrative plays little role in Sand's famous non-novel: Each character has a secret sin, and one by one, the players step forward to offer an aria of confession and to elaborate scenarios of expiation and redemption. A compulsive gambler, Trenmore has robbed an old man, a crime for which he was condemned to five years in forced labor. Pulcherie, the actress and courtesan, has squandered her gifts and sold her body for pleasure. The object of every man's desire, Lélia, Pulcherie's sister and double, is punished for a narcissistic incapacity to love. Her confessional arias include a daring allusion to her sexual frigidity, a symptom that certain contemporaries promptly attributed to the author.

For reasons that may seem mysterious to us now, Sand's "metaphysical" novel and its talky protagonists caused a sensation. With *Indiana* and *Valentine,* readers and critics alike had been led to expect the author's bold reappraisal of sacred institutions like marriage and class. Now that Sand's established success and celebrity had given her a bully pulpit, she appeared to accept Christianity and the existence of God as a given. The real drama plays out in the ways individual characters reconcile the messier earthly passions with love of God, how they grapple with sin, redemption, and the eternal question: What must we do to be saved? Against the background of a Christian cosmology, Sand's secular cantata introduces individual conflict: sex and love, pleasure and conscience, free will and obedience to divine law. Finally, the novel reaches for existential debate between our essential humanity and an identity whose source lies in action alone.

Lélia instantly became one of those books that had to be owned and discussed—if rarely read. No literate Parisian could admit to *not* having an opinion about the issues, the characters, the meaning of the novel, and, not least, the author. Hostile reviews, which unfailingly related the fictional sins to the scandals in Sand's own life, assured the novel's success: *Lélia*'s first edition of fifteen hundred copies—a hefty printing for the time—sold out immediately. Adverse criticism proved to be the best advertising. With so many "modern" ideas undermining the social order, *Lélia* did not just record, but contributed to, the end of civilization.

"Shall I give you my honest opinion?" wrote the critic for *La France litteraire*. "This book strikes me as dangerous . . . it teaches skepticism, the egoism of unhappiness, how to live without our most cherished beliefs, and it's particularly ill-timed now—just as ill-timed as Alfred de Musset's constant denunciations of Christianity."

9

Two for the Road

Lélia's REVIEWER had paired George with her brand-new lover, the poet Alfred de Musset. Only in Paris would a book review do double duty as a gossip column. Although Sand and Musset were cast together into the pit normally reserved for the damned, their sulfurous match had not been made in hell, but by Sand's new friend, promoter, and mentor: the powerful critic Charles-Augustin Sainte-Beuve.

George had certainly traded up her circle of male supporters, but it would be unfair to attribute the change entirely to opportunism or ambition. When Jules Sandeau was dismissed, his friends, George's Berrichon "family" of young men with more dreams than drive, disappeared with him. Predictably, they had sided with Jules, but then, having failed to conquer Paris, they drifted home, to become doctors and lawyers in the provinces.

Henri Latouche, George's first editor, had also been replaced.

His possessive jealousy made it awkward for even the fiercely loyal Sand to maintain their friendship. He issued *samizdats* against all other editors and critics with whom George now enjoyed cordial relations. His mischief making was so notorious that Balzac, another former protégé, warned Sand of the impossibility of maintaining ties with Latouche without forfeiting those of all other literary powers in the capital.

In place of the old guard, George's inner circle now consisted of two men: The critic Gustave Planche, forgotten today, was a force to reckon with in his time. Sand vigorously denied persistent rumors that they were lovers, Planche's personal filthiness being the strongest argument against this gossip. Whatever the case for an intimacy beyond friendship, the critic was every young writer's dream come true: He scrutinized George's contracts, advised her on every aspect of the writing of *Lélia,* then corrected the proofs. Nor did his collaborative role give him pause about reviewing the novel—ecstatically—as soon as it appeared. In the many publications to which he contributed, Planche heralded Sand as a mirror of the age and its New Woman, even persuading her rivals, like Balzac himself, to join George's chorus of admirers. Planche's own character assured that the influence of this brilliant and productive man would wane steadily. Strongly antiromantic, with a rigid critical "system" for evaluating literature and art (almost all of which he found wanting), he fell into a predictable cycle of critical attacks, followed by wrath and retaliation from his victim. Then Planche would respond with bitter claims of persecution. What had he done to deserve such treatment, besides having dismissed as worthless almost all contemporary artists and writers—except George Sand?

Sainte-Beuve, born the same year as Sand, was as diplomatic and political as Planche was savage and self-destructive. Writing mostly for the *Revue des Deux Mondes,* Sainte-Beuve's silky, well-turned phrases often made it a puzzle to know exactly what he thought about the work under review; his criticism thus required the kind of parsing that insured his power.

His personal life was more ambiguous still. Small, bald, plump, and homely, Sainte-Beuve's large head and truncated neck gave him "the air of an elderly child." He suffered from hypospadias, a malformation of penis and foreskin, which affects urination. Although sexual function was not technically impaired, physical embarrassment had clearly taken its toll on Sainte-Beuve's love life. Nonetheless, for several years before he and Sand met, the critic had been part of a triangulated relationship that was the talk of Paris. While his best friend, Victor Hugo, found diversion outside marriage, including (but not limited to) his official mistress, the actress Juliette Drouet, Sainte-Beuve provided quasi-official consolation to the poet's wife, Adèle. Whether the two were actually lovers remains uncertain. He left no doubt, however, about his devotion to the plain and charmless Madame Hugo, who at least protected him against more sexually challenging women—like George Sand. Sainte-Beuve's real satisfactions lay in areas other than the erotic or even romantic: One of the few critics who "had to be read," he was the first professional to merit the title "man of letters," and at thirty, he wielded a sovereign influence over Paris's cultural life. He knew everyone who counted and loved putting people together. And in his many friendships, especially with younger literary aspirants, he played a "governessy" role, that of the "wise older child" who acts as surrogate parent. From all Sand had heard, Saint-Beuve was just what she needed in her life now—confidant, confessor, advisor, publicist, with little likelihood of amorous complications. So George, in her breathtakingly direct fashion, asked the soon-to-be-banished Planche to introduce her to his friend and replacement, Sainte-Beuve, who was duly presented at 19 Quai Malaquais early in 1833.

Like most men, Sainte-Beuve found himself mesmerized by George's dark, "devouring" eyes and her strange, hungry silence (the latter quality especially admired by those who liked to hear themselves talk and who thus interpreted her silence as avid listening). Less accomplished *Parisiennes* might be known for their sparkling conversation and charming feminine chatter; George saved her brilliance for the written word. She felt no need to impress in male company, except by allowing men to shine.

For some time, Sainte-Beuve had had his eye on the young woman behind the changing pseudonyms. He seemed to have taken it as a matter of course that she was now interviewing him for the role of her "director of conscience."

In these months, George felt herself at an impasse: After the runaway success of *Indiana,* she suffered the inevitable letdown, followed by anxiety about the new novel, *Lélia,* then in the press. She was feeling the burden of expectation, the "what next?" syndrome coupled with the knowledge that in the spiteful literary cenacles of Paris lurked those waiting for her to fail. The parting with Sandeau and its bitter aftermath had left her with wounds to heal—alone. There was no erotic equivalent in her life to the smooth apostolic succession from Planche to Sainte-

Beuve. She sank into such profound melancholy that her new confidant's first step was to arrange for George to see Victor Hugo's physician, "Dr. Louis," famous for his "depression" pills.*

Next, turning to his protégée's literary fortunes, Sainte-Beuve prepared to bestow his imprimatur upon *Lélia*; writing in the influential *National,* he would crown it a great "philosophical novel," thus elevating the work to an immediate place in the French canon—where it remains today. Now, however, Sainte-Beuve played a distinctly unphilosophical role in Sand's life. His friendship had hastened the healing process so successfully that George was "ready for love" once again, she said. It fell to him to undertake the job of "talent scout"—to put it politely—finding his friend a new lover.

Sainte-Beuve set to work with a will. He produced several likely candidates, along with letters of recommendation that would be the pride of any intellectual's folder: Lofted as a "virtuous" man, Théodore Jouffroy was a philosopher, teacher, and encyclopedic writer on a variety of subjects. His special interest in psychology would seem to point to a meeting of minds. (Sand found him a "finished man" and thus uninteresting to her, an "unfinished woman.") Sainte-Beuve next presented Alexandre Dumas, whom George already admired from afar. Somehow that did not take, either; perhaps the playwright was already too taken with his own celebrity and success. Then Sainte-Beuve remembered another friend, a younger man, so incomplete as to be

*It would be fascinating to know what medication was prescribed for depression in 1833. Possibly it was morphine based, but this must remain conjecture.

embryonic; he was also beautiful, aristocratic, and troubled, but most important, everyone agreed that his was the talent to watch.

Alfred, Vicomte de Musset seems to have been one of those charmers whose very transparency—looks, speech, manners all of a piece—veils complete mystery. Small and delicate, with wavy golden hair and cornflower-blue eyes, he aspired to a Byronic style, favoring swallowtail jackets with high velvet collars; as a volunteer officer in the national guard, he was often seen in a uniform featuring a gray tunic festooned with gold braid and gilt buttons, paired with sky-blue trousers fitted like a dancer's tights.

At twenty-three, Musset's talents were so boundless that he still hadn't decided where they would lead. He had tried and abandoned law, medicine, and painting. The death of his father in the cholera epidemic of 1832 had left him and an older brother dependent on their mother and her tiny income. If poetry hardly promised to rescue the family finances, the rapture that greeted Musset's first published work, a collection of poems and snippets of historical drama called *Tales from Spain and Italy,* at least suggested that he had found his calling and was about to realize his most original gift, a "romantic irony that softened the raw emotions of youth."

Escorted by Sainte-Beuve to Quai Malaquais, Musset, too, initially failed to win Sand's favor. She dismissed him as "too much of a dandy" and not her type—a phrase that could be carved on the tombstones of most of love's casualties. However much George might disavow her supposedly paternal blue-blooded half in favor of her mother's plebeian blood, Musset's own contradictions intrigued her. His combustible mix of refinement and coarseness (conversation peppered with obscenities), reserve and self-exposure reminded George of no one so much as—herself. She was further titillated by his bad-boy reputation. Wreathed in an aura of nobility and debauch, the poet was known to be addicted to champagne, opium, and whores. Whether as cause or result of these excesses, his nerves were shot.

After the first awkward visit, Alfred called on Sand again—alone. This time, he found a more intimate, less sphinxlike George. Attired in her favorite "at home" costume, a yellow silk Turkish robe, which fell open to reveal billowing trousers, she received her visitor from the floor, where she lounged on pillows, harem-style, smoking a hookah. Kneeling at her feet, Musset traced with an idle forefinger the gold embroidery on George's *babouche,* the daring, backless slippers with upturned toes. His first note, enclosing a drawing of her, was redolent of an eighteenth-century world with its delicious play of persiflage and candor. Between this visit and the following, Alfred's reading of *Indiana* inspired him to poetry. In verses probing the author's own erotic experience, he asked:

Sand, when you wrote this, where did you see
That terrible scene where Noun
Half-naked, abandons herself with Ramon[d] in Indiana's bed?

He could never attain the kind of high-minded friendship she offered—"Too moral for me," he declared. Instead, he suggested that they should be buddies. (Humor was never Sand's strong point; she failed to recognize that he was making fun of her.) But she let him tear one of her gowns to pieces to make a harlequin costume he needed for a ball.

It was too late for teasing. A few more visits elicited a confession.

"George . . . I've got something ridiculously stupid to tell you," Musset wrote. "You're going to laugh in my face, decide that I've been lying all along and show me the door. I'm in love with you. I've been in love with you since my first visit. . . . I know that in telling you this I only stand to lose you as a friend, but the truth is that I'm in terrible pain. I have no will left."

Far from rejoicing in her new conquest, gloating over "fresh meat," as a recent writer has accused her of doing, George was sincerely troubled. Everything she had heard about the poet gave her pause.

Aware of her suspicions, Musset responded by warning her himself. "Love only those who know how to love," he urged. "I only know how to suffer. Farewell! I love you as only a child can love." Clever man! The last were probably the only words that could have succeeded in lowering George's guard. With her, the maternal and the erotic were one. A few weeks later, Musset moved into Quai Malaquais.

On August 25, a month after Sainte-Beuve had introduced them, George wrote to him with the news: "I've fallen in love with Alfred. And this time, it's serious. I've given my heart as never before, to the point that I should be frightened. Instead, for the first time, I've found frankness, loyalty, tenderness—I'm intoxicated. This is love and friendship such as only a young man can offer. I had no idea such a thing even existed!"

Gossip was the stuff of Sainte-Beuve's largely vicarious existence. As George well knew, she might as well have slapped a poster on every wall in Paris.

Almost as soon as she and Alfred became lovers, George decided that the poet must come with her to Italy—a place both had always longed to visit. But first, they tried a brief getaway closer to home. It was on this three-day excursion to the romantic Forest of Fontainebleau that Alfred revealed his darker side. Walking off alone at twilight, he lost his way in a rocky, desertlike area known as the Franchards. Darkness fell and by the time a frantic Sand found him, many hours later, Alfred was wandering in a delusional state, shrieking in terror about seeing in the mist a spectral figure whom he had recognized as his sinister—and dead—self.

Far from taking this as a warning, George pressed on with her plans for a lengthy Italian stay, with Venice as their destination. She dropped her son, Maurice, off at the Lycée Henri IV, where he would be a boarder, hiding her own tears as the sobbing ten-year-old was led away by his tutor. Her daughter, Solange, remained at Nohant with her father. Casimir seemed to be thriving as lord of the manor, unencumbered by any officially resident lady. He applauded her decision to go to Italy; she needed the trip, "for pleasure and instruction," he said.

Only a few obstacles remained: Boldly, George called on the dowager Vicomtesse de Musset. Casting their illicit honeymoon as a health cure, George promised to take perfect care of her son. Finally, there was the problem of money. Alfred hadn't a sou to call his own. For an advance of five thousand francs, George promised her publisher a novel with an Italian setting, to be delivered by the following May 1834.

They were off, with the first stop Bordeaux. Then, boarding a steamboat in Lyon, they proceeded down the Rhône. En route, they fell in with a fellow writer, one as hidden in his double life of government functionary as Sand and Musset were defiantly exposed. Henri Beyle, to become immortal under his pseudonym Stendhal, was on the way to resume his duties as French consul in Civitavecchia, a backwater in Tuscany.

The lovers' troubles began in Genoa. While George was felled by traveler's stomach, Alfred disappeared with a ballet dancer. Arriving in Venice, George and Alfred moved into rooms at the Albergo Reale (the present Hotel Danieli), the once and future destination of well-off tourists. Sand fixed her first fleeting nocturnal impressions of the crumbling mirage that was the post-Napoleonic republic—"just like a Turner painting," she reported. But they did little sightseeing together. A few days later, George succumbed to a more virulent attack of the symptoms that had assailed her en route: fever, diarrhea, extreme weakness. Musset's fastidious nature was not equipped to deal with intimacies that included intestinal upheavals. He had not come all this way to hover over a sickbed, ringing for tea and a clean chamber pot. He disappeared for days at a time, exploring the city's famed casinos and wine shops and discovering that the Fenice theatre, too, featured dancers who were forced to moonlight and who made much of a young and handsome client.

Fearful of his besotted, dependent state, Alfred used sexual adventures to assert his freedom: "An artist needs change for inspiration," he informed George. The adorable child had become a sullen, rebellious adolescent. Convalescent now, the doting mother lectured, scolded, or patronized him. Alfred struck back, giving another excuse for his infidelities: George was prudish, withholding—"frigid," he complained—the sin she had ascribed to Lélia. For all her talk of frenzied transports and the worship of body and soul, she could neither give nor receive pleasure; she never abandoned herself to "hot slutty sex," he griped to a friend. It was all a horrible mistake, he told George.

"I was wrong and I'm sorry, but I don't love you." She was devastated. Too weak to leave her room, she stared out at the gray, smelly canal, waiting for him to return.

Now, the curtain went up on the famous "Venetian Drama." Returning early one morning, feverish and hollow-eyed, Alfred collapsed, much sicker than George had been, with unmistakable symptoms of typhoid complicated by a recently acquired venereal infection: pain, vomiting, high temperature. Used to nursing young and old, George took charge as best she could. But knowing no Italian and with no friends in Venice, her fear turned to panic. Alfred was failing. If something wasn't done immediately, he would die. In answer to her desperate inquiries, she was referred to a young doctor, reputed to be of exceptional brilliance. Trained in Padua and Pavia, Pietro Pagello, now attached to the Saints Giovanni and Paolo Hospital, had served his apprenticeship in a city infamous for periodic outbreaks of typhoid, along with every other infectious disease. He prescribed medication costing twenty francs a day, but it may have been the doctor's presence that turned the tide. Pagello was in constant and reassuring attendance during vigils that lasted through sleepless nights. In Alfred's case, delirium was accompanied by hallucinations—recalling to George the terrifying spells she had witnessed during their Fontainebleau excursion.

Slowly, the sick man began to recover, but the feverish rages continued, directed now toward his lover and his doctor. He claimed to have seen George seated on Pagello's lap and, worse, to have observed them drinking from the same teacup! These accusations were denied, but George did acknowledge that she had, in fact, torn up a letter she was writing to Pietro in Alfred's presence and tossed it out the window. He raved that she was writing a love letter to the young doctor. George countered that it was no such thing and that she had only disposed of the pages to avoid upsetting the patient further. (She failed to mention that she was later seen collecting the scraps of paper from the edge of the canal below.) Whatever Musset saw—or imagined that he saw, passion now spoke for itself: George had fallen in love with Pagello. In the drama of their situation, this was hardly surprising. No very remarkable fellow under ordinary circumstances, Pietro had proved a savior and faithful friend in crisis—and unlike Alfred, a man to be relied on. Just to be sure, Sand wrote the doctor a letter in the form of a questionnaire: "Will you be someone I can lean on, or my master? Will you console me for the grief I've suffered before we met? Will you know why I'm sad? Will you always show me sympathy, patience and friendship?" (Apparently, Pagello checked "yes" in the right boxes.)

The recovering poet was more frightening than the dying one. He alternated tirades of accusations—claiming that George and the doctor were conspiring to have him committed—with abject confessions of guilt and threats of suicide. Night and day, scene followed scene. George was unable to work, and they were running out of money. But she could hardly return home, leaving Alfred alone and penniless. Finally, they agreed that as soon as he felt strong enough to travel, he would go back to Paris; George would stay in Venice and get on with her writing. On March 29, a subdued trio said their farewells. The mood was one of reconciliation and forgiveness: Musset pronounced the doctor a fine fellow, and the three pledged lifelong love and friendship for one another. Then George accompanied Alfred to Mestre to begin the long voyage home. Returning to Venice with seven centimes in her pocket, George moved out of the Reale and into Pietro's tiny apartment in the insalubrious *sestiere* of San Luca. With Pagello out during the day seeing patients, she could return to the discipline of work.

No sooner than it had begun, this idyll, too, started to sour—or dull. The moment they had parted, Sand and Musset had begun to miss one another desperately. "Who will take care of you, and who will need me as you do?" she wrote to Alfred mournfully from Mestre. For his part, once he found himself alone, Musset felt free to express the masochism, the taste for suffering "the voluptuous jealousy" that, together, George and Pagello had aroused. He confessed to "finding no peace until he heard the bell announcing the doctor's visit." George should be sure to tell Pagello how much he loved and missed him, too.

Venice was an island frozen in time. Without the stimulus of her native language, of friends, of the literary and political worlds of Paris, George felt marooned and her writing faltered. Now that he was gone, she yearned for Alfred. She missed the children and Nohant. Pagello was fascinated by George and flattered that he had inspired the passion of a famous and brilliant woman. But he had his own more prosaic destiny to fulfill. Nonetheless, both love and a sense of honor required that he accompany her home. Besides, he had always wanted to see Paris.

10

Double Exposure

SEPARATION, MEANWHILE, freed the lovers from the need to torture each other. With too much time for reflection, Musset's journey from Venice, accompanied by the Italian manservant hired by George, had proved a *via dolorosa* of loss, guilt, and contrition. In letters that followed Alfred from Venice, Sand transformed their mutually lacerating passion into the perfect love of brother and sister, brother and brother, or mother and son; allusions to incest and gender reversal kept things lively. Once he arrived in Paris, George plied Alfred with errands and commissions; these included picking up the proofs from the publisher, correcting them, and then nagging the gentleman for payment. By way of reward, she dangled the hope of reconciliation. She was already looking forward to their reunion over the summer holiday, she wrote to Alfred: "How we will love each other then, my little brother, my beautiful child."

Alfred eagerly embraced this shrinking image of himself. Seeing his slight form in a Geneva shop window, he asked George, "Is this the man you loved, the man you thought you could lean on? Love something like me! I shudder to think of it! You thought you were my mistress, but you were my mother. We didn't make love, we committed incest!"

Stakes kept rising in the contest of who had wronged whom more.

"My child, my child, it's *me* that needs *your* love and forgiveness," Sand replied. "Don't say a word about my forgiving you! Where I'm concerned, don't even think that you've any cause to reproach yourself."

Arriving in Paris on April 10, Alfred learned, to his astonishment, that everyone had known of their separation for at least two weeks before he had left Venice. He found his "camp" (led by his older brother, Paul) baying for tell-all accounts of his sufferings at the hands of the she-devil. Instead, his supporters were privy to a one-man public ceremony of self-flagellation. It was all his fault, Alfred proclaimed ceaselessly. Sand was blameless: forbearing, generous, a saint, in fact, and their dear friend Dr. Pagello had saved his life. To his defenders, Musset's protestations only confirmed him as a gentleman and an aristocrat, noble in his martyrdom, who, along with enduring every indignity that could be visited on a sick man, refused to blame his vampire of a mistress. Among close friends, he alternated an attitude of stoic suffering with outpourings of grief and guilt. In his letters to George in Venice, Alfred professed horror at the ugly stories being spread about her and, worse, at learning the identities of those spreading them. (He spared her nothing, however.) Prosper Mérimée, it seems, was a prime source, spreading "disgusting" gossip (revenge, no doubt, for Sand's unfortunate morning-after report about their night together). George wasn't surprised to learn that Marie Dorval had failed to defend her "zealously." The vilest slander was traced to Gustave Planche, who was still brooding over his replacement by Sainte-Beuve and who now claimed firsthand knowledge of Sand's "worst" offenses. Even George's landlady joined the fray, Musset wrote, repeating vicious gossip about George to Alfred's mother, the aged vicomtesse.

Familiar scenes of happier days reopened Musset's wounds. Visiting the apartment at Quai Malaquais, he smoked the remains of Sand's stubbed-out cigarettes left in a saucer eight months before. As he inhaled the stale smell, he felt grief, he told George, but also "a strange joy." He "stole" a broken comb from her bathroom. He insisted that she hear these sordid things: Why should she think him any better than he was? He felt great pride that she had told him every detail about her relations with Pagello; such proof of trust would be his happiest memory.

Five months later, on August 14, Sand with Pagello in tow returned to find a Paris divided into warring camps: "Sandistes" and "Musset-istes." Friends, acquaintances, and those who had never laid eyes on either party had all taken sides. After Sand's lyrical letters invoking their joyous reunion, however, Alfred was unable to accept the reality: Their affair was over. He immediately wrote to George, saying that he must see her. They met three days later, but the shock of the encounter and of being told (whether the statement was true or not) that she was happy with Pagello undid him. His capital of heroic behavior was spent; he was falling apart, the prey of violent impulses that frightened everyone, including the poet himself. He took to mixing opium and alcohol, a version of freebasing; then, joining friends, he would repair to a brothel. At the moment of climax, he wrote to Sand, he felt an overwhelming urge to strangle the young whore he had chosen. (He had become obsessed with finding the youngest girls available—the only women who would not deceive him, he told George.) His companions in these forays dined out on the latest episode of Alfred's drug-induced craziness. Probably on the advice of friends, he decided on a health cure—abroad. He implored George to grant him "one hour and a final kiss."

The last good-bye came in writing, when he also pledged: "I shall not die without having written my book about you and me (above all, you). I swear this on my youth and genius.

"Posterity will repeat our names, along with those of other immortal lovers: Romeo and Juliet, Héloise and Abélard: the name of one is never spoken without the other." Musset would keep his literary promise, but posterity would pair George Sand with others of greater genius.

With Alfred providing a spectacle of romantic passion run amok—the drugs, homicidal impulses, masochistic scavenging, coupled with vows of eternal love and hymns to his own youth and genius—how could Paris fail to be disappointed by Pietro Pagello? Plump and placid, the doctor's attempt to ape the fashionable dandy only made him a laughingstock in the capital of style, while his ignorance of French and of all things literary occasioned more smirking on the part of all their friends. Had Sand thrown over Musset for this spectacularly banal fellow? For that matter, the new couple no longer seemed quite as besotted with one another. As George now discovered, Pagello did not travel well; unable to communicate, patronized or ignored by Sand's friends, he turned possessive, cranky, and critical. "As soon as he set foot in France," Sand complained, "he no longer understood a thing." Or perhaps, he understood too much.

George had planned her return in order to surprise Maurice at his school's Prize Day. In the eight months that she had been away, her son's anger had taken the form of answering his mother's letters seldom or not at all. She had retaliated by reminding the boy that it was a long way from Venice to Paris; she trusted he would reward her for cutting short her stay on his behalf by winning the honors she expected from a child of hers. But there were no prizes for Maurice. Then, on August 24, she left Pagello under the wing of Jules Boucoiran, Maurice's former tutor and her former lover. Accompanied by her mother, Sophie, and Maurice, Sand repaired to Nohant for a joyous reunion with Solange, now six—and Casimir. The ever-compliant husband had even invited Pagello to join them, but these civilized French mores were too much for the provincial young doctor, and he declined.

In her Nohant retreat, along with enjoying family, neighbors, and the landscape she loved, Sand planned to complete some unfinished work and to catch up on reading, sending for books on Christian theology, along with the Koran. Her old Berry circle of admirers, forgiving George for deserting Sandeau, now rallied round. To a man, they were appalled by the mudslinging that pursued her from Paris and were concerned by how devastated she was by the attacks. To her own surprise, she felt torn between her genuine love for the "good and generous" Pagello and her rekindled feelings for Alfred. Through September, both men deluged George with passionate, reproachful letters. To the closest of her Berry friends, the lawyer François Rollinat, she confided thoughts of suicide: "I wanted to play the strong man, and I was broken like a child."

It was Aurore, the motherless child, who was both the cause and victim of much of George's confusion and suffering. She clung to an ideal of the trio, not as erotic stratagem or to appease an insatiable vanity, but as a doomed attempt, endlessly repeated throughout her life, to reconstruct the family. Complaining to Musset about Pagello—his lack of faith in her, his weakness—she solemnly explained, "I loved him like a father and you were our child."

Four days after Sand's departure for Berry, Musset left for Baden, the fashionable spa famous for remedying the effects of living—if not loving—too well. Even luck at the gaming tables, along with such reliable distractions as champagne and the better class of pleasure-loving ladies, failed to console Alfred. At their last meeting, George had "covered him with the kisses for which he had waited five months." He knew that he must get on with living, with work, with other loves. But he also realized that he was more attached to suffering than to life.

"I can't live without you. That's all," he told George.

Meanwhile, Sand's idyll with Pagello was over. Unwisely, she had shown the doctor Alfred's desperate letters from Baden. Reading them, he assumed, reasonably enough, that such resurgence of passion after their reunion in Paris could only have been unleashed because George had given Musset hopes of reconciling. Was Pagello wrong? Sand's belief—always to be disproved—was that true love, enduring love, wished only the happiness of the beloved. How could that glorious night in Venice—when the three of them had joined hands, pledging an unbroken eternal circle of affection—been forgotten? Was it all a bad novel, turned into a bad dream? Apparently. Now, everyone was angry. One turned on her; the other abandoned her. If it weren't for the children, she told Alfred, "I would gladly throw myself into the river!"

Having said his farewells to Sand, to his mother, to friends, and to Paris itself, swearing never to return, Alfred now wrote to George from Baden to say he was coming back—and soon! By October 13, he was in Paris to greet Sand on her return from Nohant. Once more, at Sainte-Beuve's urging, George agreed to see him.

At the beginning of January 1835, their affair resumed where it had left off: Musset moved back to Quai Malaquais, and the two began tearing each other to pieces—yet again.

But there was one difference: By all accounts, Alfred was now violent most of the time. Far from assuaging his jealousy, Pagello's departure for Italy served to focus Musset's sexual obsession. When precisely had George and the doctor first betrayed him? He demanded an exact chronology, "day by day, hour by hour," Sand reported. He harangued and grilled her relentlessly, trying to catch her out. (In fact, he seems to have been tipped off that George was lying to him when she swore they had only consummated their passion *after* Musset had left Venice.) When George now declared her "right" to refuse further interrogations, to maintain a "veil of secrecy" around her relations with Pagello, Alfred went berserk. Resuming intimate relations with George, after a long period of false calm lulled by exchanged vows of brotherly and sisterly love, had flung him back into a psychosexual maelstrom. "He felt compelled to claw and flay his own wounds," George said. Sainte-Beuve now declared himself to blame for his poor judgment in urging George to see the volatile Musset again, and he admitted his mistake to all of Paris. Friends and enemies hung on each installment of the drama; no novel serialized daily in the newspapers could compete with the scenes of *l'amour fou* imploding in their midst.

There was one brief coda. Terrified by his own destructiveness, by the evidence that he might destroy George after all (she had begged him to leave, but not before killing her!), Alfred fled, this time for good, he swore. Now Sand became the supplicant: Sane or crazy, she couldn't live without him. She cut off her long, wavy black hair and sent it to him. (Her friend Delacroix painted her with cropped head, pale and hollow-eyed, her lips appearing to tremble.) The message was clear: "Baby, come back."

With George now in his thrall, Musset abandoned himself to a final psychotic episode. There were mutual threats of murder and suicide. Finally, George's instinct for self-preservation prevailed. It was finished.

If Sand was devastated by the turn taken by this second and third act of their Venetian drama, she did not seem distressed by its public airing. Before leaving France with Musset, she had declared herself happy to have her love for Alfred "held up to the light of day."

Less immediately apparent to the principal players and their Greek chorus of contemporaries was the literary posterity of their passion. Both writers mined the raw material of their twenty-one-month affair—even as it was happening—to produce a new kind of nonfiction fiction, the literary equivalent of cinema verité. In poetry, plays, novels, confessional, and travel writing, they both wrote revealingly of the other and of themselves in "the Affair." In most instances, the writers' attempts to fictionalize their roles expose more than any other documentation could do.

To a recent literary historian, the Sand-Musset affair exemplifies a peculiarly French romantic self-consciousness. *The Love Affair as a Work of Art* is the title of Dan Hofstadter's enchanting look at a number of these literary passions. More accurate, if less poetic, would be the description of Sand and Musset's love affair as a work in progress, one that is constantly being "revised" by the participants and their descendants (Maurice did considerable bowdlerizing of his mother's letters). Dead or alive, the two lovers remained each other's muse, just as Alfred had predicted, beyond the grave.

It's been said that there's nothing like poverty to clear the mind and the agenda. In Musset's case, we should add misery—the poet's real muse. Normally indolent, or "blocked," we would now say, Musset found that his despair at losing George, and especially the gnawing sense that it was all his fault, goaded him into writing. A year after their relations had ended, Musset's novel, *La Confession d'un enfant du siècle,* was published. Here, in scarcely veiled fictional form, the poet laid bare the lacerating self-indictment and exoneration of Sand to which his friends had played audience since Alfred's return from Venice. To George herself, Musset had described his new literary project a month after he had left Italy. "It will be an altar to you," he wrote of the work he had just begun. Musset's *Confession* survived the curse of timeliness to establish itself almost instantly as the bible of the first "lost generation" of post-Napoleonic youth. Missing his shot at glory, Musset's dissolute alter ego Octave, like one of Stendhal's heroes, casts his failure at love and life within a larger protest against soulless, bourgeois modernity.

His theatrical masterpiece, *On ne badine pas avec l'amour* (You Can't Trifle with Love), was begun before Musset's departure with Sand for Venice and finished in the tumultuous months following his return. A doomed pair of lovers, Perdican the cynical and debauched student and the convent-bred heroine, Camille, spar for dominance. By the closing scene of Act II, however, Alfred makes good on his promise to George in Venice. In his future writings, he had pledged, he would "open a vein" to immortalize her. Here Musset performs a double act of literary bloodletting, quoting almost word for word from one of George's letters to him on the sublime abyss of love. Dispatching his disillusioned lover, Camille, back to her convent, Perdican instructs her to repeat the following:

"All men are liars, false and faithless, hypocrites and gossips, as full of pride as they are cowardly, contemptible in their lust; all women are deceitful, artful, vain, prying and depraved, the world is a bottomless sewer where wily serpents crawl and writhe on heaps of slime. But there exists one holy and sublime thing—the union of two of these horrible deformed creatures. As often as we've been fooled, hurt, tortured, pushed to the edge of the grave, we can at least look back and say: I've loved."

In "October Night," the fourth and final poem of his cycle *Nuits* (Nights), the poet complains to his muse about two women who, in betraying him, robbed him of the innocence of youth. The second of these perfidious lovers is clearly Sand. ("It's your voice, your smile, your corrupting gaze which taught me to curse even a hint of happiness.") His muse, however, argues persuasively that by teaching him to suffer, his faithless mistress had transformed the child into a man.

As soon as Alfred left Venice, Sand, desperate for money, her contractual commitments to her publisher overdue, resumed writing. In a fever of productivity, she completed *Jacques,* an epistolary novel as daring in concept as it proved summary and offhand in execution. It would not be the first time that the pressure of deadlines derailed her best ideas. Seventeen-year-old Clemence, another idealistic heroine fresh from the convent, marries a paragon of a suitor. Rich, twice her age, brilliant, handsome, and virtuous, Jacques is "too good for his bride," who promptly falls for an empty-headed fop and leaves her husband after six months of marriage. Rich in possibilities, the dynamic of this intriguing triad is never explored—neither in its "sexual or moral" implications, complained Balzac, who dismissed the novel as "hollow and false."

Supposedly dashed off in a week, *Leoni Leone* (1835) re-genders the great eighteenth-century tale of sexual obsession, *Manon Lescaut* (1732), the last book Sand had read before leaving with Musset for Italy. In George's retelling, the amoral, luxury-loving courtesan is transformed into Casanova, a satanic and schizophrenic figure of glamour whose very craziness exerts a fatal hold over his besotted mistress. The manuscript was dedicated tersely in pencil in Sand's racing hand: "To Alfred, from George."

Sand, who outlived Musset by nineteen years, had the last word, and her use—and misuse—of the survivor's advantage has been the subject of much recent debate. In the last twenty years, the close study of both George's handwriting and the content of certain letters—mentioning events she could not have known at the time, for example—has revealed that Sand doctored, changed, or simply rewrote sections of both Alfred's letters and her own. The kindest interpretation of these forgeries has been that Sand altered their "story" to more honestly reflect the feelings of those involved. In *Elle et lui* (She and He) (1859), written two years after Musset's death, Sand presented her version of their explosive passion.

In this novel of alternating narrative and letters (Paul de Musset accused George of quoting his brothers' letters verbatim), Sand's love triangle transforms the two writers into painters, Thérèse and Laurent, while the Italian doctor becomes an American (possibly the first non-native in European fiction) "Dick" Palmer. Here, Sand merely followed Musset's *Confession,* whose debauched hero, Octave, nobly hands over his virtuous lover, Brigitte Pierson, to the stolidly adoring Henri Smith.

Sand's publisher François Buloz sensibly saw that the subject of *Elle et lui,* first serialized in the *Revue des Deux Mondes,* would be a gold mine, reviving older readers' fascination with Sand's affair as it had happened over twenty years earlier and kindling new interest in the author's spicy past. He remained uneasy, however, about Sand's self-portrait as Thérèse. By making her heroine less "saintly," he tactfully suggested, George would make the character more believably human.

Incensed both by Sand's self-canonization and selective use

of the truth, Paul de Musset now got into the act. Marrying his late brother's last mistress, Aimée d'Alton, he and his wife collaborated on what they claimed to be the true story of the affair: *Lui et elle* (He and She), published in 1860, the year after Sand's novel. Painting George in the blackest light, their version contains as much invention as do George's fictional changes of reality. Novel, memoir, letters—they were all true and all false.

IN THE 1890S, when Sand and Musset, along with most of those who could remember their carryings-on, were long dead, the scandal of their passion was revived by the posthumous publication of their correspondence—both sides—and by Sand's *Intimate journals.* At the high-water mark of Anglo-American Victorianism and its continental equivalent, the excesses revealed by the letters caused far more shock than would have been heard had they appeared in the laissez-faire heyday of the July Monarchy, a half-century earlier.

Henry James had always been repelled and fascinated by Sand the novelist and, still more ambivalently, by Sand the woman. He would devote no fewer than five essay-reviews to the French writer—more than to any other single literary figure—the number of pages alone confirming a certain obsession. James himself suffered from a kind of terminal discretion; the very notion of causing scandal in one's private life, then airily exposing and exploiting every episode in what he would refer to as "the Great relation" (his euphemism for sex), retailing each savage quarrel and ecstatic reconciliation, all this aroused in him shudders of horror. At the same time, the high seriousness of Sand's engagement with social and moral issues forced him to accord her a respect he granted few fellow writers. These conflicted feelings were compounded by envy of her success and not a little misogyny: Women writers were not supposed to stray from the decorous and safely domestic.

Now, reading the Sand-Musset letters as they appeared, James again felt buffeted by familiar waves of attraction and repulsion. Drawn to the savagery of the relationship itself, of sexual passion divorced from any civilizing impulse, he nonetheless recoiled from the exposure of love as physical violence: "They entertained for each other every feeling in life but the feeling of respect," he wrote. Putting himself in the position of a "stupefied spectator," he was alert to a new phenomenon: the ways in which the "eloquence" of both writers fed a complicit agreement. The opening of veins, in Musset's image, took place on a public stage, but the audience also consisted of readers who bought Sand's books—as they had never bought James's. How much was commerce, and how much was art in their drama? "It is all rapture and all rage and all literature," James concluded.

"The lovers are naked in the market-place and perform for the benefit of society."

11

A Political Education

In March 1835, in the garden at Nohant, George Sand swore off love. At thirty-one, she was too old, she said, for the cycle of joy and hope followed by deception and disappointment. Sainte-Beuve had prescribed one "cure" for her sickness: the "acceptance of imperfect love." Useless advice for one who dealt only in absolutes. She was now reading Plato for the first time and she reached for the philosopher's famous image of shadows on the cave wall to announce that she, George Sand, would never again mistake illusions for the real thing. Sainte-Beuve came back with a better solution: God. Recalling the certainties of her convent conversion, George was more receptive. Finishing Plato's *Republic*, she turned to the latest writings on Christianity. But she quickly grew discouraged. It was too late. She had strayed too far: God had abandoned her.

Buloz, her publisher, professed alarm at Sand's recent reading: "George going mystical on us! We can't have that!"

Parisian cynicism was no help. Failed in marriage, in love, and in the eyes of God, she wondered to what larger cause could she devote her life. Writing books was not an answer. George never saw herself as an artist, still less an acolyte in the "religion of art."

Friends from her old Berry circle, recently married and now heads of families, urged her to reconcile with Casimir. "Turn yourself into his mistress," one advised. She was revolted—morally and physically. Prostituting herself to save the marriage—the advice only strengthened her growing resolve to do the opposite and obtain a legal separation decree to end the tangle of uncertainties about money, property, children, and sexual freedom.

Divorce had been legalized in France after the 1789 revolution, only to be abolished by Napoleon. A court-ordered separation agreement, however, signed by both parties, could provide the same terms except for the right of remarriage (now requiring a papal decree). As with divorce itself, skilled legal representation made all the difference. And there was no difference of opinion in all Berry as to who was the best advocate.

By the time he and Sand met in 1835, the fame of Louis-Chrysostom Michel had already spread from local courts to Paris, where the lawyer was renamed with the honorific Michel de Bourges. His legendary pleading before the high court was only the public arena for his powerful behind-the-scenes political role: South of the Loire, Michel reigned as undisputed leader of government opposition, where he "exercised on liberals of the region an influence quasi-despotic." No less a figure than the poet and legislator Alphonse de Lamartine called Michel a "man of granite." Among Michel's circle of disciples, he counted a number of Sand's young friends. They may have become bourgeois in their domestic and social lives, urging George to make up with Casimir on the grounds that a woman—even George Sand—was always better off married. Nonetheless, like Sand's close friend, the lawyer François Rollinat, they kept the faith with youthful republican ideals, proud to count themselves members of Michel's inner circle of young firebrands.

Exceptional by every measure, Michel also personified a social mobility rare within France's rigid class system, which was little changed by half a century of upheaval. Son of an impoverished lumberjack who had been killed in the region's counterrevolutionary violence, Michel's driving intelligence and ambition had propelled him through lycèe and then law studies in Aix-en-Provence. Physically, too, he was a hard man to miss. Lest anyone forget his origins or present politics, he dressed in coarse smock and wooden clogs. Hypersensitive to cold, he swathed his outsized bald head and high forehead (cruelly described as resembling two crania joined together) with three madras head scarves, which gave him the look of a Breughel peasant—but for one detail. Underneath this rustic garb, Michel's immaculate shirt was of the finest linen, a reminder that he had married a rich widow from a prominent Bourges family.

His disparate costume was one distraction from his ugliness; at thirty-seven, the man with the stooped figure, nearsightedly peering through spectacles, already looked middle-aged. The other distraction was his voice: soft and low before rumbling its way to a crescendo of "savage" eloquence, Michel's voice held every courtroom spellbound. His conversation was no less hypnotic in its effect—especially on women. Introduced, probably by François Rollinat on April 7, Michel and Sand were so entranced by one another that they walked the streets of Bourges, deep in argument from early that same evening until four o'clock the next morning, when dawn silhouetted the sprockets of the great Gothic cathedral against the pale spring sky.

Two days later, Michel gave George a ring. On the interior of the wide gold band, enameled with red and blue interlaced flowers, is the date: April 9th, 1835—most probably to commemorate the end of words, when, like Héloise and Abélard, "they spoke no more that day."

Lovers they had become, but talkers they would both remain. Michel confessed himself awed by the genius of *Lélia*; then, having acquitted himself as an admirer of the author, he now undertook the political reeducation of the woman, his mission to rescue George from what Marxists would later decry as "false consciousness." She must be weaned from the pap of romantic, do-nothing humanitarianism, the rosy belief in the arrival of social justice—someday—in the far Utopian future, the complacent republicanism that involved no risk or sacrifice or real change. He introduced her to the men who were actively seeking to overthrow the present regime, writing, teaching, and organizing, all in an effort to educate the people about their rights and duties in the new social order to come. Among Michel's associates, Pierre Leroux, a printer and journalist, most impressed Sand. Hungry for action, Leroux had left the periphery of Saint-Simonianism, bored by its navel-gazing communes of bourgeois rebels, for the harder and more subversive work of instructing the masses.

At the end of April 1835, George joined Michel in Paris, where the lawyer was preparing for the court drama that would make him one of the most famous men in France. In a case known as "the Monster Trial," Michel's clients, 131 insurgents from Lyon and most of them from the ranks of starving silk workers, were accused of conspiring against the Crown. The radical lineup on the defense's bench included Garnier-Pagès, Ledru-Rollin, Carnot, Barbès (all tamely immortalized today as Paris street names), and Leroux himself; most would become Sand's friends and allies.

Inspired by the presence of George at the trial, Michel surpassed himself, his acolytes declared. They had never heard their leader so deadly in argument, so incandescent in rhetoric. He could convert any juror or judge—but not, in the long run, his fiercely independent lover.

Increasingly, Sand would recoil from Michel's fanaticism. "I just met Robespierre today," she joked to a friend, but in the course of their stormy affair, she found that this was no joke. Michel saw himself as the heir of Babeuf, the eighteenth-century intransigent radical who was so committed to a primal, egalitarian future that he terrified the assassins of the Terror itself. Though he was executed in 1797 by the Directory, his legacy lived on, in the tradition of *Babouvisme,* the take-no-prisoners zealotry whose end—a society swept clean of privilege—would always be strangled in an apocalyptic destruction of people and property. Stalin and Pol Pot were Babeuf's true descendants. Behind Michel's declared idealism, George sensed the spirit of class vengeance and a genocidal impulse toward his fellow citizens that frightened her.

For the moment, they kept talking as they walked the dark streets of Paris. Unlike their strolls through Bourges, which had been accompanied by an exalted exchange of opinions and ideals, George now found the mentor she had earlier called "a god" alarming in his fury and vision of days of wrath to come: Scorched earth, he proclaimed, was the precondition of a just society. Crossing the Pont des Saints-Pères, Michel conjured a vision of the river running red with blood, and as he and George reached the Right Bank, he vowed that the palaces rising before them would be reduced to ashes, along with their occupants. To make his point, he smashed his cane against the ancient ramparts of the Louvre, breaking the stick into pieces.

Needless to say, God had no place in Michel's cosmology. Life was a jungle, where human beings were at the mercy of one another. What did it matter, George wondered, if the executioners and their victims were aristocrats or anarchists? Or the reverse. But there was undoubtedly a deeper cause for Sand's growing discomfort with Michel's politics: uncertainties about her own class. Her lover sought revenge on behalf of the "people," his own disenfranchised and murdered peasant father and the new urban proletariat. He taunted George for being a "lady of the manor" living in a château where being kind to the servants counted as proof of social conscience. But who was she, really? A descendant of kings or a whore's child, "of father unknown"? Was her Christianity only the superstition of an ignorant irrational woman—like her mother? Michel mocked her fears of a revolution without God as another form of ruling-class hypocrisy; an allegiance to privilege masked as faith. In fact, Sand's reformist impulse had early been directed toward the church, which under Pope Gregory XVI collaborated with monarchs throughout Europe in seeking to silence the rising voices of republicanism.

She could no longer play worshipful subject to Michel's despotic philosopher-king. Here George faced a new dilemma: The more she withdrew from him ideologically, the more she was besotted with Michel sexually. Her thralldom tightened when, from the gallery during the trial of the Lyons insurgents, she listened to his incantatory words, the oratory that held rapt the royal judicial lackeys and the jurors alike. His passion before the bench made all other men seem pallid creatures. There was a near riot among the plaintiffs and their supporters when all 131 of the accused were acquitted. To save the government face, their advocate was sentenced to a month in prison and a ten-thousand-franc fine.

Michel's sentence was largely symbolic: The tribunal ordered him remanded to the Castle of Bourges, with such minimum security that he was free to plead before the high court there on behalf of his client in the case of *Dudevant v. Dudevant.* With not a flicker of embarrassment, Baroness Dudevant's lover now made a stirring case on behalf of the wronged wife (seated in full view of the court in a simple white, hooded dress) who merely sought to regain her dignity and property from a debauched and wastrel husband. He pointed to his client, an irreproachable young matron who had brought a considerable estate and fortune as a dowry, only to see it dissipated by her spouse, who, while living in luxury and profaning their home in orgies with the maids, had banished his wife with a miserable allowance, further defaming her as "the lowest of prostitutes." Meanwhile, Casimir's case was fatally weakened by his efforts to maintain his marriage to a spouse he had declared a fallen woman and an unfit mother. His ultimate capitulation, however, had to do with money, not morals. As his brother-in-law Hippolyte reminded him, he hadn't a sou of his own and if he continued to be obstructionist, he would end with nothing.

Thanks to Michel, Sand was now a rich woman. The rents from Nohant, awarded to her in the agreement, along with custody of Solange, came to ninety-four hundred francs annually, before any earned income from her writings.

From the moment they became lovers, George and Michel had talked of a life together, one that promised a perfect union. Now that she was free, Michel began to retreat. George could no longer deny what she had long suspected: Her lover would never leave his wife to live openly "in sin" with her. More, he valued his sexual liberty above any monogamous relationship. She had heard the Bourges gossip that he had found a new mistress, a soprano "of repulsive obesity," Sand reported nastily, and who couldn't even sing! Whatever her vocal shortcomings, Michel's new love was unlikely to challenge him politically.

When George accused Michel of humiliating her with his infidelity, the lawyer was ready with his defense. He was well aware of *her* recent liaison with a handsome, young Swiss novelist, Charles Didier, newly arrived in Paris, where he had already cut quite a swath through the ranks of literary ladies. As Michel knew, George swiftly carried off the prize, moving from Quai Malaquais into Didier's apartment. Her defense: Michel was ever less available, and sexual abstinence was bad for her health.

She gave little cause for concern. Didier was invited to Nohant for a week, which he declared "the happiest of his life."

Now that they were quits, Sand and Michel's affair ground to a slow and, for George, agonizing end. Much of their correspondence has been lost or destroyed, but the letters that survive, along with passages devoted to Michel in *The Story of My Life,* suggest that her lover had wearied of her, her sexual demands, and her insistence on constant debate. He wanted an acolyte, not an equal. Older, powerful, supremely self-confident, he had been both father and teacher. Finally, Michel was the one man in Sand's life she could not dominate. Her voice in the letters—adoring, accusing, abject—is the voice of all abandoned women. What happened to us? Where did I go wrong? Why did you stop loving me?

She needed a new prophet, and fate had a way of providing Sand with what—or who—she needed in timely fashion. The lawyer's defection had further convinced her of the chasm separating men and women, but also of another divide, never to be bridged. On the one side were the secular radicals like Michel, who, denouncing all authority, had gained in number and influence from the betrayals of the July Monarchy. On the other side were those who, refusing to renounce their faith, demanded that the Church be "born again" as champions of the poor and powerless. Scarcely had Sand, only half in jest, decided to renounce "Great Men" than she came under the spell of a great artist who was also a passionate believer.

A musical prodigy, Franz Liszt was born in the rural reaches of the Austro-Hungarian empire, where his father managed one of the Esterhazys' far-flung estates. Moving to Vienna to further his son's musical education had reduced the family to penury. They had no choice but to put the young virtuoso to work, and Liszt was touring European capitals before he reached his teens. By the time he arrived on the Paris musical scene in the early 1830s, the twenty-year-old was already a celebrity. His electrifying performances were only part of the Liszt legend: His bony frame made him appear even taller than his six feet, while the angular form; shoulder-length, ash-blond hair; long, pale-green eyes; and white face gave him an otherworldly appearance, making the power that could smash more than one piano in the course of a performance all the more shocking. Women swooned in his wake, scouring backstage for the pianist's burnt-out cigars as relics.

In fact, Liszt was immune to temptation, being passionately in love. He had just persuaded Marie de Flavigny d'Agoult, a beautiful, golden-haired aristocrat and heiress to a German banking fortune, to leave her husband and young daughters to make a new life with him. But his head remained unturned for another reason: The matinee idol possessed a deep humility based on faith, a piety unshaken by adulation. Along with music, this was his deepest bond with George Sand. Mutual friends, Sainte-Beuve among them, suspected that Sand and Liszt might be made for one another. But the musician, possibly put off by Sand's extravagantly public loves and furious professionalism, was never tempted. His blue-blooded Botticellian Venus was all that his romantic nature required—at least for the present. He valued George all the more as a friend, a passionate fan of his music, and a fellow believer in a church based on Christ's teachings and his example. It was this conviction that led first Liszt, then Sand, to become disciples of the most controversial figure of nineteenth-century Catholicism.

Priest, philosopher, and social reformer, Hugues-Félicité Robert de Lamennais established himself early as a pied piper to young and ardent Catholics of liberal sympathy, and a thorn in the side of Rome. Imbued with a revolutionary vision inseparable from his religious vocation, the Breton from Saint-Mâlo saw the revival of the church's spiritual roots as key to the regeneration of society. His conviction was expressed through an ongoing "*J'accuse,*" an inventory of crimes committed by the church terrestrial. Through his writings and those of his followers, Lamennais came to inspire such fear in the Vatican that he managed to make himself the subject of two papal encyclicals; these condemned the renegade priest for a range of sins, from disobedience to fomenting a dangerous egalitarianism, if not mob rule. The first vehicle of Lamennais's radical ideas was his journal *l'Avenir* (The Future), which attracted a group of left-leaning writers and dissident young theologians as contributors and became required reading for all those refusing to choose between God and social justice. When the journal was suspended by the church in 1834, Lamennais retaliated with *Paroles d'un croyant* (Words of a Believer), a blistering attack on all authority—popes and monarchs alike. Severed from the church by the time Liszt introduced him to Sand, Lamennais devoted his prestige and eloquence to the cause of a new Christian socialism—what would now be called Liberation Theology.

For the first time in her adult life, Sand felt spiritually and intellectually at home, and the philosopher soon became a close friend and adviser. At first, not even Lamennais's fundamental misogyny could defend him from a woman as fascinating as Sand. For George, the priest answered her need for a worshipful relationship to a prophet—but one without the complications of sex.

Friendship had its consolations. A refuge from Michel's intellectual bullying followed by abandonment, Lamennais's ardent vision of community in Christ, of a return to primitive Christianity, took Sand back to her childhood faith and even to her pantheistic woodland altar to Corambé. For the first time, a priest's inspiriting demand for a society where brotherhood and belief united humanity brought her closer to another artist; Liszt's faith and genius affirmed Sand's hope that a fellowship in art could be a holy community.

Still, her happier state of mind left the question of women—as artists and sexual beings—unresolved: Marriage, unchallenged and unchanged, seemed immovably the fate of all her sex. Indeed, on this issue, Lamennais himself soon betrayed her. The former priest might be high on the Vatican's enemies list, but where women's rights were concerned, he was more Catholic than the pope. Among other writings that Sand offered gratis to Lamennais's new publication, *Le Globe,* was a series of articles in the form of fictional letters to a young woman, without dowry or prospects, from her (male) spiritual adviser. In "Letters to Marcie," he urges that, instead of lamenting her future as an old maid, the despairing girl (based on George's friend Eliza Tourangin) rejoice in her independent state—counsel illustrated by copious examples of the horrors of marriage.

Among other crimes, Sand accused men of suffocating women's intelligence in order to dominate them; Lamennais's disapproval of this piece was merely reflected by his—unauthorized—cuts. What terrified the former abbot above all, however, was Sand's encouragement of "the demon of [female] lust." When George proposed that her next installment be titled "The Role of Passion in Women's Lives," followed by one raising the issue of divorce, Lamennais wrote her a frosty note canceling publication of any further articles in the series, and he even took to denouncing her to mutual acquaintances. Another idealized friendship had foundered.

Where marriage was concerned, no man shared Sand's conviction that this most unjust of institutions must be radically reformed before a just society could come into being. As she would often do, George now sought a solution in fiction, in the hope that life might indeed copy art.

Mauprat, begun in 1835 and set in a prerevolutionary France of the 1770s, reflects Sand's faith that a changed social order could transform relations between men and women. In the novel, two branches of the same ancient family represent a brutal feudal past and an enlightened future. Bernard de Mauprat, abducted from the "good" Mauprats as an orphaned seven-year-old, has been brought up as a bandit by the savage, illiterate "Cut Throat Mauprats," a father and seven sons who terrorize the region. At seventeen, Bernard is "saved" by the love of his cousin, Edmée, and, with her help, abandons his criminal family to their deserved destruction. Although betrothed to another, the pure and beautiful Edmée chooses Bernard as the likely candidate for a moral makeover. She undertakes his education, and the former delinquent becomes virtuous, learned, and responsible. With the help of Patience, a hermit and "noble savage" in the mold of Jean-Jacques Rousseau, Edmée creates the ideal husband. Perfected as individuals, the romantic and sexual passion that unites the young Mauprats assures a union of equals in an idyllic pastoral setting. The happy couple becomes a force for collective good. Utopia begins at home.

12

The Long Good-Bye

Legally, in 1836, Nohant was not yet hers. Utopia would have to wait. Final negotiations with Casimir having stalled, in late July, Sand decided to accept an invitation from Liszt and his countess to visit them in Switzerland. Since her travels in the Pyrénées more than a decade earlier, she had always longed to explore the Alps, whose high-voltage scenery led the Romantics to claim it for their own. Setting off with the two children and a maid, Sand arrived in Geneva on September 4. Her departure had been so hectic that George had failed to alert Liszt and Marie of her family's imminent descent. On arriving at Geneva, George learned that her friends were in Chamonix, where the visitors now followed. Their reunion at the Hôtel de l'Union seemed nothing short of miraculous, occasioning giddy celebration. Then, together, the combined band of wandering Bohemians (Sand had chosen a page's costume as her travel wardrobe) traveled back to Geneva by way of Fribourg, where Liszt thrilled his friends by playing Mozart's *Dies Irae* on the organ of the city's great cathedral.

In Calvinist Geneva, anticipation of Liszt's arrival crackled with news that the famed virtuoso was living in sin with a beautiful noblewoman. The glamorous couple had immediately attracted an entourage. Liszt had brought a protégé with him: Hermann Cohen, a slight young pianist known as "Puzzi." A local savant, Colonel Pictet, was in constant attendance. Sand's presence drew more callers among the city's cultural elite, sparking conversations on art, philosophy, and religion, Dante and Jean-Jacques, God and Plato. Pictet fell deeply in love with George. The children were buoyed by the animated talk, the laughter, and the unaccustomed attentions of their mother: Maurice filled notebooks with drawings and caricatures. Nine-year-old Solange, rescued from frequent beatings at the hands of a Nohant maid, basked in the indulgence of all the grown-ups.

In high spirits, George gave everyone nicknames: Collectively, Liszt and the other men were "the fellowes" [sic]; Marie d'Agoult was promoted to "Princess," or more familiarly, "Arabella." Meanwhile, Sand baptized her own tribe "the Piffoëls," from the slang word for nose, *pif* ("schnozz"), a tribute to the prominence of this Sand-Dudevant feature. So apt did this sobriquet strike her that George endowed a newly invented literary altar ego with the title "Professor Piffoël," whose role was to listen and advise his confidante on her love problems. Unable to let go of Michel, George tried to fit her subjective misery into a larger context: the doomed pursuit of "progress" in the relations of men and women.

When Sand wasn't exploring her sorrow and anger with Professor Piffoël, she and Liszt inspired each other in work. The composer dedicated *Rondo Fantastique* "To Monsieur George Sand." She responded with a "lyrical tale," *The Smuggler*, which purportedly transcribed Liszt's music into prose.

Another equation was eternal: The triangle equals trouble. As odd woman out, Sand envied the "perfect love" of Franz and Marie, and she deflected her jealousy by first exalting, then denigrating, each of them in turn. Promoting d'Agoult from countess to princess had a whiff of "too-grand-for-us" and excluded her from the magic circle of art. She and Franz were so "attuned" to each other, Sand spitefully told Marie, that she, George, crouched under the piano when he played, the better to physically experience each vibrato. Even though Michel had put her off brilliant men, she forgave Liszt for being more intelligent than she was and loved him, anyway.

Then, it was Franz who was unworthy of his golden-haired princess: "Lucky him, to be loved by a woman who is beautiful, generous, smart—and faithful. What else do you need, you thankless man! If only I too was loved."

Marie was hardly reassured by Sand's tributes to her, starting with the dedication of her latest novel, *Simon:*

> *Mysterious friend, be patroness of this modest little tale.*
> *Patrician, excuse the rage of the rustic storyteller.*
> *Madame, tell no one you are his sister.*

Called "the first republican novel," *Simon* also marked Sand's first politically engaged fictional narrative. At the same time, the work celebrated her passion for Michel de Bourges. Its eponymous hero, a self-made lawyer of radical ideals, was based on her lover; the novel was begun when she was filled with hope that their union could overcome their differences. Thus, *Simon*, like the simpler *Mauprat,* seals its Utopian vision with a happy marriage. By the time the novel was published, her dream of the exemplary couple was over. "*Simon* ends with a wedding," Sand noted drily, "making it no more nor less a fairy tale than those told by Perrault or Madame d'Aulnoy."

Worse than disillusion or even despair, George now feared that the torch she still carried had consumed her. Reminding Liszt that he has a "treasure" in his mistress (now pregnant with their first child), she mourned: "I, too, possessed a treasure—my own heart—and I did nothing but waste it."

Michel was to blame for another kind of waste: Forsaking all others, she had allowed her vital sexuality to wither. Earlier, Sand had defended herself against the lawyer's accusations of betrayal, announcing that he was to blame for her fling with Charles Didier: "I'm still young . . . my blood burns." Now, in Geneva, she was surrounded by attractive men—younger than Michel, she informed him. At a glance, any one of them would be glad to console her. What stopped her? She was revolted by the thought of lying in the arms of anyone else: "When I awake bathed in sweat, it's you that I've been dreaming about, it's you that I cry out to, when nature sings her most passionate hymns and when the sharp mountain air penetrates my pores with a thousand needles of desire." Images of pleasure mingled with pain were not figures of speech, but reminders that their sadomasochistic lovemaking fueled Michel's continuing hold over her: Like holy stigmata, she cherished traces of him in the bruises and welts on her body.

They had talked of his coming to Geneva; when this proved impossible, Michel seems to have promised to meet her in Lyon, on her way home to Nohant. She and her family left Switzerland around October 1. They waited for almost a week in a Lyon hotel, the children growing cranky and bored. Michel neither appeared nor sent any word. On October 13, they arrived at Nohant, where Sand deposited both Maurice and Solange, leaving for Paris less than two weeks later. She had given up her old apartment on Quai Malaquais, and resisting Charles Didier's entreaties to move back with him, yielded happily to Liszt and d'Agoult's invitation to join them at Hôtel de France, 23 rue Lafitte, their Paris headquarters. An establishment of opulently furnished rented apartments, the hotel suggested an exclusivity that was assured by its cost and by the neighboring mansions of the Restoration's richest bankers, soon to include Baron James de Rothschild.

Now that she was a pariah to her former world, that of the blue-blooded salons of the Faubourg Saint-Germain, Marie d'Agoult was determined to replace the aristocracy of name and pedigree with that of talent, if not genius. Her timing was perfect: She harbored intellectual aspirations of her own, while Liszt, subordinating his brilliance as a composer, had yielded to the more profitable career of concert virtuoso. This was the moment to cultivate those who might be of help to both of them.

"The capital of the 19th century," Walter Benjamin called the city at the bend of the Seine. Here, ambition in every sphere, homegrown and émigré, converged. Literary and musical Paris flocked to the Countess d'Agoult's free-flowing soirees.

George could only afford one room on the ground floor, sharing a reception area with Liszt and Marie installed in splendor directly above. "Those of my friends you don't like," she joked, "will be received on the landing."

As it happened, the guest lists of the two women proved entirely compatible. Among the distinguished men of letters were Heinrich Heine, émigré poet from Dusseldorf, and Sand's friends Balzac, Victor Hugo, and Sainte-Beuve. Of the music establishment, Their Eminences Rossini and Meyerbeer made appearances, along with newcomers in the ascendant: Hector Berlioz, the Young Turk of vast orchestral ambition, and Frédéric Chopin, a Polish exile whose two Paris concerts had announced a rival to Liszt. Orbiting these stars, there swirled a large cast of supporting players, including journalists of unkempt appearance, loud voices, and radical politics. George and Marie, at least, thrived on the constant tumult of egos and eloquence clashing in loud political argument, critical judgments on the latest offerings in art, music, and theater, leavened by rowdy jokes, laughter, and freely flowing wine.

In January 1837, George returned to Nohant, which was now restored to her by law. Finally, she was free to realize her Utopian vision of artists and activists. But the beloved community was to have included Michel, and it was painfully clear by now that the jurist would be an occasional presence, at best.

As soon as she settled in, Liszt arrived—without Marie. Only when Franz played did she feel "consoled"; listening to his music, she found that "all my pain turns to poetry, every instinct exalted." Still, George's most powerful emotions were not addressed by Liszt's cascading arpeggios. Although his music occasionally "hits an angry note," she observed, "it couldn't reach my hatred."

"I'm devoured by hatred . . . but hatred of what? God, why can't I ever find a person worthy of being hated?" (not Michel, she quickly added). "God, just do me this one favor, and I won't ever ask You to help me find someone worthy of being loved!"

At the end of January, Marie arrived. She was distressed to find that George still clung to Michel, encouraged by the "crumbs of hope" he occasionally tossed her way in the form of last-minute trysts proposed when the jurist had court business in nearby La Châtre or Châteauroux. Then, a few months later, he agreed to a reunion on their famous anniversary of April 7, in Bourges. George rode through the entire night, only to spend the dawn hours and beyond arguing politics with her lover. Deriding Michel's labors on behalf of an egalitarian future as "moonshine," George sneered at the radical "brutes" whom he insisted on treating as brothers.

Sand refused to see that she was the one escalating their old political conflict into all-out war—a war she was sure to lose. "A woman's love is not an unworthy thing," she reminded Michel, "but these men whom you've raised from the muck, and now believe to be worth more than you, will never be your equals."

Michel's reply says everything about the end of their affair: "Every single day and hour I'm in a state of war—at home, for you and because of you—Fine! That's only fair. Nothing worthwhile in this life is given to man without a struggle. If I could only find in your arms a refuge from this misery. But no! You demand—insist—that I make war against you, too. Enemies to the left, enemies to the right. I have to tell you—this is an untenable situation. I must have peace."

For George, to define herself in terms of a peaceful haven of domestic and sexual refuge from the world was to turn herself into a "fawning, flattering, servile creature." She would be a partner—even a combative, disputatious one—or nothing. Unable to dominate Michel, George decided that he ceased to exist for her. For the first time, *she* broke a date with him, ending her note not with *"au revoir,"* but with *"adieu."*

In our day, Sand has been accused of exceptionalism, the belief that the problems of "ordinary" women did not apply to her. Along with a disdain of feminism, she disapproved of divorce, rejected women as unfit to vote (a right granted to Frenchwomen only in 1945), and angrily demanded of a group of active feminists that they remove her name, placed in nomination as a candidate for the first woman deputy to the National Assembly. Women were not ready for public office, she believed, and to accept the nomination would be to suggest otherwise.

Even in her private life, however, Sand *was* exceptional, not the least in her relations with men. In the end, she always managed to set the terms—a gamble that she was willing to lose and often did. Still, she won by losing; at the last minute, she always escaped the bluestocking blues. She silenced the cries of despair and outrage voiced by women—including George herself—who had staked their very existence on independence, on the equality (if not superiority) of their sex, on demands to be treated and loved as a partner, only to find themselves in thrall to an unworthy man. We want to avert our gaze from the scrawled pleas of Mary Wollstonecraft to Gilbert Imlay, promiscuous American adventurer and shady businessman with whom she was besotted to the point of suicide. Or stifle the irritating Margaret Fuller, hectoring Ralph Waldo Emerson to love her, to see her as more than ideas in a hoop skirt, to appreciate her as a woman, not a sexless disciple.

These other exceptional women beg to be loved *more*—because they are more intelligent, more honest, more self-respecting. Assuming their own worth, they are therefore worthier of being loved. How could you love that fat soprano, painted courtesan, boring heiress—and not me?

Any Paris shopgirl could have answered that question without a beat of hesitation. A man did not care about a companion. Only two needs accounted for his attraction to a woman: social advantage or animal passion. One need meant leveraging ambition through marriage to the "right" woman; the other meant yielding to lust with the "wrong" one. A man's right was to enjoy both. Refusing the prostitution of either was to banish a woman to the margins of society.

Only Sand's talent and success, her force of will and ironclad ego, trumped all the cards stacked against her.

At Nohant, Liszt had turned to serenading his princess (the family was summoned to admire the beautiful naiad leaning against a tree in the moonlight). George found diversion in new recruits to her circle of young acolytes and, as always, in work.

Charles Didier, still smitten and trying again, arrived on the heels of the latest matinee idol, George's new lover, a thirty-eight-year-old actor known only by his stage name, Bocage. Byronian in dress and style, Bocage's interpretation of the starring role in Dumas's drama *Anthony* had been the talk of the Paris season, and his courtship of George took the flattering form of persuading her to write for the theatre. Among the locals was the ever-devoted François Rollinat, along with Maurice's most recent tutor and George's recently dismissed lover, Eugene Pellétan. Another new face came with the allure of an Old Testament prophet: A young Creole playright, Félicien Mallefille, with burning black eyes and long, curly beard, was shortly pressed into action on both fronts.

Marie d'Agoult wondered how anyone could take George seriously. One minute she described herself as suicidal, "cast into nothingness" by Michel's defection; the next, she could be found cavorting in unseemly fashion with her young admirers. Neither of these moods interfered with work; in less than two months, she completed *Les maîtres mosaïstes* (The Master Mosaic Makers), one of over twenty novels or stories by Sand set in Italy. This tale of a family of medieval artisans who created the shimmering interior of Saint Mark's was dedicated to Maurice, perhaps as compensation for abandoning him for Venice (and Musset). Indeed, the novel has some of the simple, uplifting quality of what is now categorized as young-adult fiction, in which knotty problems are neatly resolved to the satisfaction of all.

As a marker of how far Sand had come and as proof of her industry and productivity since the publication of *Indiana* five years earlier, she was now at work on the first edition of her "Complete Works," commissioned by Buloz. There would be many subsequent editions that would be more or less (mostly less) supervised by the author and, for certain texts, seized as a welcome opportunity for Sand to revise Sand.

Undertaken with enthusiasm, the new edition of her most famous novel, *Lélia,* soon turned into an unexpected minefield. From the first, the project was freighted with too much emotional baggage and conflicting goals. Moving from earlier disclaimers, she now bowed to the reality that the eponymous heroine would always be conflated with the author. That being the case, she determined to recast her alter ego: Lélia, the formerly frigid ice princess, was transformed into a passionate woman with a sexual life and a partner of her own. This change required a reconfiguration of male characters, as well. The result is a wan, attenuated version of the 1833 novel (adding a third volume to the earlier two), a change that reflected Sand's confusion in her life as much as in her art.

Further, the new *Lélia* caused endless quarrels with Buloz over payments, lateness, and format. When wrong, Sand's default position was always that the best defense is an offense. Now, missing deadline after deadline, she blamed the publisher. Then, striking a conciliatory tone, she offered a new work of fiction in place of *Lélia,* always assuring him that after "this one," she would get back to the promised revision.

At the beginning of August, leaving the newly anointed Mallefille in charge of Maurice and the Nohant household, Sand took off with Bocage for a honeymoon in the Forest of Fontainebleau. As an act of exorcism as well as a romantic getaway, she booked them into the same Hôtel de Bretagne where she had stayed with Alfred de Musset, whose *Confession d'un enfant du siècle,* published the year before, had bared every detail of their mutual lacerations. Writing to Alfred, George noted, with fairness, the "truth" of all he had written; she hadn't realized her suffering had been so terrible that she had "forgotten" most of it until reading his thinly disguised fiction.

Hardly had George and Bocage settled in when two successive bulletins, each bearing bad news, disturbed their idyll: The first informed George that Casimir had been sighted creeping around La Châtre; fearing that he was planning to abduct Maurice, Sand dispatched Mallefille to investigate what turned out to be a false alarm. The second bulletin notified Sand of her mother's worsening illness. For several weeks, George rushed back and forth between Fontainebleau and Paris. She claimed that Sophie Dupin's last words, before slipping into a final coma, were a request to her daughter: "Please comb my hair." She had always been "as immaculate in appearance as she was flirtatious in manner," George eulogized her mother. And she also recalled Sophie as "subtle, intelligent, artistic and generous. Angered by little things, big-hearted where it counted." Even now, though, George could not soften the pain her mother had inflicted upon her: "She made me suffer as no one else has ever done; dealing me the worst blows of my life."

The lingering trauma of these blows was guilt. Sand blurred the circumstances of Sophie's last hour, leaving it unclear whether the author was actually present, a witness to her mother's "good death," watching as Sophie slipped away for a little nap and convinced that she would wake in a few minutes.

Or whether George had earlier raced back to Fontainebleau to rejoin her lover and now appropriated what she had been told by others about Sophie's last moments. The image of the beloved daughter, blessed by this final deathbed intimacy—combing her mother's hair—may have been Sand's most moving fiction.

13

The Music Makers

In Paris, at the Hôtel de France, George had begun to weary of emerging from her single room to find still in progress the same party that she had left the night before. Looking back, though, she recalled one great compensation: "We heard wonderful music there." The cacophony of voices fell silent when Liszt or a musical guest settled at the piano. One evening, in the late fall of 1836, the host's fellow musician and performer was Frédéric Chopin, and it was here that George and the Polish émigré met and where she heard him play for the first time.

For months, she had begged friends to introduce them, but from all he had heard of Baroness Dudevant, Chopin was in no hurry to make her acquaintance. George Sand was already notorious when the composer had arrived in Paris five years earlier. He had probably never read a line of her writing, but he would have heard about her shameless revelations of women's sexuality—and implicitly, their entitlement to pleasure equal to their obligation to please. Utterly conventional and ultraconservative in his political and, especially, his social views, Chopin anticipated with distaste Sand's strident expression of radical theories, including impious denunciations of marriage and religion. He envisioned her as mannishly large (Chopin was under five feet tall), coarse in manner, with her somber, trouser-clad form wreathed in her own cigar smoke like Laöcoon half-obscured by the serpent.

He found her even more repulsive than he had imagined—and more frightening. Still, she was not the looming giantess of his fantasies; for a large-breasted and wide-hipped woman, George was startlingly small. But everything about her was dark: the wings of jet hair and swarthy skin; the huge, slightly bulging black eyes—"devouring," some said—whose fathomless gaze under a swoop of inky brows cast a spell over men.

Her silence was still more unnerving; she hardly spoke. For Chopin, used to the musical sibilants of Polish women and the *Parisiennes'* twittering soprano, Sand's muteness was unfeminine—unmanning, even.

"Is that really a woman?" he asked a friend, neutering the threat, as they strolled home that evening from the Hôtel de France. "I seriously doubt it."

Even Chopin's family in Warsaw had heard of the notorious female novelist with a man's name. Writing to them now, he noted in passing that he had recently made this lady's acquaintance. At the same time, he shed the armor of the Parisian boulevardier to confess his dread—of what, precisely, he could not say, only that "something about her repels me."

Marie d'Agoult had her own motives for playing cupid. She did not want George to remain a destabilizing odd woman out; she did not trust her or, for that matter, her own volatile lover. If their friendship was to continue, it required the symmetry of a companion for George. When Liszt and d'Agoult next called on Chopin, they brought with them, unannounced and uninvited, Madame Dudevant. Before the visit was over, Chopin's disapproval had started to crumble, yielding to Sand's ardent love of music. He discovered in her a fellow musician of talent, who played the harpsichord and guitar and collected folk songs of the Berry region. In Paris, she had attended nearly every concert and opera; indeed, her passion for music and theatre, she explained, had dictated her off-putting masculine dress. Unable to afford expensive seats in the orchestra or loges and, as a woman, forbidden to sit in the balcony, Sand had initially adopted this disguise to see and hear all that Paris offered.

Chopin was mollified, at least to the extent of including George in an invitation to a musicale he was giving at home.

"I'm having a few people over today, among others, Madame Sand," Chopin wrote on December 13, 1836, to a Polish friend passing through Paris. For this occasion, George compromised. Instead of her black trousers and frock coat, she wore billowing white pantaloons and a red sash—the sexually ambiguous costume of a houri *or* a pasha and, more important, the colors of the Polish flag.

There was no more ardent champion of a liberated Poland or friend to its émigré artists than George Sand. She had signed every manifesto urging the government of the July Monarchy to come to the aid of "the Christ of Nations," as exiled Poles called their martyred homeland. She befriended her writers and poets who had been robbed of their native language, and she did all that she could to promote the country's greatest poet in exile, Adam Mickiewicz, hailing him as "cousin to Byron and Goethe."

Sand was certainly aware of her host's mythic conquest of Paris. Two years and only two concerts after he had arrived from Russian-occupied Warsaw via Vienna, Chopin ranked among those few artists who moved in every circle that counted. Ignoring protocol, older, established musicians called on him. More exceptional for a musician, Sand observed, was his social ascent: This son of a French peasant-turned-schoolmaster did not merely ape his betters, in the way of poor Dr. Pagello; he set the style for the new dandy—pale lavender gloves, exquisite manners tinged with a melancholy, ironic wit.

He was a fixture at the grandest houses; at balls, receptions, dinners, and especially salons, that Parisian tradition perfected in the previous century, where hostesses vied to create intimate gatherings whose regulars represented a fizzy mix of talent, beauty, brilliance, and wealth. Here, Chopin was welcomed as a lionized guest who never failed to charm and amuse; if he could be prevailed on to perform, as he did at the Hôtel de France, he hypnotized every listener. George would have been one of the musically knowledgeable who drew close to the piano to study the wizardry of Chopin's technique and his famous inventions in fingering, third finger crossing the fourth, that made his impossibly difficult compositions appear effortless.

Buoyed by the Parisian passion for the sounds of the new pianoforte and by the vogue for all things Polish, Chopin's compositions were sellouts in sheet music. His principal source of income—and imposing it was—came from lessons. His fee was twenty francs—highway robbery from a mere piano teacher. But when the instructor was a genius (hadn't a German named Robert Schumann said so in an important review?) as well as a sought-after guest and, since he was to be entrusted with wives and daughters, utterly reliable as to morals, it was a bargain.*

Knowing all this, George was still astonished by what she found on this first visit to Chopin's apartment. He had recently moved to rue de la Chaussée d'Antin, in the heart of fashionable Paris, newly established on the Right Bank. Although small, the light-filled rooms, papered in white and oyster gray, gave an illusion of infinite space. White silk and muslin hangings set off precious objects offered as tributes to his musical triumphs: a silver-gilt tea set and a Sèvres dinner service had been presented to Chopin following each of three concerts he had given before the royal family.

Her host's visible hunger for luxury, starting with the composer's cabriolet and coachman that waited on the street below, was foreign to George and a startling contrast to her fellow artists. Aside from her grandmother's few treasures saved from the Revolution, Sand had been brought up in the tradition of *bricolage,* of making do, of endless repairs to what was usable. Ushered in by a

---

*Estimates of the French franc between 1830 and 1848 and its equivalent in today's U.S. dollars, English pounds sterling, or euros vary dramatically, ranging, for example, from $2.50 to $4.80. For a more useful idea of the franc's value during this period, we should note that the average daily wage of an unskilled Parisian worker was one franc. Thus, Chopin's fee for one lesson would have represented about three weeks' wages for a laborer, who often also has a family to feed.

manservant, George goggled at the brand-new furniture, daringly upholstered in pale brocade and whose cost, Liszt gossiped, was already giving the composer attacks of "worry and nerves." For the musicale this afternoon, the rooms were perfumed by hothouse flowers, and for refreshments, Marie d'Agoult passed around ices from the most fashionable caterer in Paris.

The "few people" Chopin had casually mentioned in his invitation turned out to be a crowd in which the obscure guest (one newly arrived fellow Pole) was outnumbered by the distinguished: Besides Liszt and Sand, there was Heinrich Heine, poet and waspish cultural critic who reported from Paris for his Hamburg newspaper; best-selling novelist Eugène Sue; Chopin's adoring fan, the rich aesthete Marquis de Custine; and Count Albert Gryzmala, dashing and mysterious former soldier, revolutionary, womanizer, diplomat, and, most recently, financier and art collector. At forty, "Gryz" was Chopin's father figure and his only Polish intimate to move in the same lofty circles.

As host, Chopin declined to take the spotlight in performing; he would only agree to play a duet with his most celebrated musical guest. Together, he and Liszt dazzled their listeners with a sonata for four hands by an admired contemporary, the now forgotten Ignaz Moscheles. To their rapt guests, they played as one. Enthralled, Sand yielded to her worship of genius, doubled now by their duet for four hands: the familiar brilliance of her friend Liszt and the revelation of Chopin's playing merged into "angelic" sounds, detached from the forgettable music.

Envy was foreign to George; she took only pleasure in friends' talent and success. In anticipation of Liszt's earlier visit to Nohant, she had sent to Paris for a piano, and she used her connections to further the literary efforts of Marie d'Agoult. Chopin would complete their magic circle. She saw the four of them, a Parnassus unto themselves, at Nohant, writing, reading, walking, and making love and music.

The sacred symmetry that Sand envisioned never came to pass. Liszt's passion for the fragile and demanding d'Agoult was starting to cool. And Chopin could never sustain a friendship of equals with a fellow musician. Reserved, proud, mysterious, he inspired love by withholding its expression: He gave, Liszt observed, "everything but himself."

Sharper warnings followed: Chopin had nothing but contempt for most of his fellow émigré Poles—their political factionalism, religious zealotry, or plain provincialism brought out his worst snobbery. His dislike was reciprocated. Even a peer in talent and recognition, Adam Mickiewicz, honored by his adopted country with a Chair at the Collège de France, took a dim view of the composer. Now Mickiewicz held it as one of the duties of friendship to warn George against Chopin: The man was a "moral vampire," he said. His advice came too late.

In the six weeks following the musicale, Sand and Chopin saw each other six times. Spanning the old year and the new—1837—the season of festivities and bright beginnings ought to have smiled on the new couple, a union deemed predestined by most of their friends. New obstacles now loomed, the principal one entirely foreign to George's experience of men. All that attracted her in Chopin and set him apart from the others—his genius, his intellectual subtlety, his delicacy of perception, his refinement and reserve, his fastidiousness of manner and dress—were inseparable, so it appeared, from the shame, disgust, and guilt he felt about sex.

Sand was horrified: In a forty-page letter to Albert Gryzmala, Chopin's father confessor, she revealed the outrage she felt on discovering that his friend had been so revolted by earlier sexual experiences as to recoil from the physical as a defilement of love. What unspeakable woman had done this to him?

Whores and a virginal fiancée had perpetuated his adolescent confusion. Two years earlier, the composer, then twenty-five, had fallen in love with the sixteen-year-old sister of a friend. Encouraged on the one hand to see Maria Wodzinska as a future wife, he was, on the other hand, entrusted to protect her well-chaperoned purity. Learning of Chopin's poor health (including rumors that he was dying in Paris), the young woman's family appears to have withdrawn their approval of the match.

He had confided the story of his great "sorrow" to George, leaving unanswered the question of whether he was still in love with the younger woman. In the same letter in which George elaborated her concerns about Chopin's sexuality to Count Gryzmala, she also set forth her doubts about her own role in the composer's life *if* his affections were still engaged elsewhere. Sand clearly saw the symbolic roles that she and Maria played at this point in Chopin's life: the innocent child sweetheart, an icon of old Poland, whom he could romanticize from afar, and the Frenchwoman, independent, sexually experienced, powerful, and demanding—one representing his past, the other his future. Although his reply has not survived, Gryzmala seems to have reassured and encouraged Sand to proceed with her mission of reeducation.

But Chopin was not reassured. George's imperious certainty that swept aside all obstacles to desire filled him with dread as much as longing. The reserve and distance he maintained between himself and the world was no romantic pose; always sickly, his energy limited, he saw preserving and protecting himself as crucial to his art. And what Sand demanded was nothing less than that he abandon this wary stewardship and yield his fears of loss and of waste (connected certainly to sexual terror) to embrace her own belief that extravagance—in money, politics, friendship, work, and love—promised not death but rebirth.

Now it was Chopin who turned to Gryzmala, sending him an urgent message. He must see his friend immediately, no matter the hour. They met late that same night in the fashionable Maison Dorée Café. The older man dismissed the case for caution and delay. In the spring of 1838, nearly two years after their first meeting, Chopin and Sand became lovers.

Félicien Mallefille, the incumbent in George's life, took it badly. The playwright began behaving like a character from a boulevard drama; staking out a place near the Hôtel de France, he took to stalking the lovers. When he waylaid her one night, waving a gun, it was clear that Sand's vows of a love that ended only with death had been taken literally.

Others whom she cared about also showed symptoms of neglect: Maurice complained of constant pains whose indeterminate source raised the specter of rheumatic fever. Solange, nearly ten, wrote weepy letters from her pension. The children's unhappiness, Mallefille's continued threats, and Chopin's dread of the impending cold weather, bringing seasonal bouts of flu, grippe, and morning attacks of coughing, decided George to flee Paris for a winter in a mild and sunny climate.

Chopin and Sand's four-month interlude in Majorca has taken on a mythic life of its own: They set out to worship the Apollonian miracle of the sun that cures the incurable, conferring strength, health, and immortality. Instead, the largest of the Balearic Islands has come to stand for the perfidies of climate, as the setting for the longest-playing trope on consumption consuming the artist, of fatality hastened by carnal passion, on the flesh laid waste. Majorca has become a vampire tale with Sand in the starring role, keyboard streaming with Chopin's blood. As it happens, that was Hollywood, not history.

In reality, Majorca was the place where George was transformed from sexual outlaw to nurturing parent, beginning the slow drip of dependence. Here Chopin, orphaned by exile, was reborn into the Oedipal dream: the favored older son who shared his mother's bed.

Theirs was no wild flight of lovers. Like diplomatic missions, they traveled separately, Chopin escorted by a friend, and Sand accompanied by the two children and a maid. The two groups met in Perpignan and, taking the boat from there, arrived in Palma on November 8, 1838. No sooner had she found the only house to be rented on the island than Chopin succumbed to a respiratory infection. Visits by three local doctors only succeeded in spreading the word that his illness was indeed tuberculosis. A recently passed Spanish law decreed that those infected be promptly evicted, and the costs of burning and replacing all household effects be added to their bill. The carriers were banished to the remote beauty of an abandoned Carthusian monastery in Valldemosa, perched among mountain crags where the nearest neighbors were the eagles circling overhead.

Food and medicine were sold to the pariahs at extortionist prices. A local peasant woman cooked for them, but the rancid olive oil added chronic diarrhea to Chopin's respiratory problems. Now, Sand's competence and grit became crucial to their survival. She dealt fiercely with every problem, human and material. She was desperately behind in finishing her new novel, *Spiridion*, but the demands of housekeeper, teacher, and nurse left her no time to write. She took over the cooking, and in between kitchen duty and tutoring the children, she set in motion the superhuman feat of getting Chopin's Pleyel piano shipped from Paris. Three weeks of pleading, threatening, and haggling on Sand's part were required just to release the instrument from the extortionist customs officials in Palma. There followed further negotiations to arrange for the transport of the delicate mechanism—with its hundreds of movable parts—before it arrived at the monastery gate on January 11. Now Chopin could continue work on the twenty-four preludes of Opus 28, along with other pieces begun in Paris.

Ultimately, the climate's treachery defeated them. (Is there any crueler lie than the dark skies and freezing rain of Goethe's "lands where the lemon trees bloom"?) The northerner's dream of a life-restoring south more often ends in death—in Venice; or in Rome, like Keats; or, like Lawrence, on the Côte d'Azur. It was

Sand who had brought Chopin on this "catastrophic voyage," she said; now it was Sand who saved and, for a time, strengthened him.

Fear only made George stronger and more decisive. Each attack left Chopin weaker than the one before. Soon after the New Year of 1839, she knew he would not recover in these primitive, hostile conditions. By the middle of February, he was coughing blood; he was feverish, refusing to eat, and too weak to leave his bed. She booked passage for them on the next boat leaving for the mainland, and packing up her little household, they made the agonizing descent to Palma. In the cart and again on board the boat, Chopin coughed up "basins of blood." After a week in Barcelona, he was well enough for the trip to Marseilles. There, installed in suites in the best hotel, Sand supervised Chopin's convalescence as minutely as she had nursed him during the worst of his sickness. She found a competent and solicitous doctor, while she continued to hover over his diet and rest.

Like a Mozartian duet in which the hero and heroine sing of their love at opposite ends of the stage, Sand and Chopin wrote to friends, extolling, in identical phrases, the perfection of the other.

"My God, if you knew him as I do now, you would love him even more," Sand told Charlotte Marliani, wife of the former consul to Majorca, who had so ill-advised her about its restorative climate. And to his friend Gryzmala, Chopin confided: "You know, you would love her still more if you knew her as well as I do at this moment." Each was anointed an "angel" by the other, George of devotion and self-sacrifice, and "Chip-Chip," as she called him, for his "kindness, tenderness and patience."

She felt blessed that their ordeal had drawn them closer: "We became a family, our bonds tighter because it was us against the world. Now, we cling to each other with deeper, more intimate feelings of happiness. How can we complain when our hearts are so full?"

14

The House of Art and the House of Life

SETTING OUT ON THE FINAL LAP of their journey home, George felt buoyed by optimism: The place that had always healed her would confer its blessings on Chopin as well. From Marseilles, the family traveled by ferry down the Rhône to Arles; then, proceeding by leisurely relay of carriages, they arrived at the gates of Nohant on June 2, 1839.

After Majorca, they were all the more appreciative of a nature that seemed to welcome—even to embrace them. Instead of Valldemosa's circling eagles, they were greeted, Chopin wrote to Gryzmala, by the sounds of "nightingales and larks." He was even more delighted by the living arrangements in the house itself. Next to her bedroom, Sand had created a little apartment for him; a library and sleeping quarters freshly hung with festive, red and blue Chinese paper. Downstairs, the upright piano George had earlier installed for Liszt was replaced by a small Pleyel grand on which Chopin immediately set to work.

In her happiness at being home, George and the children took off on a round of excursions—as though reassuring herself that familiar sights, sounds, and smells were all still there. They were eager to experience new places as well. The warmth and sunshine of early summer seemed to urge everyone outdoors; no corner of the Black Valley was left unexplored. There were trips to prehistoric sites and Merovingian ruins and nature expeditions where Maurice, fifteen and encouraged by George, pursued his avid collecting of minerals and meteorites, butterflies, reptiles, and insects. Armed with a plentiful supply of small sketch-pads, Sand, in dense, nervous lines, drew streams lined with pollarded willows, cataracts, strange rock formations, later heightening the pencil impressions with white pigment and color, in the eighteenth-century style. Occasionally, Chopin set off with the rest, riding on the back of a gentle donkey, happy to lie in the sun when the others dismounted to investigate the area on foot.

Medically, there was only good news. Disagreeing with the Majorcan doctors, Sand's old friend and neighbor Dr. Papet pronounced Chopin's lungs to be sound. The physician predicted that Chopin's condition would continue to improve with wholesome country life: regular meals, sleep, fresh air, and George's vigilant care.

For Sand, work would always be the measure of health. She now felt confident of Chopin's recovery as, within weeks, he returned to composing and playing with a concentration and energy she had never observed before: "He enchants all of us from morning till night." Ordinarily, the composer began pieces with élan, only to falter. Then, giving up the struggle to complete them, he would lay the works aside—indefinitely. Now, he finished the first Nocturne of Opus 37, which was begun in Majorca, along with the entire Second Nocturne and the Third Scherzo. With all that he accomplished in these first months, it comes as no surprise that Chopin would compose half of his entire oeuvre in Nohant. More than restored, he seemed reborn.

Listening to Chopin at work on the scherzo, George heard an agony of creation new to her. In Majorca, he had been too ill to yield to his obsessive perfectionism; the endless repetition of a troublesome phrase, like a hammer to the head, worked and reworked; the angry, despairing sounds of frustrated effort—cunning, desperate, exhausting—to retrieve a composition that had earlier come to him, complete and unbidden, only to evaporate. This was art as blood sport, or human sacrifice. She was humbled, but also mystified and frightened. It was too foreign to her.

A journeywoman scrivener, covering reams of paper nightly while the rest of the household slept, she wrote the way others breathed. She was grateful to let editors, friends, lovers, take on revisions and corrections, while she plowed on—to the next volume or a new work. She wrote to pay bills and pay off debts, "to feed twelve mouths," to satisfy her exigent publisher for work owed him, and to extract needed advances against future novels.

"I'm working like an old rat, gnawing my brains," she wrote to Hippolyte. Now that Casimir was out of their lives, warm relations had been restored between brother and sister. She thanked 'Polite for seeing to their small income from property, a favor that freed her to write. And she later told her great friend, the other slave to perfection, Gustave Flaubert, that even had she been blessed with his brilliance, she never had his luxury of time, to chew each word, prod and pare every sentence. But she harbored few illusions about herself: She was not an artist. Her success simply enabled her to provide for all of those dependent on her and, where Chopin was concerned, to pay the tribute owed by talent to genius.

We should not take Sand's own modesty for the measure of her work. She was so fecund in ideas about plot and character, and so passionate about the issues of the day, that she was in a frenzy to get them down, to illuminate, instruct, and possibly even to change the course of events as they bore upon the lives of ordinary men and women. Style would have to take care of itself.

THEY HAD BARELY SETTLED into Nohant when, three weeks after their arrival, Sand, using a penknife or hard, sharp pencil, scratched a date on the paneled embrasure of her bedroom window: June 19, 1839. Originally, the mysterious graffito—the only known notation of its kind ever attributed to the writer—was followed by a line of verse in English. The line didn't survive, and no one has ever identified the poetry, which seems to have been obliterated first—and definitively. The carved date itself has been painted over and papered over many times. Theories about the meaning of the lost words abound: What do they commemorate? The editor of Sand's twenty-five-volume correspondence and most of her other autobiographical writing believed that the tracing paid homage to the new life of peace and happiness that opened before them, affirming the optimism she had first expressed in Marseilles: Majorca and its trials had forged deeper bonds of love and intimacy between them. Others have argued that so precise a date must signal an anniversary. Its location in Sand's bedroom (with two children in the house, George and Chopin would never have openly shared sleeping quarters) has produced two divergent views of supposed sexual significance: The day marks either the passage of a year since the consummation of their love, or the reverse, the end of George's physical relations with Chopin.

There are few clues from either of them to shed light on the meaning of the graffito. Nineteenth-century medicine held sexual activity to be dangerous for consumptives. Sand, however, was persuaded that Chopin was free of the disease, and she believed, almost alone among her contemporaries, in sexual fulfillment as natural—indeed, as the *most* natural, both physically and spiritually, expression of human love. She had come to take Chopin's frail constitution for granted; he would always feel "not quite ill or yet entirely well." As soon as he felt the least bit energetic, he was in high spirits, and even in the grip of melancholy, "he threw himself upon the piano to compose some of his most beautiful pages," she recalled.

George's principal worries were allayed by Chopin's generally improved health and steady productivity, but she continued to fret over his moodiness. She feared his slide into an enveloping ennui, the paralyzing boredom and melancholy whose only antidote is diversion in its true sense, the turning away from care. He needed spectacle, opera and theater, concerts and cafés, balls and soirees, but most important, he needed other people:

friends, acquaintances, and strangers—the swirling, shifting, human panorama of Paris.

Life at Nohant, with its country rhythms, was "austere," Sand acknowledged. Estate manager, housekeeper, children's tutor, breadwinner writing into the night to make up missed deadlines, she could not help failing him as an available companion; her other obligations often left him without company when he least wanted to be alone.

With the distractions and demands of managing Chopin and Nohant, Sand's writing in the wake of their return was not her most ambitious, consisting largely of completing unfinished work for which she owed the publisher for advances long outstanding: *Spiridion,* a "monastic" novel, was begun, suitably, at Valldemosa. Its eponymous hero, a converted Jew, has moved from his inherited faith to Orthodox Christianity and from there to Deism. The end of his spiritual quest is to pass the torch (in the form of a secret and sacred text) to a younger disciple, Master Alexis: Its words will free yet another acolyte, Angel, to leave the order, embracing life as the ultimate religious act. A novel without women, the elder and younger monks bear more than a passing resemblance, respectively, to Lamennais, the priest in conflict with his church, and Leroux, the former Saint-Simonian attempting to forge a new religion, while both men reflect stages of the author's spiritual journey still in progress.

Two more novels with Venetian settings, *The Last Aldini* and *The Seven Strings of the Lyre,* a wan retelling of the Faust legend, fared badly with readers and critics alike; the same proved true of *Uscoque,* a tale of Barbary pirates. The most famous—and unlikely—fan of this novel was Dostoyevsky. Most would have agreed with Liszt, who, influenced by an increasingly venomous d'Agoult, described these novels as "painful" reading after *Indiana* and *Lélia.*

One work from this period, *Gabriel,* a novel-in-dialogue, has received little attention until recently, when its theme of androgyny has invited fresh scrutiny. Begun in Marseille during Chopin's convalescence, *Gabriel* examines the psychosexual questions of gender as biological determinant or social construct. In order to allow Princess Gabrielle to inherit the title and kingdom, her grandfather has raised her as a boy. For three months of each year, however, Gabriel/Gabrielle is allowed to return to her female self, a period during which she attracts the ardent attentions of a suitor, Astolphe, allowing Sand further play with received notions of "masculine" and "feminine." Are different qualities required to rule a kingdom or to give and accept love? (It can be no coincidence that Sand borrowed the name Astolphe from Chopin's openly homosexual friend, Astolphe de Custine, who was most certainly in love with the composer.) In *Gabriel,* Sand explores all the ironies and complexities of dual identity—anatomy, dress, sex, and politics. It's tempting to speculate as to why the novel was ignored for so long. One reason may be its hybrid form (theatre piece or prose fiction?), which raised problems of genre. Another was the absence of a vocabulary among Sand's contemporaries to tease out the most troubling issues; her peers relegated the novel to the safe zone of fable or fairy tale. Praising *Gabriel's* "psychological" acuity, Balzac alone seems to have grasped the "hall of mirrors" phenomenon of gender that Sand strips bare of encrusted assumptions to reveal its fluid realities.

Clouding the bright start of the new decade, 1840, was the problem of money. Nohant, Sand calculated, cost twice as much—fifteen hundred francs a month—as living in Paris. In the country, she often descended from her study to find no fewer than twelve guests for dinner, among them, friends or neighbors who didn't hesitate to invite themselves. Deciding that another long stay there was unaffordable, she and her family skipped Berry in the summer of 1840. In November, George signed the contract for a new edition of her *Complete Works* for an advance of twenty-eight thousand francs. But a year later, she was forced to take out a loan of ten thousand to meet expenses.

Money troubles urged her to more serious consideration of the theatre—which she had discussed earlier with her lover, the actor Bocage. George's publisher, François Buloz, had recently been promoted from royal commissioner to director (the equivalent of board chairman) of the Théâtre Français. In this capacity, he too urged Sand to write for the stage, pointing out the huge earnings that success had won for playwrights like Dumas père.

In early spring, Sand began work with Marie Dorval on her first play, *Cosima,* or "Hatred at the Heart of Love"—a subject in which both author and star could claim a certain expertise. They both hoped that the drama would revive Marie's languishing career; the actress had fallen victim to the cruelty of age and her massive weight gain. Neither Sand's current prestige or Dorval's once-magnetic name saved their collaboration: On opening night and before the final curtain, *Cosima* was booed off the stage. With her resilience and professionalism, George cut her losses and withdrew the play after seven performances.

Chopin, too, was deep in debt. He had sold the six compositions he had finished since Majorca and had given up his expensive apartment in Chaussée d'Antin, but in Berry, he was deprived of his only reliable source of income: lessons. He feared that his pupils—and their families—would forget him.

During their last summer in Nohant, Chopin had taken on the task of finding them housing—officially, separate—in Paris. Gryzmala and another of Chopin's Polish acolytes were armed with instructions (including floor plan) of George's requirements, starting with her preferred addresses, with "peace and quiet" at the top of the list.

In 1841, Pigalle was still a tranquil village, and at 16 rue Pigalle, they found paired pavilions at the back of a luxuriant garden that promised an oasis hidden from the street. Chopin's and Sand's second-floor apartments, located above workshops and reached by an exterior iron staircase, had the feel of adjoining tree houses. Chopin and Maurice occupied one wing; George and Solange were across the garden. Delacroix had agreed to take on Maurice (now eighteen) as one of several studio assistants; his mother hoped that the master's genius and industry would move the indolent boy from artistic "leanings" to a real career.

Once installed in her freshly decorated Paris quarters, Sand's entertaining, informal as it was, took on the fixity of a salon. No longer a planet in the orbit of Liszt and d'Agoult, she shone alone. From late afternoon on, the largest room, painted a pale coffee color, filled with friends; Balzac especially loved the tubs of flowers and other plants sent from Nohant, the walls hung heavily with paintings, and, in the middle, Chopin's piano, as richly carved as a baroque altarpiece. The novelist nosily eyed his hostess's bedroom and reported to his mistress, "no bed, two mattresses on the floor, à la turque."

For months, George, abetted by friends, had been working to convince Chopin to brave the ordeal of a concert. He had not played in public since the spring of 1838, before their stay in Majorca. His horror of performing before strangers—akin to feelings of violation—had worsened with time. In spite of these fears, intensified by the debilitating bouts of illness he had suffered since his first Paris concerts, Chopin's practical side (encouraged by George) reminded him of the profit, both direct and indirect, sure to flow from a return engagement, from the sale of tickets to the increased value of new works through audience word of mouth and glowing reviews. Then, there was the challenge from his only rival: In March 1841, Liszt had returned to Paris after a triumphal tour that included a musical milestone; in Rome, he had given the first performance by a single virtuoso.

Whether the decisive factor was Liszt's brilliant success, Chopin's constant need of money, or the reassuring certainty that Sand would manage the entire event, he let himself be persuaded. George was jubilant. "A great, no the greatest piece of news is that little Chip-Chip is going to give a grrrand concert" she proclaimed to their friend and protégée, the famed singer Pauline Viardot. Chopin had agreed only because he assumed the event could never be arranged on such short notice, at the end of the musical season, Sand reported. But he had not reckoned on her efficiency. Scarcely had he uttered "the fatal 'yes,'" George added, when, as if by magic, everything was done, with three-quarters of the tickets sold before the actual date of the concert had been announced.

Chopin panicked, she told her Viardot: "He doesn't want posters, he doesn't want programs, he doesn't want a big audience; he doesn't want anyone to talk about it. He's so terrified by the whole thing that I suggested he play in the dark, with no one present, on a dumb keyboard!"

Sand conquered fear by appearing fearless. She refused to accept the reality that anyone—let alone a man who was also a great artist—could succumb to terror. Her mocking surrealist scenario of Chopin's ideal concert—the hall dark and empty, the keys mute—was a measure of her well-honed skill in facing down her own terrors.

She had thought of everything—even a pacifier. Only now did George reveal that the forthcoming concert was public in name only. Tickets had been "placed"—offered only to those already part of Chopin's world.

The occasion was more brilliant than any manager—including George herself—could have hoped. Masses of hothouse flowers at the foot of the red-carpeted double grand staircase at the Salle Pleyel welcomed the glittering throngs, before their ascent to the concert hall on the floor above. "The most elegant women, the most fashionable young men, the most celebrated artists, the richest financiers, the most illustrious peers, indeed all the elite of society, all the aristocracy of birth, fortune, talent and beauty" attended, Liszt reported.

For this performance, Chopin spared himself nothing; he would never play a more arduous program, including the four mazurkas of Opus 41, the second Ballade in F Major, Opus 38, the murderous Third Scherzo, and the two polonaises of Opus 40. "The 'bravos,' the 'encores,' the ladies fainting away"—by every measure, Sand reported, Chopin's "Great Concert" had been his greatest success. And it was not lost on those who knew them both that the works performed by Chopin on this historic evening had all been composed since his liaison with Sand. Along with her organization of the event and her role in his restored health, the occasion was also revealed as his homage to George. Lover, companion, nurse, host, and now impresario—all these gifts had never been bestowed so lavishly on an artist. Freely given, they nonetheless bore a price. Chopin's world narrowed, and his dependence on George deepened.

15

Separate Tables

THE GREAT CONCERT ended a hectic Paris season. In the late afternoons, Sand's salon in rue Pigalle continued to fill with visitors. And almost every night, when the last guest had gone, George and Chopin went out—together or separately. Both their agendas were crowded by complimentary tickets from fellow artists—singers, musicians, actors, and playwrights–inviting the couple to performances (George herself never hesitated to ask for house seats when these were not forthcoming). No friend to aristocrats generally, she nonetheless warmed to Chopin's talented Polish princess and pupil, Marcelina Czartoriski, even going so far as to attend her benefits and balls at the vast Hôtel Lambert to aid fellow exiles in need. When it came to the salons and receptions at which the composer appeared regularly, Sand was otherwise engaged. She found the splendid entertainments provided by his grander patrons, Baron James de Rothschild and his wife, Betty, uncongenial. It's unlikely that she was missed. Those who hoped to add a literary lioness to their social mix were invariably disappointed by the famous writer. What passed for sparkling conversation drove her into silence.

Paris was killing her, George now claimed, starting with her exhausting social life. She complained about the dirt, the noise, the crowds, the drafts and the damp—the latter causing all kinds of illnesses unknown to her in Nohant: grippe, flu, quinsy throat, and chronic headaches.

These last symptoms may have been due more to overwork than any noxious effects of city air. Within a year, she had completed two new novels. The first, *Horace,* is the only one of Sand's full-length fictions to be set in Paris, and it reflects her soured feelings about the capital as the source of corruption of every kind. Situating her story in the recent past, George used her own memories of the "Three Glorious Days," the uprising of 1830, when the corpses of slaughtered students hung from the Saint-Merri tower—only one of the infamies that laid bare the betrayals of the July Monarchy—followed by the devastating cholera epidemic. The victims of both had been visible from her window on the Quai des Grands-Augustins.

For her protagonists, George opposed a hero and antihero. Driven by poverty, Paul Arsène is forced to give up a promising career of painter. Returning to his father's trade of shoemaker, he sees life at the bottom with the eyes of one who had briefly escaped. Fired by new awareness, he becomes a radical leader, organizing the masses to revolt and to work toward a new world order. Paul's friend and double, Horace Dumontet, son of well-to-do peasants, squanders his mother's savings, which had sent him to Paris to rise through the study of law. Instead, Horace becomes a slothful dandy, dilettante, and Byronic caricature of the romantic artist: "If I give myself to love," he proclaims, "I want it to wound me deeply, to electrify me, to break my heart or to exalt me to the seventh heaven . . . what I want is to suffer, to go crazy." Along with images of revolutions past, memories of Musset hover over Horace, with not a little parody of the author herself.

Increasingly, George's salon welcomed critics of power and privilege—those whose targets were the same men and women on whom Chopin was dependent and whose company, in truth, he preferred. The same disheveled young journalists whom Sand had introduced to the established *culturati* at the Hôtel de France had grown up; a few had become as notorious as Sand herself had once been. In certain quarters, Louis Blanc, firebrand and tireless writer, had made himself feared as well as famous through his influential radical study, "The Organization of Labor," written as an idealistic blueprint for a republicanism that would represent all citizens. The celebrated message of his proposed solution, "From each according to his capacity, to each according to his needs," was not lost on the nervous new money shoring up "the Citizen-King." Blanc's agenda implied nothing less than income redistribution: The anti-Christ was here. Like Chopin, Blanc was six years younger than Sand and would soon become her lover as well as confidant and colleague. With George, a meeting of minds—when the encounter involved a vigorous, impassioned young man and a seeker of social justice—was apt to stray from the cerebral.

At that point, a related article of faith thrust yet another cast of characters into Sand's life. She became a convert to the belief that artists, writers, and especially poets were waiting to be discovered among peasants and urban proletariat alike; they had only to be identified and encouraged before poverty stifled their gifts. Soon, rue Pigalle and Nohant welcomed a literary locksmith, along with a baker and a weaver; George established long-lived friendships with Charles Poncy, a stone carver whose copious poetic works she helped publish, and the cabinetmaker Agricol Perdiguier. It was to Perdiguier—activist, writer, amateur historian, and future deputy—that Sand confided her proto-Marxist vision: "The future of the world is in the hands of the people, and above all the working class. In time, the masses will emerge from the blindness and crude ignorance where the so-called enlightened classes have held them in chains." Perdiguier saw his mission as nothing less than the development of class consciousness among skilled workers—stonemasons and carpenters like himself—through the revival of artisans' guilds, called *Devoirs*. Perdiguier's own training as apprentice cabinet maker had required a walking tour of France, in which the young workers stopped at designated hostels in a sort of secular pilgrimage, before being qualified as master craftsmen.

Sand was intrigued by this disappearing tradition of the guilds, the romantic, on-the-road character of an "ambulant apprenticeship," as she called it, of young workers traveling together: singing, drinking, brawling; the rival *Devoirs* resembled Freemasons' lodges characterized by secret passwords and handshakes. Her fascination with this culture, its folkloric roots, and its practical application to the present took the form, first, of helping to publish, with her own preface, Perdiguier's recollection of the apprentices' songs, games, scraps of memoir, along with his thoughts on this disappearing chapter of history. Now, Perdiguier himself became a model for Pierre Huguenin, the tall, blonde, and handsome hero of her new novel, *Le compagnon du tour de France* (Comrade-Carpenter).

So inspired was George by her subject, she all but completed the novel over a single weekend, which the author herself spent on the road. She had decided to accompany her new friend, Pauline Viardot, to a series of concerts the singer was giving in Cambrai in northern France. While Pauline rehearsed in the city's opera house, George found that a quiet hotel room was more conducive to uninterrupted writing than was the bustling Nohant household and its demanding occupants.

As an example of one of Sand's revealing failures, *Le compagnon . . .* tells us why the subject and author were made for each other but also why the novel falls short of its ambitions: George tried to elevate her hunk of a hero to the level of a Louis Blanc. A visionary, Pierre sees beyond his personal circumstances to the larger possibilities for laboring mankind. The author's efforts to yoke a coming-of-age narrative to Pierre's rising political consciousness falter; like many of Sand's heroes and heroines, he is never allowed off the ideological leash, to become a full-blood character. He's radical! He's irresistible! He organizes subversive labor associations and falls in love with well-born ladies, but Pierre remains lifeless, a recruiting poster for romantic socialism. Anticipating this critique herself, Sand's preface defends her own "idealism"—exemplified by Huguenin's impossible beauty—against the "realism" of Balzac. The way things are, she declared, repelled her; she wanted to show what they should be.

Both *Horace* and *Le compagnon . . .* were promptly rejected by Sand's publisher. Defender of the established order and fervent monarchist, François Buloz owed his recent honorary appointment as royal director of the Théâtre Français to court favor. He had had earlier qualms about publishing Sand's attacks on marriage and assertion of women's sexuality in his *Revue des Deux Mondes.* These controversial decisions had been vindicated by the success of the serialized novels—gobbled up by the very bourgeoisie whose institutions the author had challenged. In turning revolutionary criminals into heroes, like Paul Arsène in *Horace* or suggesting in *Le compagnon . . .* that artisans should organize to secure better working conditions, Sand had gone too far: She had now put her publisher at risk for undermining law and order (indeed, there were statutes forbidding all "associations" of workers as seditious). Both manuscripts could also be read as implicit attacks on the monarchy and its rising service class of millionaire industrialists. This elite had already been made jittery by the rumored revival of the suppressed "Workers' Movement." For the first time, a labor organization threatened to endorse the real meaning of "union," one that would embrace both skilled artisans and the unskilled urban proletariat.

Enraged by this fresh evidence of Buloz's cowardice and favor currying, George now acted on a plan she had been meditating for months: founding, with the collaboration of like-minded friends, a journal of their own. Born of many late-night meetings, *La Revue Independante*, with Sand as publisher, was launched with the help of Louis Viardot, Pauline's new husband, who contributed his managerial skills—first of theatres and now of his wife's career, together with deep pockets and republican sympathies. They were joined by Louis Blanc, along with a new recruit to George's inner circle.

Sand had first met Pierre Leroux when the young radical was an acolyte of Michel de Bourges. Leroux now became George's protégé, rising rapidly in her esteem and confidence until, in a reversal of roles, it was Sand who exalted the visionary genius of Leroux, her mentor and master.

Printer, writer, educator, inventor, prophet (with a strong component of con artist), Leroux is one of those figures whose character, motives, and accomplishments still elicit debate. Son of a lemonade vendor in the Place des Voges, Leroux and Sand, daughter of a bird seller on the Quai des Mégisseries, forged deep and lasting bonds, starting with their class origins. With characteristic honesty, George acknowledged that only her grandmother and the advantages provided by this relative accounted for the social divide between them. A brilliant student, Leroux, unlike Michel de Bourges, never found patrons to further his education. Forced to leave school as a child, he followed the path of other self-taught radicals, becoming a compositor and printer and thus mastering the means of getting out the word.

Leroux's theology, a mystical pantheism, owed much to both Buddha and Saint-Simon and, echoing the Christian Trinity, was based on a system of triads: God is power, intelligence, and love; he manifests himself in man, through sensation, sentiment, and knowledge. This unexceptionable faith, wedded to an egalitarian social gospel, spoke to Sand's own eclectic and capacious

Christianity. She had already been so impressed by Leroux's prophetic utterances that she dedicated *Spiridion* to him.

Among the other articles of faith in Leroux's system that spoke to Sand was his belief in the education of working men and women. Like George's first love, Stéphane de Grandsagne, Leroux was the author of several popular encyclopedias whose goal was to be accessible to the less literate. Like Sand, Leroux had lost faith in Saint-Simonianism, but for different reasons. Believing marriage vows to be sacred, he rejected that sect's espousal of free love: Without complaint, he had assumed the lifelong burdens of an insane (or possibly, retarded) wife and of children too numerous to be counted. His domestic straits may explain why he proved to be a sinkhole for other people's money: Loans (many from George) solicited for all kinds of grandiose projects and plans vanished with nothing to show for the lenders' investment—other than staving off starvation for the Leroux family.

La Revue Independante's first issue, in November 1841, featured the opening chapters of *Horace,* ninety-six pages of the manuscript rejected by Buloz's *Revue des Deux Mondes.* With an organ of her own, together with fiery and committed comrades, George could take on the world.

WHEN HER NEW ASSOCIATES weren't noisily gathered at rue Pigalle, Sand was out, at meetings or raising money for the new venture. She had fewer evenings available for Chopin. He might have missed George, but he was only too happy to avoid her new friends and their distasteful ideas, foremost among them the rejection of the one true church and their obsession with elevating the lower classes.

In Nohant, intrusions by Sand's political allies were rare; radical journalists like Louis Blanc had neither time nor money for leisurely country visits. In contrast, the only prosperous backer of the new journal, Louis Viardot, was always welcome, in large part because his wife, Pauline, and baby daughter had become, for both Sand and Chopin, a part of their family.

In August 1841, the Viardots arrived in Nohant for a two-week visit, when Pauline helped Chopin christen his new Pleyel grand piano. At twenty, the contralto, fresh from a triumphal tour, was as complete a musician as either of her hosts had ever heard. Her father had been a famed voice coach, and the untimely death of her sister, the legendary soprano Maria Malibran, had deepened Pauline's sense of vocation. Besides her thrilling voice, she was a talented pianist and inventive composer. She shared with George a special interest in collecting folk songs from her native Spain and, now, from Berry, even providing vocal settings for Chopin's mazurkas. That August, to the delight of all, he accompanied Pauline as she sang her way through all the Mozart operas, along with Handel, Gluck, and Haydn arias.

George adored Pauline for her depth and generosity of spirit that was at the polar opposite of the diva. The young singer was her "Fifille," the nickname expressing Pauline's place in her heart as a beloved older daughter, and when the Viardots' first child was born the following December, George would act as honorary grandmother and babysitter for little Louise when her parents were on tour. Most important, Pauline was probably the only friend that Sand and Chopin held in equal affection and esteem.

Consuelo, the life story of a singer whose real-life inspiration was the incomparable Viardot, remains Sand's only novel whose heroine is not an idealized portrait of the writer. The fictional Spanish artist's career takes her from charity orphan in one of Venice's famed singing academies, to Habsburgs and Hungary and includes revolution and romance along the way. Consuelo's talent and success collide with her high moral scruples to create the novel's dynamic. Because Sand had a flesh-and-blood model before her, the protagonist pulsates with life; we believe in Consuelo's art and her passion. This authenticity explains why *Consuelo* is one of Sand's most loved novels—as opposed to the much-studied and little read *Lélia.* Ennobled by marriage as the Countess of Rudolstadt, Consuelo reappears in a long, rambling sequel of that name, which drew heavily on the activities of freemasonry and the conspiratorial world of secret societies. Thus, the invented character's drama plays out against a panorama of historical events and personages, starting with the singer's first teacher, the great Venetian composer and choirmaster, Porpora. For both works, Sand insisted on scrupulous research and documentation; she depended on friends to trawl the Bibliothèque Nationale, finding, copying, and speeding to Nohant quantities of material on a Mozartian eighteenth-century universe.

In the fall, Chopin went to Paris on business—alone. Even from afar, he basked in George's concern for his well-being, a solicitude that embraced all aspects of his life: from her management of what Sand playfully called his *frélicatesse* to her shrewd financial advice. Since Pigalle was too remote a bohemian outpost for his grander pupils to come to him, Sand now persuaded

Chopin to raise his fees for lessons from twenty to thirty francs for going to their houses (and they would have to send their carriages to fetch him and bring him home). "I had a hard time convincing him to do it," she said, "but with his poor health, he really has to earn much more to work less."

Then, early in the new year of 1842, Chopin gave another concert in the Salle Pleyel. Playing his own works, old and new, he assured his place at the pinnacle of musical Paris and, not the least, earned five thousand francs. Amid the swans and the peacocks in the audience, only one entrance created a stir: "The real star of the evening was George Sand," noted the reviewer for *La France Musicale*. "As soon as she appeared with her two charming daughters, all eyes fixed upon her."

But the reporter was mistaken. Only one of the girls, Solange Dudevant, now fourteen, was Sand's daughter; the other, eighteen-year-old Augustine-Marie Brault, called Titine, was a young stepcousin whom Sand was helping to study music in Paris. The observer's confusion is part of Solange's story and the unhealed wound that bound mother and child.

16

Children of Paradise

SHE WAS BORN IN 1828 and named for Solange, the patron saint of Bourges, capital of Berry. But Solange Dudevant was not blessed by divine or, for that matter, much human favor. The birth of her brother, Maurice, five years earlier, had brought only joy to the love match of the young parents, Casimir and Aurore Dudevant. Conceived in discord and estrangement, Solange was an unwanted child, probably not fathered by Casimir, but by Stéphane Ajasson de Grandsagne, Aurore's neighbor, girlhood friend, and lover.

When the Dudevants parted and Aurore was granted Nohant by court order, Casimir retired to his property in Guillery in Gascony. Under the terms of the separation, Maurice was to spend vacations with his father, who also retained the right to make decisions about his son's education. Solange, although given Dudevant's name, rarely saw him, and her mother was now reborn as George Sand.

To both children, Sand was the sun around whom everything in their universe—friends, family, neighbors, servants, even pets—revolved. They basked in her brilliance and warmth, her sense of fun. With a child's enthusiasm, George threw herself into games and jokes, riding and painting, trips and skits. They vied for her attentions, divided, inevitably, among so many.

Maurice alone had no need to compete for Sand's love. From birth, he was enveloped in his mother's adoration, a passion absolute and unconditional. Her maternal pride in his character and talents (distinctions not always discernible to others) was expressed often enough, but George also recognized that her infinite tenderness for the boy, her pain when they were apart, had more in common with another kind of love. When Maurice was four and Sand had returned to Nohant after a short absence, she described their reunion to Casimir: "I can't be away from him without grieving. I miss him so much, especially at night." Back together, George reported, "we are both still in the newness of our rapture, like two lovers reunited. We can't be out of each other's sight. We go to sleep together and when we awake, side by side, it's like a dream. The poor child throws his arms around me with such joy!"

In the next few years, there were many more such absences. Solange hardly knew either parent. Then, it was her brief moment in the sun. When she was three and a half, her mother took her to Paris, where the little girl became part of Sand's freewheeling *vie de bohème,* sharing a series of apartments on the quays overlooking the Seine with her mother and George's lover, Sandeau, and playing exotic pet to their childless circle of artists and journalists. In this largely masculine company, the pretty and clever child learned early that attention and affection were more easily won from men, albeit a shifting cast of uncles and big brothers.

Sand's troubled feelings toward Solange emerged early. Before the little girl was three, her mother described her as "fat and lazy." Solange had a quick mind, a startling memory for facts, and could already read "with real understanding," George allowed, but these proofs of exceptional intelligence only led her parent to expect more of her—harder work, higher achievement, larger ambition—and to be always disappointed. When Solange was four, Sand complained of her "strong will and extremes of emotion—especially her violent temper"; her mother feared the child showed signs of instability.

Before Sand disappeared to Venice with Musset in December 1833, she delivered Maurice, now ten, at his father's insistence, to the Lycée Henri IV, where he was enrolled as a boarder. His career there was as unhappy socially as it was undistinguished scholastically. Solange was dispatched to Nohant, where she was left to the supervision of the servants.

When their mother returned to France nine months later, she found that the saucy, high-spirited five-year-old had become cringing and submissive: Solange, it turned out, had been regularly beaten by Julie, the maid. To emphasize the inherited nature of her charge's wickedness, her tormentor had also filled the child's ears with gossip about her mother's sins. Sand's response to the brutalizing of Solange was to remove her daughter to Paris, where the six-year-old was enrolled in a select boarding establishment for girls near the Etoile, then a semirural area of expensive villas. Directed by two English sisters, the Pension Martin, Sand reassured her friends, was a "jewel box" of a house, filled with sunlight and fresh air, surrounded by a large garden, and run according to the healthy child-rearing precepts of Jean-Jacques Rousseau. Sand made known her firm expectations of the Martin ladies: They were to teach Solange self-discipline in both behavior and in application to studies, but also to discourage dependence—no whining, complaining, crying, or clinging to other adults as a mother substitute.

There was no further question of fathers, real or surrogate. Due to his "erratic" behavior in the months following her flight to Venice, Sand had forbidden Casimir to take Solange out of school on holidays. Then, without warning, in the summer of 1837, while Sand was still in Paris, Dudevant abducted the nine-year-old from Nohant. Over the feeble objections of the servants and the hysterical screams of the resident governess of the moment, Casimir galloped off to Gascony with his daughter.

As soon as Sand was alerted, she staged a daring kidnapping raid of her own. She enlisted the help of the Gascon authorities, who, storming Dudevant's property in the dead of night, ordered him to turn over the child to his estranged wife. Sand and Solange, with their official escort, then galloped back to Paris.

This dramatic rescue only confirmed Solange's sense of her mother as all-powerful; George's displays of love were as yearned for as they were infrequent. The absent mother became the emotional lodestar of her life, the focus of Solange's sense of privation and of her most intense longings. To her own daughter now, George passed on the legacy of the withholding, dismissive mother she had mourned and adored in Sophie Dupin. The female child's tragedy of unrequited maternal love seemed doomed to repeat itself.

From a series of boarding establishments, the little girl's letters echo with pleas for Sand to write, to visit. Solange had waited so long. "Please come on New Year's Day," she begged; she had made her mother a basket for the traditional gift-giving holiday. But Sand did not come, and Solange gave the basket to her godmother. Later, and most achingly, she pleaded to be allowed to come home for a visit, especially when the others were together at Nohant. Her requests, with their run-on sentences—"I love you don't forget me"—were followed by notes sodden with grief and, always, disappointment.

Disappointment is the duet voiced by mother and daughter—disappointment addressed to one another, but also to others. Sand complained of Solange's indolence, her carelessness, her poor progress, as revealed by the badly written letters (the Martin sisters' knowledge of French was sketchy); she scolded the child for complaining about her health or conditions at school—Solange was exaggerating or telling lies merely to worry her mother and garner sympathy. But just as often, George didn't bother to specify faults; instead, she harped on her daughter's "bad character" and urged her to pray to God for help in overcoming her flaws. Finding that the English ladies were too tenderhearted, she demanded an end to leniency; they must punish Solange for every instance of poor performance—both academic and behavioral—by forbidding holiday outings. But when Sand herself needed confirming evidence that she was the ideal mother to both children, she showered Solange (safely out of her sight) with written endearments—"dearest chicken," "darling angel"—and assurances of how keenly she was missed.

When Maurice's misery at school took the form of mysterious aches and pains, Sand invoked the family doctor's advice: the first step toward a cure was to remove the boy from lycée and return him to his mother's care. "This child breathes with your breath," George quoted the doctor as telling her. "You are his tree of life, the only physician that he needs." Mother and son went off to Nohant, "where, for six months, we didn't leave each other's side," Sand recalled.

From the Pension Martin, Solange wrote adoring letters to her mother and brother. She so longed to be "seated between [them] at table" and begged for news of their doings. Then, to the girl's joy, Sand decided that her clever daughter required greater intellectual challenge than what the English ladies could provide. Solange, too, was dispatched to Nohant, where both children would share a tutor, Félicien Mallefille, soon to enjoy promotion as their mother's lover. In her description of the requirements for his successor, Sand revealed an objective judgment of each child's capacities, along with her own progressive notions of an education based on ability and interests, not gender—the schooling she herself had received, first from her grandmother, then from the eccentric Monsieur Deschartres. For six hours a day, Solange, nine, and Maurice, fifteen, would share lessons in arithmetic, French, and geography. As the more able student, Solange alone would receive instruction in English, history, and music. Maurice, Sand noted vaguely, would be free to follow his "artistic disposition."

More important than learning or pedagogical skills, the tutor would need natural authority to control Solange: "The Girl is a demon who requires constant surveillance," not physically (a maid attended to that), but "morally, everywhere and at all times. . . . He must be serious, firm and rigorous, never showing signs of weakness"—and "no intellectuals," George stipulated.

Where Solange was concerned, Sand wanted a jailer, not a tutor. What did she fear? That the precocious ten-year-old would do her mother one better, that instead of waiting until she was sixteen, like Aurore, the rebellious, pubescent girl would entice one of the locals—or her tutor—to exploit her?

Their mother's new lover, Frédéric Chopin, was a complete stranger sprung suddenly on the children. When the little group convened in Perpignan to board the boat for Majorca, Chopin had never met Solange or Maurice. Under the circumstances of hardship and illness, the composer became part of the family. No greater tribute survives of Chopin's delicacy and tact, deferring always to their mother as head of the family; he never tried to replace their father. Nor, with Maurice, did he even presume the rights of an older brother. The composer possessed the rare ability to inspire trust in two troubled children, one still a child, the other an adolescent boy, all rivals for George's love.

His friendship with Solange was something apart from the others. From the beginning, a nameless bond joined them: Unloved child and homeless artist, they were both exiles; wherever they found themselves, they were there on sufferance, rewarded for performing, for charming, for summoning a sympathy that, once granted, deepened loneliness. Neither could satisfy the restless, voracious, imperial mother: her dynamism, her need, her ideals of work and love—of self, family, humanity,

God, art. In her churning wake, they would be washed up, broken, on some distant shore, easily replaced.

"I love you don't forget me." Chopin would not forget.

Twice more, as soon as she appeared to flourish, Solange was moved from one pension to another. In each case, Sand decided that the directors were lax with punishments and too lavish with praise and high marks. They had ignored George's warnings of her daughter's "flawed character," "moody, capricious, domineering, jealous and hysterical." The girl was also a liar—the only accusation that Solange, outraged, denied. After assuring her mother of how hard she was working to correct her other flaws, Solange added: "I don't have to say that I'm no longer a liar because I never lied; that's a fault which you accused me of having which I never had."

In the spring of 1841, Sand wrote to the director of the child's third and last pension to suggest that canceling weekend outings as punishment for laziness and poor behavior was insufficient: If the thirteen-year-old's schoolwork was less than exemplary, she should be kept after the others had left for summer vacation.

Cruelty—cold and gratuitous—snakes through Sand's letters to her daughter, and always, her remarks have a vengeful, retaliatory thrust. In truth, she found Solange's presence disruptive and accusing and dreaded it; she was the one human being who could make George feel a failure. This was her daughter's unforgivable crime. Now, she held up to Solange the idyllic picture of life at Nohant without her, the loving tranquillity that her arrival would shatter: "Here's how we spend our time, your brother and I. Since it's been pouring rain for the last two weeks, we go to my study after breakfast at 10; there your brother paints watercolors, with a concentration and perseverance which I'd be happy to see you apply to something, even if it were only needlework. While he draws, I paint flowers and butterflies. Evenings we go back to work from 8 to 9; he copies engravings while I read to him."

Lest she slacken in her efforts to improve, Solange was kept in suspense about whether she would be allowed to join the family until two days before Maurice was to bring her from Paris to Nohant on August 15. "Now, I hope you're happy and that you're coming resolved to change your character." And George again listed the sins the girl must "destroy in herself."

Solange had just missed Pauline Viardot's visit, and Sand made plain what a poor substitute the real daughter was for her "Fifille": "Everyone here who saw her—even for a moment—adored her instantly, not just for her talent and intelligence, but above all, for her goodness and simplicity, her devotion to others. If you could only be like her some day, I would be the happiest of mothers."

In the first joy of her return to Nohant, Solange charmed everyone, but not for long. Restless, bored, sulky—she yawned, threw aside a book, fiddled with her hair, played with the dogs, and bothered anyone who was engaged in any purposeful activity, Sand said. Only Chopin welcomed her interruptions. He understood the emptiness of ennui, the invisibility of the less busy—or less loved—in this bustling household. He readily succumbed to her childish jokes, her teasing and flirting, her beauty.

The plump, pretty child had become a smoldering nymphet, with sleepy blue eyes and a provocative pout. Seeing her, Marie d'Agoult, another golden goddess, waxed lyrical: "When the wind blows through her long blond hair tumbling in natural curls over her Roman shoulders and the sun's rays illuminating her face, skin dazzling white with a brilliant flush of red, I see a young dryad escaped from the forest upon whom the gods smile; birds, insects, plants and flowers bow as she passes." And artists.

If she was using him as a mirror, an audience, a stand-in for a dress rehearsal of seduction, Chopin did not care. The dark and angry mother, observing them together, cared.

PITILESS TOWARD HER OWN DAUGHTER, George's sympathy for the powerless was aroused by another unwanted child. A few kilometers from Nohant, a retarded girl, not yet fifteen and probably pregnant, had been found wandering a back road with nothing but the clothes on her back. Fanchette, it turned out, was a foundling; she had spent her entire life in the asylum in La Châtre, whose directors had clearly given unofficial orders to get rid of her. While at the institution, she had been sexually abused—"passed from hand to hand," Sand reported—by those charged with her protection. The scandal and subsequent cover-up by the local establishment, including the clergy, were immediately exposed by Sand in a pamphlet called, simply, "Fanchette." Now, for the first time, George realized the extent of government repression on the level closest to most citizens; no printer in the region would publish her report. Galvanized by outrage, she immediately set about gathering support for an alternative local newspaper, to be called *L'Eclaireur de l'Indre* (The Watch on the Indre).

In the two years since she had helped found *La Revue Inde-*

pendante, Sand's political convictions had moved farther to the left. She was ever more convinced of the evils of wealth and the conspiracy of the powerful to deny all rights—especially the vote—to the powerless. The Fanchette affair summoned her to a larger reformist role. The provinces were worse than Paris; here, feudalism still lived. Among a less literate, scattered population, information was scarce and slow to arrive from the capital. Official authority was absolute and unchallenged. The new venture must be as independent as possible from the timidity of local suppliers and services like printers. The timing seemed perfect. Her friend and mentor Pierre Leroux had long wanted to establish a printer's cooperative; with the help of Sand and other friends, he and his family now relocated to nearby Boussac. As editor, Leroux recommended a talented young journalist from Tulle, in the Corrèze. Unlike Sand's other new associates, Victor Borie came from a middle-class family that had enabled him to complete studies in economics. After a brief stint as regional commissioner of weights and measures, he soon made a name for himself in local newspapers, where he covered agricultural issues. A polished writer, brilliant popularizer, and, by all accounts, a witty and delightful conversationalist, Borie, like George, had moved steadily leftward. At the ripe age of twenty-five, he was thrilled to be in charge of a new antiestablishment publication whose publisher was the famous Madame Sand. They established the editorial offices of *L'Eclaireur* in nearby La Châtre. When the authorities predictably took action to suppress the paper, Sand and her colleagues were prepared; they struck back with a campaign of exposure that silenced the embarrassed officials in the region.

Now, Nohant, too, was overrun by homespun local activists, as Sand again began the struggle to raise money and solicit subscribers. Among those "patriots" whom George named as supporters of the new journal, Chopin was down for fifty francs. But that was the extent of his sympathies. Endless meetings now crowded the family rooms, sending the composer in retreat to his quarters upstairs.

Sand's indignation had rescued Fanchette. But the exploitation and attempted disposal of a retarded orphan had also revitalized George. Her depression at the prospect of a looming fortieth birthday lifted. Orchestrating public outrage, she was energized by a new cause, a new journalistic project, and, in the compelling person of Victor Borie, a new lover.

17

A House Divided

At the end of July 1842, Chopin and Sand made a brief trip to Paris to find another apartment for the fall. The charming paired pavilions off rue Pigalle turned out to be cold and damp; climbing up the steep outside staircase to his rooms left Chopin short of breath. They loved the neighborhood, which still had the character of a village, but one now inhabited by a yeasty mix of artists, musicians, and writers, leavened by actresses and dancers kept in palatial new villas paid for by their rich protectors. The first group had led the marginal *quartier* climbing toward Montmartre to be reborn as "the new Athens."

Square d'Orléans, where they moved in September, was the new Athens in microcosm. An oasis off the bustling rue Saint-Lazare, its eight buildings were constructed around a central courtyard, where, surrounded by trees and grass, a graceful fountain played. Its expensive apartments, some with separate studios, were home to other successful artists, including the dancer Marie Taglioni. But Sand and Chopin had been lured there by George's friends, Countess Charlotte Marliani, a warm and motherly older woman, and her husband, Emanuel. The newcomers took two apartments: George rented the roomiest, which was soon to be famous for its billiard table, while diagonally across the courtyard was Chopin's smaller retreat. Maurice had his separate bachelor studio on a higher floor; Solange was given a tiny maid's room off her mother's apartment to use on school holidays when good behavior earned her a visit home. These separate quarters were symbolically joined by their friends' larger apartment, a measure of Charlotte's nurturing role in Sand's life: "The kind and energetic Marliani," Sand later said, "made us a family." With Sand paying the cost of food for her own little household, they all gathered together for dinner each evening at her friends' table.

George may have been grateful to Madame Marliani for "making" them a family, but she also conceded the appeal of the depersonalized, urban atmosphere of the square, calling it "a kind of phalanstery," after the communal ideal promoted by the Utopian social philosopher Fourier. Exalting the collective also suggests her relief from the strain of intimacy: The Square d'Orléans offered escape from isolation in the country with Chopin.

She was struggling to complete a projected two-volume work of memoir and travel, *Un Hiver à Majorca* (A Winter in Majorca). Memory had neither softened the hardships of that time four years earlier nor recalled the strengthened bonds of love she had expressed on their return: *Winter* is an angry and bitter book. "Monkeys" was Sand's most benign designation for the Majorcans; they were ugly, filthy, thieving, superstitious primitives whose fanatical Christianity was equaled only by their aggressive absence of charity. With no proof of Chopin's consumption, had they not driven the composer from Palma to the insalubrious and remote monastery of Valldemosa?

A Winter in Majorca was first translated into English in 1956, by the poet and novelist Robert Graves, a longtime expatriate living on the island with his family. In his introduction, Graves points out Sand's many inaccuracies of fact, while defending the islanders against her accusations, which he considers proof only of her snobbery, provincialism, and total insensitivity to the local culture. The most acute of Graves's observations, however, concerns his sense that Sand's venom directed at the barbaric "natives" was displaced rage toward Chopin. The islanders' hostility, which resulted in banishing Sand and her group to Valldemosa, had imprisoned her with a querulous, ungrateful invalid. His sensibilities were exacerbated by the most petty annoyances: "A true calamity did not oppress him so much as a small vexation. . . . No connection could be found between his emotions and the causes that provoked them. Our stay at Valldemosa was therefore torture for him and torment for me."

Because *Winter* was published in 1852, when Chopin had been dead for three years, Sand was then free to suggest that his irritability was not involuntary. He could control it when he wished: "Though sweet tempered and charming in Parisian society, Chopin when sick and confined to the exclusive company of a few intimates, drove these to despair."

When those few intimates were reduced to one—George—her loneliness felt unbearable. Succumbing to depression as she neared her fortieth birthday (in 1844, a date that marked a woman as elderly), she was made more desolate by the sense that she had no one in whom to confide her grief at aging; all those close to her were dependents, starting with Chopin. From its promise of a retreat together, Nohant now joined two solitudes.

"We're alone here, Chopin and I" runs like a refrain through Sand's letters in the summer of 1843. It was not the shorthand of intimacy but a cry for help. They worked and slept like relay runners; as one rose, the other went to bed after the night's labors. Sand missed Maurice, who was in no hurry to leave the good life in Gascony, where he was staying with his bon vivant father. Chopin's letters to friends in Paris—especially to Polish intimates—sound a note of abandonment.

Delacroix arrived in July, accompanied by his cat, "Cupid," which traveled in a specially fitted basket. For the ten days of his stay, the household reclaimed the atmosphere of old: music making, painting (Sand had made a studio for their friend in a third-floor addition), and writing alternated with hiking, eating, drinking, and ceaseless talk. After Delacroix left, as though on cue, Sand's old loves reappeared: The first of these was Michel de Bourges, now tubby and balder. His silver-tongued eloquence had turned to harangue, and Sand, as much as Chopin, was not sorry to see him leave after a long and bibulous lunch.

Another of George's former lovers, the actor Bocage, was a different matter. Since her separation from Casimir, Sand had rarely lied about her sexual history. With Chopin, she would not have even needed to equivocate; delicacy, discretion, and tact were his very measure—at least, in the great world where he moved with such grace. In private, such questions as he might have had would be silenced by inhibition and fear. He would be the last man to interrogate the woman he loved about her past. He would have known of her most famous affair—with Alfred de Musset—and perhaps he had heard allusions to others. But he was unprepared now for George's own casual revelation about the handsome actor, occasioned by her leaving a letter from Bocage where Chopin could not fail to see it. Sand continued to be careless in that way. Now, to her professed astonishment, dreadful scenes erupted: suspicions, accusations, and denials, followed by icy silences.

"As for a certain younger man's jealousy about a certain old lady, it's subsided for want of nourishment," Sand wrote to Bocage. "Still, I can't say that the sickness is entirely cured or that one doesn't have to be very careful about hiding the most innocent things. The old lady was wrong in believing that sincerity and trust were the best remedies. I warned him simply to stop going on about the letter of a certain older man for whom she indeed still harbors silent feelings of eternal loyal friendship."

Arch and coquettish, embarrassingly seductive in its reminder that the writer is one "old lady" who can still reduce a younger man to fits of sexual jealousy—the tone of Sand's letter would certainly fan any suspicions Chopin harbored that old passions, far from settling into the friendship of old lovers, as she maintained, had reignited. A rift was opened—never to be mended. For Chopin, his Aurore could no longer be trusted; for Sand, her "Chopinet" had joined the gallery of other lovers, crazed by jealousy, sniffing, Othello-like, for evidence to confirm their fears.

Lovers weren't the only ones whose jealousies she ignored, while acting to exacerbate them. At the end of October, Chopin and Maurice—"my two little boys," Sand called them—set out for Paris together. Shortly after they arrived, news that Chopin was sick sent George into a frenzy of anxiety tinged with guilt, and she wrote to Maurice: "Please let me know whether Chopin is ill; his letters are so short and gloomy. If he does feel sick, can't you stay in his room? Be another me," she urged, then underlining her next words, added: *"He would do the same for you."**

This same year—1844—that George faced down the forty-year-old woman who stared back from her mirror, Maurice turned twenty-one. Along with a quiet coming-of-age party, he celebrated his majority by the successful conquest of Pauline Viardot and by a campaign of murderous hostility directed at Chopin. It may be that Sand was the only one who failed to anticipate the inevitable rivalry between son and lover.

Then, in May of this same year of anniversaries, Chopin learned of his father's death three weeks earlier in Warsaw. The composer locked himself in his darkened rooms refusing to emerge; Sand's pleadings met with silence. In the face of Chopin's inconsolable grief, George invited his favorite sister, Ludwika, and her husband, an agronomist turned judge, for an extended visit to Nohant. This was the wisest and most humane distraction she could have offered and one that was characteris-

---

*The first editor of his mother's letters, Maurice Dudevant-Sand, as he later called himself, suppressed the last three sentences of this quote.

tic of Sand's sensitivity to others' grief and loss. And she was unexpectedly rewarded. For Ludwika and George, it was love at first sight.

She had expected a devout, disapproving provincial, and instead George had encountered a woman "totally superior to her age and her country, and of an angelic character." For her part, Ludwika expressed only gratitude for the care and love that Sand had lavished on her brother for almost a decade. Guarding his health and talent, George had saved his life and nurtured his art. His sister's presence, and the instant and profound sympathy between the two women he loved, restored Nohant to its state of privileged happiness.

Ludwika's departure for Paris and Poland at the end of August left Sand "brokenhearted"; she would now tease Chopin by asking why he couldn't be more like his sister, in every way his superior. After Ludwika's return to Warsaw, Sand entrusted her brother and neighbor, Hippolyte, to send Ludwika the manuscript of *La mare au diable* (The Devil's Pool), her masterpiece; it was dedicated "to my friend, Frédéric Chopin."

The magic circle of love uniting the three seemed to widen and deepen. When Chopin returned to Nohant in September, he found mother and daughter affectionate and peaceful. Solange was even eager to work, and he taught her a Beethoven sonata.

George, meanwhile, put up forty pounds of jam made from the late-ripening local plums. No one was allowed to help her in this labor. To conserve the fall's rich harvest was a way of husbanding the joys of late summer and autumn; she was certain the fruit would see them through the lean times to come.

"It would be impossible to savor so much happiness in one

month," Sand wrote Ludwika, "without preserving some, without healing old wounds, without laying in new stores of hope and trust in God."

It was Eden before the fall.

By the end of November, the rooms at Nohant were unheatable. Chopin returned to Paris, where he discharged chores and commissions for George. He chose fabric for a new black dress, sorted her mail, and took her plants indoors. His servant, Jan, had polished her mirrors to a blinding brilliance, he wrote. And he allayed her concerns about his eating habits by reporting on the friends who fed him faithfully.

Nonetheless, when George returned to Paris in mid-December, she found the "patient as usual," coughing, and with intermittent attacks of neuralgia and asthma. In fact, the city had never seemed to her so noxious. She felt suffocated. After six months in the country, she was unused to the noises of a large apartment complex. Unable to sleep, she was so exhausted, she told her new confidant, Louis Blanc, she feared she might be dying of brain fever.

Her finances, however, looked blooming; installments of her latest novel, *Isadora,* the story of a courtesan, were about to appear in *La Revue Indépendante,* the journal she had helped found. This dazzling creature of fashion and sin was the favorite heroine of late romanticism. Thanks to the new millionaires of the July Monarchy, their ranks had multiplied, and their rise—and especially fall—provided novelists and readers with a teasing mix of high life, erotic titillation, and morality tale. Dumas,

Balzac, Zola, and Flaubert created memorable temptresses who continue to inspire fascination, fear, and pity; the iconic "Camille" coughs on, in opera and on film, and who can forget Zola's Nana, furs and jewels gone, a terrifying hag, scarred by smallpox? Sand's forgettable Isadora remains forgotten.

At the same time, George signed a two-book contract with Louis Blanc, whose new newspaper, *La Reforme,* one of the great radical journals of the time, would serialize both novels: *The Miller of Angibault,* to be followed by another book, as yet unwritten. Her income assured, Sand planned to take Chopin away from Paris before another bitter winter set in. The worst of the season spent in a warm climate, followed by a long summer in Nohant, would give him eighteen months' respite from the cold, she wrote to Ludwika.

On their return to Nohant, the plan was vetoed by Maurice. Twenty-two now, he had finished biding his time; both mother and son were eager for him to assume the role of man of the house. Meanwhile, his adoring mama could keep him at her side while he tried to learn the day-to-day responsibilities of a gentleman landowner. In return for easing her burdens in the business of rents and leaking roofs, Maurice persuaded Sand to yield some of her authority as well. His first act was to fire Jan, Chopin's manservant. Next, he convinced her to retire Françoise, the robust, middle-aged housekeeper, along with the old gardener, who had reigned over everything grown on the property since the final years of the first Aurore Dupin. Their replacements, Maurice made clear, would answer to him alone.

The young master preened in the attentions of his lover, Pauline Viardot, who had settled in for a long visit at Nohant.

Sand certainly knew about Maurice's pursuit of her beloved "Fifille" and seems to have smiled upon his conquest. Before the singer moved on, the enchanting Pauline would provide Maurice with the ideal sentimental education. George always preferred to have matters under her control; in Nohant, she could monitor the affair.

At the end of summer, Madame Viardot returned to her family and career. But Sand had seen to her replacement. George's young cousin Titine arrived on September 10 escorted by Maurice from Paris. At the end of January 1846, she was still there, and when they returned to the capital, Titine moved into Square d'Orléans with Sand and the children. No longer a visitor, she had become a resident member of the family.

Augustine-Marie Brault—Titine—remains a blank canvas. Recent accounts exalt her as "prettier and cleverer" than Solange—a Cinderella scenario to account for the angry daughter's antipathy to the poor relation, but Solange, in fact, was described by all who knew her as a lush beauty, of superior, if undirected, intelligence. Her hatred and jealousy, then, were aroused not by Titine's attributes but by her mother's displaced love.

What attracted Sand was the vitality of this child of the people; in contrast to Solange's languor, Maurice's passivity, and Chopin's sickly ennui, her young relative's purposeful energy—the driving ambition of a penniless girl who had to make her own way in the world—promised a transfusion of George's proudly declared "plebeian blood" into a line threatened by moral anemia. As for Titine, she was only too willing to become whatever her new family wanted her to be. Sand yearned, first, for another daughter. From there, Titine might be groomed into the ideal daughter-in-law.

Like everything else about this unhappy scheme, Titine's alleged "adoption" remains a murky affair. The young woman's parents were a disreputable couple: Adèle Philbert, who was Sand's stepcousin and Titine's mother, had borne several children by different men. When she married Joseph Brault, a sporadically employed stonemason, he chose to legitimize Titine, possibly because she was, in fact, his daughter. Meanwhile, her mother, so gossip claimed, returned to her sluttish ways, often taking the child with her on assignations. When Sand undertook the girl's rescue, the father shrewdly decided he had found a buyer for his daughter—and right in the family. For an undisclosed sum, in the form of ongoing payments to Brault, Sand adopted Titine.

For Solange, her replacement at this time came as a catastrophic shock. For the past year, relations between mother and daughter had been happier than ever before. Solange was devastated; her only recourse—one that at least had Sand's wholehearted blessing—was to find a husband and to leave home as soon as possible.

To Maurice, Titine was a consolation prize provided by his mother to compensate him for the loss of Pauline. But the twenty-year-old girl was after larger game. Titine cast her loyalty with the man of the house and against those who challenged his shaky authority. In turn, Maurice, as he made clear in his open flattering and flirting, was prepared to act as her defender. If he chose to take liberties, permitting himself intimacies with her in front of the others, that was his *droit de seigneur.* Titine was mindful of her father's promise: If she played her cards right, she might one day be the young Baroness Dudevant.

As head of a household of fractious children, Sand tried to appear neutral. Privately, she was relieved to see her adored son and future heir assert himself, grasping the mettle of masculine authority. Moreover, after exalting Titine to friends as "perfect . . . beautiful, charming virtuous, hardworking," George had painted herself into a corner. If she now sided with Solange and Chopin (who detested the interloper so much he refused even to refer to her by name), George would be admitting that she had been wrong, that the daughter she had chosen over her own child was, in fact, a nasty, vulgar little tart. George did, however, decide that marriage was out of the question.

The father, who essentially had sold Titine to Sand, now denounced George for "prostituting" his daughter, for buying her as a whore for Maurice. The source of Brault's affronted paternal feelings was a letter from Sand, in which she tactfully explained why Maurice could never marry Titine. Her son was far too young, and his affections were engaged—however irregularly—elsewhere. Reading George's obvious second thoughts on Titine's suitability as a daughter-in-law, Joseph Brault decided that he had been robbed and his daughter violated. Not trusting in gossip alone to spread the scandal, Brault would soon manage to publish his own seamy version of events in a pamphlet that enjoyed wide distribution in Berry. Sand sued—successfully—to have the pamphlet suppressed, but the damage had been done. Added to her local reputation of communist, adulteress, advocate (and practitioner) of free love was this fresh evidence of depravity.

Ever practical, George set about finding another husband for Titine. To reassure the next candidate of her adopted daughter's desirability, she increased the girl's dowry to thirty thousand francs.

18

Lucrezia Floriani

In early spring of 1846, Sand started work on a new novel, and by April, it was far enough along for her to sign a contract for its serialization in *Le Courrier Français,* the installments to begin in late June and run though the end of July. Then, on May 5, Sand left Paris for Nohant—alone. Over the next three weeks, she rewrote the novel from beginning to end, a labor of revision without precedent in her work. She finished the new version on May 24, making a "fat volume," in time to greet Chopin's coach from Paris when it arrived in Châteauroux the next day.

Although Sand usually read each day's work aloud to Chopin, she would not seem to have done so with the new novel—neither in its original nor in its revised version. Only when Delacroix arrived on August 16 did George read from the manuscript—with both men as her audience. The painter had harbored growing reservations about Sand's recent themes: inflammatory exposures of class injustice and dangerous visions of social leveling. But now, for the first time, he was shocked by what he heard.

Lucrezia Floriani is a double portrait of two mismatched lovers. Floriani, an actress and a playwright, has left the stage at the peak of her career, retiring with her young children to her childhood home on a remote lake in northern Italy. At the same time that she retired from the stage, she retreated from love. Never married, Floriani's affairs always ended badly, the only happy outcome being four children by as many fathers. Into this matriarchal paradise, fate delivers a mysterious traveler, Prince Karol de Roswald. Inevitably, Karol and Lucrezia succumb to the fatal disease of love. The narrative that follows traces the fever chart of their affair.

As revealing of its author as any of her autobiographical writings, Lucrezia is Sand, sanitized and sanctified, George as she saw herself and wanted others to see her. Lucrezia's only sin is loving too much—too generously, too purely, too selflessly. Prince Karol, a German noble with a Polish name, stands as Lucrezia's polar opposite: aristocratic where she is plebeian, reserved and inhibited where she is open and expressive, morally rigid and conformist where she is independent and indifferent to convention.

At twenty-four, Karol is also without sexual experience. After years of dismissing the erotic with fear and disgust, his fall from innocence is shattering. From initial repulsion toward this woman of scandalous reputation, Karol progresses to friendship until, on their becoming lovers, he succumbs to obsessive passion. Locked in the solitary confinement of his own making, Karol's love for Lucrezia, exclusive and devouring, demands her as a fellow prisoner. Her attempts to flee her captor, and his crazed pursuit, end with Floriani dead of a stroke. Her real death, though, had been a long and slow one. In our last image of Lucrezia, the woman we met in full bloom has shrunk to a withered crone of forty. Her end is her deliverance. In place of love, Sand sacrificed her heroine to loyalty and compassion. She would not accept a similar fate.

Sand's novel barely held the fig leaf of fiction over the private hell of its real-life protagonists. "The weariness of boredom," Delacroix said, stamped every page. He was "in agony" for Chopin as they both listened to George's low, velvety voice in its hypnotic monotone describe Karol/Chopin's "stubborn adoration of Lucrezia and his progressive derangement, all painted," Delacroix said, in the "transparency of truth." For this hero, the painter noted, "a woman only exists, relatively speaking. Thus, when Lucrezia stopped loving Karol, there was no oblique way she could express her feelings; she can only reach him harshly and brutally." Chopin, meanwhile, voiced only admiration for the new work. "He hadn't understood a thing" their friend concluded.

Lucrezia Floriani was Sand's first foray into the roman à clef and, helped by the author and composer's public image as a couple, was guaranteed to fan speculation, gossip, and debate about the boundaries between life and art. More than a decade later, George would return with *Elle et lui* (She and He), a chronicle of her Venetian escapade with Musset. Romantic hybrids of memoir and fiction have spawned robust descendants in our own tell-all era, along with similar indignation, denial ("All characters are purely fictitious"), titillation, threats of lawsuit, and—even—murder. These works continue to provoke argument about genres, invented documentary and truthful fiction; the morality and motives behind the pillaging of intimate relationships (including the use of real letters) and the exposure of another to the glare of public scrutiny, against which the unpublished victim has no defense.

Whether fueled by malice, envy, or sincere distaste for art that copied life so cruelly, the outrage of Sand and Chopin's friends took aim at what Sand had revealed—not invented. Loud clucking was heard from her old mentor Sainte-Beuve; Heine hedged his bets ("She has treated my friend Chopin outrageously in a divinely written novel"); and, of course, Liszt, who spoke for many in their circle in decrying the "vulgarity of confessions." Henry James would later shudder at the writer's self-exposure (and by a woman!)—her nakedness, not merely *in* but *for* the marketplace, the commercial motive that he decided explained her candor. In contrast, the reaction of Sand's contemporaries to *Lucrezia* was provoked by the contrast of her self-portrait, fully robed, halo in place, as a Madonna with Child(ren), while Chopin was stripped, flayed, and crucified.

On the last day of October 1846, Chopin left Nohant for Paris. The autumn had been so unseasonably warm that the Loire had overflowed its banks, forcing the composer, along with another departing guest, to turn back. Eleven days later, Chopin set out again—alone. The earlier false start followed by another round of good-byes sounds a warning tocsin. This was a final leave-taking: He would never see Nohant again.

In fact, he was not much missed. Determined to escape, Solange had decided to fall in love, accepting the adoration of her first suitor, a sweet, gangly young knight and neighbor, Fernand de Préaux. George worried that he hadn't a sou; he was as unworldly as the wild boar that he hunted, she said. Still, she couldn't wait for the troublesome daughter to be settled—elsewhere. Approved as fiancé, Fernand's first official visit was to take place two days after Chopin's departure. Meanwhile, the bride-to-be reveled in her new status. The others, forced by the sudden cold and unheatable upstairs rooms to spend most days and evenings below, threw themselves into nightly theatricals, loosely written by Sand, but largely improvised by the actors themselves. Relieved of Chopin's presence, animosities subsided and the family drew closer, warmed by wedding plans and makeshift footlights.

Then, on February 6, 1847, George and her "two girls," Titine and Solange, accompanied by Solange's fiancé, left Nohant for Paris. Twelve shopping days later, Sand and Solange visited the studio of a sculptor whom everyone was talking about.

Jean-Baptiste Auguste Clésinger had settled in the capital two years earlier, but he was already notorious as the talented bad boy of the Paris art world. Scandal still reverberated over his recent submission to the salon: The model for his nude *Woman Stung by a Serpent* had been a well-known courtesan whose *contraposto* pose—a thrusting display of breasts and pudenda suggestive of orgasm—was made the more impudent by the placement of the coiled snake, which pointed the viewer's gaze to the offending parts.* For the last year, Clésinger had wooed Sand in a series of letters professing his fervent admiration for her novels and begging the honor of immortalizing their author in a portrait bust. With little vanity about her looks, Sand arrived at the studio with Solange, planning to ask the sculptor, instead, to provide the traditional likeness of the younger woman at the time of her marriage, whose contract was to be signed in the next weeks. Gallantly, Clésinger insisted on offering both as gifts. A separate series of sittings was arranged.

Now, the artist mounted his siege: Certain of the conquest of the daughter, he directed his flattery to the mother, maternal approval and a handsome dowry being key to his plans. At Sand's apartment at the Square d'Orléans, there came daily deliveries of flowers, delicacies, even a puppy. In the course of a few sittings, the sculptor seduced Solange, not yet eighteen (apparently, she had been allowed to come to Clésinger's studio unchaperoned). Now, she announced that her wedding to Fernand was to be put off—indefinitely. Alarmed by the Clésinger juggernaut, friends made inquiries. The sculptor's past—in both his native city of Besançon and Florence, where he had spent several years—was littered with unpaid debts to the tune of hundreds of thousands of francs. From other artists, Delacroix learned that Clésinger drank heavily; a principal cause of his borrowing was a chronic inability to deliver on lucrative commissions. When drinking, he was notorious for brutalizing his mistress, whom he had recently

*Now in the Musée d'Orsay, this figure is one of the few private commissions by Clésinger to have survived; most of the public commissions in Paris that he managed to complete were destroyed by bombardments during the Commune of 1870–1871. Clésinger died in 1883.

abandoned, pregnant, as soon as he saw the possibility of marriage to the daughter of the successful novelist.

All this was reported to Sand, but she would hear none of it. She seemed even more smitten by the sculptor than Solange. Surrounded by weak, dependent men, she had become persuaded that the energetic, aggressive Clésinger would be the salvation of the family. She left Paris for Nohant with the girls on April 6, and a week later, the determined suitor appeared with an ultimatum: He gave Sand twenty-four hours to agree to the marriage, during which time she must also arrange to secure the permission of Baron Dudevant. Sand was even more enchanted by this last bullying tactic. Who could possibly stand in the way of this "Caesar," she sighed, who "swept all before him by sheer force of will?"

George not only agreed to the match, but also became a gleeful coconspirator. When the sculptor left Nohant for Paris, she advised him on a strategy of secrecy. No rumors must reach Solange's father until Clésinger, accompanied by Maurice (as advised by Sand), appeared in Guillery, to make his case in person. More important, she added, "Not a word to Chopin. It's none of his business." Continuing her imperial metaphor, she explained, "Once the Rubicon has been crossed, any ifs and buts can do only harm."

Chopin first learned of the forthcoming marriage through an announcement in a Paris newspaper on May 4. He was not among the invited guests at the wedding, which took place two weeks later in the tiny church outside the gates of Nohant. After being part of the family for nine years—since Solange was nine years old—he was now treated like one of the aged domestics, recently dismissed after years of service. Delacroix's revelation on hearing Sand read *Lucrezia Floriani* became prophesy: When the time came, she would deal with Chopin "harshly and brutally."

Following her shabby treatment of the composer, George did what she always did when she was feeling guilty: She fired off a round of letters justifying her actions. There was no point in telling Chopin anything, as he understood nothing about human nature or the realities of life, she told Delacroix and Chopin's friend Gryzmala. But Chopin understood everything about Solange's marriage: from the facts of Clésinger's past to his strategic wooing of George and Maurice and, finally, how Sand's obsession with secrecy, her romantic infatuation with the "artist," and the bridegroom's insistence on haste had deprived her of the counsel of friends and her daughter of a mother's better judgment.

By late June, the honeymoon was over. Clésinger had revealed himself as a liar and extortionist who, failing to mention his huge debts and lack of work, expected George to underwrite the newlyweds' extravagant Paris life—servants, lavish parties, a carriage, and daily deliveries of hothouse flowers. When his mother-in-law urged economy, he became furious, blaming everything on his spoiled young bride and concluding with no subtle threats about the future of the marriage if Sand failed to subsidize their present way of life.

Sand promptly invited "the children" to Nohant, hoping that a dose of simple country life—days of walks and visits and homemade entertainment—would restore their sense of what was needed to be happy. Instead, they arrived early in July brimming with rancor and spoiling for a fight.

By way of a dowry, Sand had made over to Solange a valuable Paris property whose rents were to provide them with an income. On learning that George planned to make the traditional cash settlement on Titine and her probable future husband, the painter Theodore Rousseau, the newlyweds were outraged. After a week of quarreling with everyone, Solange and Clésinger appeared in the front hall while the others were at dinner, demanding a family conference. Probably drunk, the sculptor bellowed his grievances to George and Maurice, insisting that his mother-in-law arrange to mortgage Nohant, giving them an allowance—to begin immediately. When Sand coldly refused, insults were traded. Solange accused Maurice of seducing Titine, with Sand's encouragement. Her cousin's dowry was blood money to wash away their guilt.* A fight broke out. Maurice struck or tried to strike Clésinger; the sculptor picked up a hammer and went for his brother-in-law. Sand rushed between them, slapping Clésinger twice in the face. He then punched her in the chest. Maurice, meanwhile, ran to his room, returning with a loaded pistol. At this point, servants and dinner guests (who included the parish priest) intervened. Sand ordered Solange, now in the first months of pregnancy, and her husband from the house, forbidding either of them to set foot on her property ever again.

Solange then wrote a frantic note to Chopin (who had had no news from Nohant), alluding to the "most appalling scenes" that

---

*Rousseau broke off the engagement on learning from an anonymous source that Titine had been Maurice's lover. His informant is assumed to have been Solange, but recalling Monsieur Brault's pamphlet, the painter could have learned from other sources that his intended was "defiled" (as he wrote to Sand).

had led to banishment from her mother's house. She was ill and stranded at nearby La Châtre with no money to return to Paris. Clésinger's name was never mentioned. As Chopin had left his carriage at Nohant, would he please write to Sand immediately, giving her, Solange, permission to take it? Her mother had refused her earlier request.

This plea arrived in the same post with a long letter from Sand, now lost. If Chopin was distressed by news from the bride, George's letter rendered him so distraught he rushed off to see Delacroix, to whom he read it aloud. In brief, Sand decreed that Chopin could return to Nohant *only* if he agreed to close his door to Solange and Clésinger. Second, he must never again mention the name Solange in George's presence; as far as she was concerned, her daughter was dead.

Delacroix was appalled. The letter, he said, was just as "atrocious" as Chopin had said. Sand's "cruelest passions, long suppressed, had finally surfaced." The composer's polite reply could not soften his accusing message: "Solange . . . can never be a matter of indifference to me." And he closed with a direct hit: "Your pain must be overpowering indeed to harden your heart against your child, to the point of refusing even to hear her name, and this, on the threshold of her life as a woman, a time more than any other when her condition requires a mother's care."

Sand's reply was all martyred virtue. She had been betrayed, first by her monstrous child and now by Chopin. After nine years of her "exclusive love," he had "gone over to the enemy," and since he had confessed as much, there was nothing else but to forgive him and wish him well. "Good-bye my friend," she wrote. "Let me know how you are once in a while. As far as we're concerned, there is nothing more to be said."

Jealousy, long festering, had imploded. To Countess Marliani, George raved that Chopin had been in love with Solange all along; his betrayal of her now only proved it. His worst blow could not even be mentioned. He had exposed as a delusion Sand's image of herself as the perfect mother. He—and other friends—had warned her about Clésinger, begging her to treat the affair as an escapade, an infatuation that would run its course, and urging her to do everything in her power to save Solange from a disastrous marriage. Instead, George had dismissed Chopin's remarks as fueled by envy, obtuseness, and snobbery, writing to everyone she knew, exalting the sculptor as a man, an artist, and an ideal husband and son-in-law.

This was Chopin's unforgivable sin: his knowledge that she had failed her child, a failure from which all her own miseries flowed. Both Viardots wrote to Sand. They protested her unjust indictment of Chopin as a conspirator who was gathering a "faction" against her and pointed to his unwavering loyalty and devotion. "If I had made mistakes, even committed crimes, Chopin should not have believed them, should not have *seen them*," she replied. "There's a certain point of respect and gratitude past which we no longer have the right to examine the behavior of those beings who have become sacred to us."

Chopin had examined and judged her. She had ceased to be sacred, and he claimed the right to love her as merely human and flawed. But this was also the excuse she had been seeking. For too long, she said, he had made her existence a "prison." Now the jailer would be banished from her life.

19

The Unmaking of a Radical

SAND HAD GIVEN UP THE APARTMENT in Square d'Orléans. It was expensive and there was always the danger of a confrontation with Chopin. When she needed to be in Paris, she used Maurice's pied-à-terre in rue de Condé. There, she was back on the Left Bank—a few streets away from where she had first lived, a young runaway wife, her hobnailed boots ringing on the paving stones, who walked the anonymous city intoxicated with ambition: She would be a free woman and a writer. Now, she was famous as both.

By the turn of the New Year 1848, rumors of insurgency in Paris had reached Berry. Cozily settled with Victor Borie at Nohant, Sand at first refused to believe the reports: It was Borie, his head spinning with excitement, George said, who persuaded her that it was true. This time, they would not wait for news to trickle from the capital: George and her old band of brothers, like the apprentice artisans of her novel, prepared to march on the capital. But the revolution had started without them. On February 22, the July Monarchy fell, literally, overnight.

Launched by the Revolution of 1830, Louis-Philippe's reign had begun as a middle-of-the-road, cautiously liberal regime, personified by its "Citizen-King" carrying his own umbrella, an emblem of the prudent reforms promised by the House of Orléans after fifteen years of Bourbon misrule. Eighteen years later, the only evidence of the regime's republican promises was an alliance with the new aristocracy of wealth over the feudal claims of the ancien régime. Money ruled, as the surge of new fortunes from real estate, banking, railroads, and industry ushered in an era of voluptuous and visible consumption hitherto confined to Versailles, but never before seen in Paris. Money commanded the favors of ministers and deputies to a degree that left few areas of government untouched by scandal. France was compared to a "joint stock company run for the benefit of those who could afford to buy shares."

Strangely, the most hated symbol of corruption was Louis-Philippe's only incorruptible minister. François Guizot, a Protestant, had been raised in Calvinist Geneva, but where social ills were concerned, the brilliant historian turned bureaucrat proved more absolutist than any royal. Moving swiftly through the administration to his present post, minister of foreign affairs, Guizot's attempts to stabilize the shaky monarchy made him the architect of its fall. On his advice, dissent was stifled, and organizations and political clubs outlawed; his infamous response to the widening gulf between wealth and poverty, "Get rich" (*Enrichessez-vous),* conveyed the regime's philosophy: Greed would continue to be rewarded, since nothing must interfere with a free market.

Class hatred erupted with mounting regularity. The failures of the potato and wheat crops in 1845 and 1846 (the wheat crop failure was followed by rioting and attacks on local landowners, witnessed by Sand and her friends near Nohant) produced an economic slump and a drastic decline in living standards for all but the very rich. In Paris, bankruptcies soared, unemployment was rife; crowds of gaunt, hollow-eyed men lined up before dawn for a handful of jobs, physical evidence that working-class Parisians were near starvation. By the winter of 1846–1847 in the Prefecture of the Seine, 450,000 had applied for government bread vouchers issued to the destitute.

As a lightning rod to deflect violence, the regime planned a "campaign of banquets" at which grievances and proposals for reform could be aired. But with growing unease at the incendiary potential of such gatherings of the disaffected, the government canceled the last one of these events, which was to have taken place on February 22.

Almost at once, betrayal ignited revolution. The next day, the king dismissed Guizot, but it was too late. Already, the famous Parisian barricades, constructed of overturned carriages, tree trunks, and the citizens' weapon of choice, paving stones, barred the way through city streets, made more impassable by housewives who strewed broken china and bottles in the vicinity. By ten o'clock on the evening of the twenty-third, a demonstration that had begun peacefully outside the Ministry of Foreign Affairs (where the unmarried Guizot also lived) on the boulevard des Capucines turned violent: A single shot fired into the crowd became a fusillade. Within minutes, fifty-three demonstrators, including one woman, were dead. Most of the bodies had been stacked one on top of another in the nearby rue Fosse-du-Remparts; sixteen corpses were piled on carts by the insurgents and paraded around the city, greeted by mobs shouting, "Death to the killers!"

At noon on February 24, the king abdicated in favor of his ten-year-old grandson. Within the hour, the royal family had fled the Tuileries for exile in England. In 1830, it had taken a week for the Bourbon Restoration to fall and for Louis-Philippe to be installed on the throne. The July Monarchy toppled in twenty-four hours.

Rejecting the royal grandson and a regency, the deputies allowed Alphonse de Lamartine, poet and aspiring statesman, to declare the Second Republic. A provisional government was installed in the Hôtel de Ville. Among the government's founding members was Sand's intimate Louis Blanc. Their dreams of a socialist France seemed about to come true.

On March 1, George arrived in Paris in time to watch the funeral procession of those killed on February 23—mostly workers and students. But she was also frantic to learn the whereabouts of Maurice, last seen rushing from Delacroix's studio in a state resembling drunken exaltation. The artist had been startled to see his normally phlegmatic apprentice fired with revolutionary zeal. Finding her son safe, George abandoned herself to the joy of discovering that it was her friends—or *their* friends—who were now in power, all learning on-the-job how to run a government. There was little Louis Blanc, Sand noted tenderly, settled into *his* Luxembourg Palace—seat of the Department of Labor he had just created. Soon, George herself felt intoxicated by the celebratory atmosphere as she was swept into a key role along with her friends. No longer an ordinary citizen, she did not witness public events standing in the street or from a garret on the quay. From the windows of Guizot's former apartments in the Ministry of Foreign Affairs, Sand chatted with its new occupant, Alphonse de Lamartine, president of the republic, as they watched the funeral of those who had perished a week before. What she saw confirmed her idealism about the people of Paris and her pride in being one of them.

"It was beautiful—simple and touching," she wrote to Titine, "400,000 people massed in the streets between the Madeleine and the July column [Place de la Bastille]; not a policeman, not a soldier, yet such order, restraint, and civility that there wasn't a foot stepped on or a hat crushed. It was thrilling. The common people of Paris are the greatest people on earth!"

Within days, Sand had become the pen of the newly declared republic, the bearer of an official pass to every government office and a contract to provide reports and analyses of events for the administration's organ, the *Bulletin de la République.* But to make sure their views were heard, George and her friends also started their own publication, *La Cause du Peuple,* to last only three issues.

This was the honeymoon period. In George's rosy view of the events of the last weeks, the revolution had been made by bourgeoisie and workers—hand in hand. Still, she had to admit that strains were already showing. Officials of the provisional government felt pulled in opposing directions by the class interests of their constituencies. These strains could still be healed, George believed, *if* leaders realized that the masses looked to the bourgeoisie to set an example, and—a still bigger *if*—the people did not feel betrayed, sold out, lied to. Only then would they remain calm, moderate, and patient.

Sand would have been less than human if her optimism wasn't buoyed by her own new power: She now enjoyed patronage privileges—dispensing appointments (and dismissals) on behalf of the government. She secured jobs for Berry friends as commissioners for Châteauroux and La Châtre. She also made sure that Michel de Bourges was removed from his judicial post. If she needed to assure herself that she was not settling any personal scores, the lawyer had recently shocked other old comrades by representing the Crown versus a dissident deputy-journalist. Nor was Sand above the temptations of nepotism. Through her friendship with the powerful, behind-the-scenes operator Auguste Ledru-Rollin, she obtained the appointment of Maurice as mayor of La Châtre. Even Pauline Viardot was rewarded; as a friend of George, she was commissioned to compose a Marseillaise for the new republic.

The dream of class solidarity—the dedication of each to the good of all—soured quickly. Old distrust had a longer history than new faith: Workers refused to hand in their arms; fear and cynicism about the role of the people were soon openly expressed by the propertied classes, who reverted to their reflexive state. "Ambition" accompanied by "outright fraud" now conspired to rob the masses of their promised participation in the new order, Sand reported. These closet counterrevolutionaries had even infiltrated and sabotaged workers' meetings to make certain the gatherings would end in disarray. It was back to business as usual. With her free entry everywhere, George knew whereof she spoke.

Returning to Berry for Maurice's swearing-in ceremonies, Sand found intact the old reactionary attitudes and provincial resistance to change. Her neighbors were, she declared, "stuck in the past." Still, she persisted: The revolution wasn't yet lost just because La Châtre wanted no part of it.

In a series, "Letters to the People," addressed to the working and middle classes and the rich, her writing soared with an exhilarated awareness of her role. The "mind and pen" of the revolution, she felt charged with the mission of keeping the frail infant alive, against diminishing hope for its survival.

As general elections, the first test of the provisional government's popular base, loomed, Sand marshaled all her powers of suasion—personal and rhetorical—to persuade the masses to "vote right," that is, to vote for those candidates who supported the new administration. Her own growing militancy stoked the dangerous illusion of the "insider"—that the world as seen from the corridors of power was the "real" world. High on righteousness, Sand was led to overstate her case. In *Bulletin No. 16,* she staked out a risky opposition between the rule of the "majority" and a quasi-mystical concept of "unanimity." She dismissed the former as merely the voice of those with the savvy to manipulate the system, as opposed to the true will of the people, whether it was expressed at the ballot box or silently. As though this distinction wasn't shaky enough, Sand went on to warn of the consequences if this "unanimity" or "galvanizing consent of the masses" was to be ignored.

"If the elections don't reflect the triumph of social realities, if they validate—as usual—the expressed interests of a single caste, wrung from the trusting loyalty of the people, these elections, which ought to have been the salvation of the Republic, will be its ruin. Of this there can be no doubt." But she went further. Should this betrayal take place, "there would be only one course of salvation for the people, who have had some experience with erecting barricades: they will take to the streets again to express their collective will, nullifying decisions made falsely in their name by their so-called national representatives. Does the rest of France really want to force Paris into such an extreme—and deplorable remedy? . . . May God preserve us!"

Readers of the *Bulletin* were not wrong in reading this apocalyptic scenario as inflammatory. More than a warning, or even a threat, Sand was seen as uttering a call for another uprising. The fire next time would see her, torch in hand, at the barricades.

George had anticipated this reaction: that she would be demonized as "communist" for exposing the corruption of the term "republican," now a tent into which crept all the "haves," including monarchists, ultramontanists, and all other defenders of the status quo. Conversely, "communist," she noted, had become code for the (nonexistent) advocates of collectivizing agriculture and for the apologists for vandalism or theft of private property.

"If by communism, you mean a conspiracy formed to seize power by means of a coup on April 16th (election day) we are certainly not communists. If, however, by communism, you mean the desire and will on the part of the legitimate voice of public conscience to abolish the poisonous inequities of extreme wealth and extreme poverty, to be replaced by the beginnings of real equality—then, yes, we are communists and not ashamed to say so, at least, to those of you who challenge us loyally, because we believe that, in your hearts, you are with us."

But Sand, too, was about to be betrayed—not by the wolfish bourgeois in republican red hood, but by her comrades on the extreme left, including most probably her sometimes lover Louis Blanc, "a little man with big ambitions," as Sand now sourly described him. Blanc and friends were indeed secretly hatching a coup to hijack the April 16 elections.

The plot failed—spectacularly. The entire national guard, the bourgeoisie, and a majority of working-class neighborhoods on the outskirts of Paris shouted: "Vive la République. Down with Communism!"

Writing to Maurice, Sand reported on "what he wasn't going to read in any newspaper." There had been as many as four different plots in eight days. In retrospect, Sand thought that Lamartine, together with his followers, could have seized the moderate center with a plan of electoral and economic reform: easing the tax burdens that fell most heavily on the poor, while saving the country from looming financial catastrophe.

Failure of the coup strengthened the right-of-center moderates. Double-crossed by her allies, Sand's famous *"Bulletin No. 16"* was held responsible for the conspirators' turning against their own elected provisional government. The right wing of the provisional government now demanded her head: Who had anointed *her* official voice of the republic, anyway? The answer was no one, as it turned out. The bureaucrats charged with oversight of the *Bulletin* could not recall ever commissioning Sand's article or even of having seen the piece before publication.

She tried to take heart from the "million souls" who turned out for the *Fête de la Fraternité* (Brotherhood Day) and whose numbers were far more meaningful than all the intrigues, plots, and betrayals that were sinking the frail bark of the republic. "The People might not understand every argument, every ideological nuance of the debates now taking place, but they feel keenly that great changes are in the works and they are all behind them," she claimed. Or maybe Parisians just loved a great fête, the way they loved a lavish funeral.

Predictably, the freshly elected assembly endorsed the newly aggressive moderates. Fears of further bloodshed and of fanatical left extremism leading to mob rule had pushed even working-class Parisians to the right. Ironies multiplied in this time of shifting alliances: It had been the efforts of the reformers to bring about a more representative electoral process, in particular, their attempts to loosen the hold of Paris on the provinces, that turned the first elected Constituent Assembly into a defiantly conservative body, sporting a few liberal slogans to sop their collective consciences. Nothing about the public face of the Second Republic would have caused Louis-Philippe to lose an hour of sleep in London. The majority of French (except possibly nonvoting women and the propertyless) wanted no part of social revolution. Political change—an end to divine right and a slightly more inclusive constitution—was revolution enough.

Louis Blanc, Sand's onetime ally, protégé, and lover, was driven into exile. George may well have thought he had it coming, for making a fool of her. Opportunists like Ledru-Rollin scurried back to the centrist fold and its lofty figurehead, Lamartine. Many Parisian workers were not so easily bought off. Led by veterans of the earlier uprising (who, unlike Blanc, had managed to stay out of trouble), they invaded the Palais Bourbon, declared the assembly dissolved and proclaimed a socialist government. Now, the national guard units stationed in the richest neighborhoods took control, arresting leaders of the insurgents—both bourgeois and working class. Lamartine and his allies felt safe in proclaiming, "We democrats have once more prevailed against both retrograde troublemakers and demagogues." It was a shock to George to realize that her old ally was talking about her. Adamant, she still predicted and believed that the people would take back *their* revolution; at a luncheon, she had warned Alexis de Tocqueville, "You'd better try and persuade your friends, Monsieur, not to rough up people in the street, and to stop their harassment and provocation. Similarly, I've urged those close to me not to rise to the bait. But if it comes to class warfare, you'll all be massacred!" She tried one more journalistic venture, *La Vraie République* (The True Republic); it lasted a month.

George's prophecy almost came true. This time, the riot had begun on May 15 as a peaceful demonstration in support of Poland, suffering under Russian occupation, but the demonstrators were also militant and vocal in their opposition to Lamartine, whose policy of nonintervention had enraged the Polish émigré community. The mob stormed the assembly, interrupting speeches and causing mayhem; yet again, another old radical leader—Barbès—was arrested. Now, it was over—for good. By evening, even George Sand admitted that the cause of a republic committed to social change was lost. There was nothing left for her to do but retreat to Nohant. She waited several more days;

although rumors had reached her that she too was about to be arrested, she refused to give the impression that she was fleeing. She took the precaution, however, of burning all her papers and, especially, her *Intimate Journals.*

THREE MONTHS EARLIER, a few days after George's jubilant return to Paris on March 1, she had arrived late for dinner at Countess Marliani's. As she started climbing the staircase, she came face-to-face with Chopin, who was descending slowly on the arm of a fellow guest. He and Sand exchanged greetings. Visibly shaken, Chopin tried to collect himself by asking whether George had heard the great news of the birth of her granddaughter, Jeanne-Gabrielle Clésinger, on February 28. Still estranged from Solange, she had not been told, so Chopin expressed pleasure at being the first to congratulate her. He extended his hand, which, Sand recalled, felt icy to the touch; then, turning away, he proceeded slowly down the narrow staircase. But when he reached the bottom, Chopin remembered what he had forgotten to say. Too weak to climb back, he dispatched his companion to run up and add that mother and baby were both fine. Sand herself now descended, asking Chopin for further details of Solange and her family. She also asked about Chopin's health. "I told her that I was doing well," Chopin wrote to the new mother. Both bulletins were premature. Jeanne-Gabrielle survived for only five days. Chopin lasted twenty months more. From Nohant, Sand had heard that he was failing and that his sister had arrived from Warsaw to care for him. She wrote to Ludwika for news, but the woman whom she had kissed good-bye with such love and regret at Nohant five years earlier had not replied. George now fired off her usual letters of self-justification: She had had no idea Chopin was so sick, she claimed. Why hadn't anyone told her? (Why did she suppose Ludwika had come from Poland?) But it was also true that most of "their" friends were, for the time being, no longer hers. Word from Nohant had described Sand as being so distraught she had taken to her bed for days. Happily for George, there was a guest arriving, ready to console her.

20

Stages of Happiness

Returning to Nohant in the middle of May 1849, George found the entire household immersed in make-believe. While Chopin had been part of the family, performances had been in the giggly, haphazard tradition of amateur theatricals, after-dinner improvisations that were closer to charades. Now, polished productions were in the works.

Tensions had evaporated with the departures of Chopin, Titine, and Solange, unleashing a frenzy of stagecraft. Maurice himself was absorbed in the creation of a puppet theatre. From the wood of local willow trees, he carved and painted the large marionettes and, with help from family and visiting friends, built the stage, scenery. and lighting. Sand contributed scripts and sewed costumes. Initially, both plot and characters were based on traditional figures in the Italian *Commedia dell'Arte*—Maurice's particular passion. But soon, figures and narrative drew on regional folklore, even local characters and jokes.

While Maurice tinkered with his wooden players, everyone else pitched in to the feverish preparations involving human actors, taking place at the same time. The program alternated original dramas or comedies written by Sand (with Maurice as occasional coauthor) and adaptations of Shakespeare or the French classics. George's work on Nohant productions encouraged her to give the Paris stage another try after her initial fiasco, and she had the inspired idea of using Nohant's theatre as the equivalent of out-of-town tryouts of her own plays before they reached the boulevard. Here, she could revise scripts, character, and plot before submitting the final version.

Still, with deadlines for the novels looming and, always, bills to pay, George could only give intermittent attention to the theatrical labors taking place downstairs. Maurice was feeling overwhelmed. When he wasn't working on his marionettes, he tried to oversee productions of Nohant's "real" theatre as well. There were props to be built, flats painted, and actors cast and rehearsed (the absence of both Solange and Titine required finding ingénue replacements). He needed other talent in residence. Eugène Lambert, like Maurice, a former assistant in Delacroix's studio, now became a permanent guest; he was still living in Nohant twenty years later. Another visitor, a young German scholar, also filled in wherever needed, including a brief stint as Sand's lover.

Then, Maurice recalled an acquaintance from his Latin Quarter circle of students and struggling young artists who ate and drank together at the same cafés and cheap restaurants. Alexandre Manceau had just completed the arduous apprenticeship required for the career of engraver: Lithography, steel engraving, monotypes, and woodcuts—all the graphic arts that in an era before photographs could be widely reproduced—functioned as the staple of book and periodical illustration.

Manceau did not enjoy the same advantages held by sons of well-off families, such as the Sand-Dudevants, who could support an unpaid assistantship in an artist's' studio. A poor boy of artistic gifts and one of eight children of a father who was variously a guard in the Luxembourg Gardens and a customs inspector, Manceau had to chose the engravers' trade, with an apprenticeship that assured a subsistence living. But what had impressed Maurice about the slight, hard-working young engraver was that, despite his modest means, Manceau was so stagestruck that he still made the time to volunteer—on the boards or behind the scenes—with any local or passing troupe that would use him. Seeing him as the ideal guest for Nohant's theatre camp, Maurice issued an open invitation to Manceau to visit as soon as his schedule permitted.

In January 1850, Manceau appeared, and immediately, his fine engraver's hand was pressed into service as a much-needed copyist: Guests had to receive "part scripts" so that they could learn their lines in advance and be ready to rehearse on arrival. Writing furiously in her study, George, as usual, was too far behind to have time to incorporate corrections into the final draft, or "fair copy" destined for the printer. She lost no time in poaching Manceau as her personal secretary, putting him in charge of correspondence and contracts, as well as literary manuscripts. By the end of March, Manceau went to Paris to take some of the equipment in his studio back to Nohant, enabling him to work in both places. By the end of April, three months after his arrival, Manceau and George became lovers.

"Yes, I love him," she wrote to her new publisher and confidant, Jules-Pierre Hetzel. "I love him with my whole being, and there's an amazing calm to my love, despite my age and his. I'm so happy I can bear anything—*even his absence* [she underlined the last three words] which was always something I could never bear." She described her lover, thirteen years her junior, with a double image of the ideal domestic pets, both an "affectionate cat and faithful dog." In the latter role, he "anticipates my every wish, putting his entire self into bringing me a glass of water or lighting my cigarette." As the more sexually experienced of the two, George used her erotic skills to "make it seem that I'm letting *him* seduce me with unprecedented ease. . . . Showing him how to please me, I let him play the innocent; I treat him like a twelve year old boy." Manceau proved an apt pupil; he aroused George to a "rage of pleasure I never experienced before," leaving her "covered with bites and bruises." In a role now familiar to her, she encouraged the younger man to lose his inhibitions and assert his masculine will to dominate her sexually; out of the bedroom, however, it was understood that he would never presume equal status. To the end of their twenty years together, Manceau always addressed Sand, and referred to her when speaking to others, as "Madame." And he never failed to provide his mistress with "all the little attentions of an agile, energetic and resourceful woman. . . . When I was sick, just watching him plump my pillow or bring my slippers made me feel better."

Still, Manceau's most manly attribute may have been the most traditional one of all: He was unique among Sand's resident lovers in his firm refusal of any financial dependence on her. With the engravers' tools he needed for his work in both his Paris studio on rue Racine and in Nohant, he either labored at night (if the theatre claimed him by day) or made brief visits to the capital to fill the many waiting commissions of his successful career.

After his promotion to consort, Manceau's new confidence led him to take charge of Nohant's principal activity, "turning the family theatre into something serious," George noted. Along with the starring roles he filled with panache, Manceau began instituting changes in all areas of staging (he could also make or fix anything). The thirty-two-year-old now revealed a quiet authority and decisiveness, along with the managerial and organizational skills of the ideal "executive producer"—all qualities that Maurice, sadly, lacked. Gradually, Manceau took on the director's role as well; blocking scenes, scheduling and overseeing rehearsals, and attending to the myriad other chores—from detail to dramaturgy—required to run a repertory company. If Maurice, now relegated to his marionettes, resented the newcomer who had taken over both his theatre and his mother's bed, he had only himself to blame.

In 1851, George embarked on a renovation of Nohant. She turned a large space downstairs, including Solange's former bedroom and the billiard room, into a real theatre with a permanent raised stage, proscenium, and, above stage left, a marionette theatre, whose height and construction preserved the illusionism created by the hidden hands and voices. Housed in the same space, each impresario ruled his separate domain.

Well before the fiasco of 1848, as though anticipating her disillusioned retreat from politics and Paris, Sand had turned to Berry for inspiration. Three novels, among a number of others, have assumed the nimbus of a "rustic trilogy": three works taught to generations of French schoolchildren as windows into a rural France that was fast disappearing, swept away by the locomotive of modernity roaring from the capital. Did it ever exist, or did Sand's fictions create this moving-picture show, akin to unspooled *images d'Épinal,* the naive colored woodcuts depicting traditional French life in the provinces? Her narratives deftly fill the space between these iconic figures. For these novels, she invented a new idiom, dialogue composed of an ingenious simulation of peasant-speak: a pure if simplified French with a few words of Berrichon dialect thrown in. Then, making use of recent research into regional folklore and customs, she wove a story linking the sanctity of labor, the seasonal rhythms of nature, and the virtues of love, charity, and community.

Written in four days in 1845, *La mare au diable* (The Devil's Pool) was serialized before being published as a single volume in May 1846. (Sometime between the preparation of the manuscript and the publishing of the book, George had deleted the book's dedication to Chopin.) In her new preface, she claimed as her source of inspiration a Holbein print depicting a weary peasant in rags, plowing the stony soil with his malnourished oxen, accompanied by the skeletal figure of Death. On seeing this image of hopeless and futile labor that would end only with the grave, Sand tells the reader she felt a sense of indignation, an immediate need to counter this message of doom with her own plot, admittedly, she notes, an idealized "parable" of what rural life ought to be. In her tale, the love of Germain, a well-off peasant and handsome, virtuous widower, serves to rescue Marie, a helpless teenaged neighbor. Marie's mother is too poor even to feed her only child; she sends the girl into service as a shepherdess, a fate that will include exploitation and sexual abuse. Here Sand's ideal of the novel as parable is, quite literally, Biblical: Carrying the virginal Marie on the back of his donkey to her new life, Germain, whose name evokes Gésu or Jesus, learns by chance of her impending martyrdom. His love proves Marie's salvation, while in marrying her, he gains a mother for his bereft children.

In *François le champi* (Francis the Waif), a rich miller's young wife discovers a small boy asleep in a meadow. Abused by her husband, browbeaten by her mother-in-law, Madeleine would be forbidden to adopt the foundling. Instead, she deposits the lad with one of the miller's tenants, an impoverished spinster; here François's saintly rescuer can safely sneak food and clothing to both the child and his foster parent without the knowledge of her own skinflint family. But now, the simple tale of innocence and virtue prevailing against cruelty and greed takes a deviant turn: The vicious mother-in-law dies, followed by her brutish son. Left a poor widow, Madeleine is further rewarded for her love, courage, and charity: The waif she saved from the orphanage, and raised alongside her own infant son, has grown into a man, becoming a rich miller and a perfect husband! Incest sanctified by innocence, Sand boldly conflates *eros* and *agape*. Named for the scriptural sinner, Madeleine provides hints of her redemption at the outset of the story. She is several times compared to Saint Christopher, carrying (with all its allusions to the Virgin birth) the boy across rushing waters, then saving him from a fatal fever with the gift of her cloak. In Sand's parable, only the cruel and greedy are punished; love—especially the love between mother and son—is always blessèd.

La petite Fadette, the last novel of the three, takes the subject of twin brothers, both in love with the same girl-child, Fadette. Into this eternal triangle, Sand has tossed the time bomb of homoerotic doubling: The stay-at-home brother, Sylvinet, is also in love with his sibling—a complication foreseen by the midwife's curse: A dire fate awaits both infants, if they are not separated at birth.

Brought up by her grandmother, an old peasant woman of reputed supernatural powers, the wild and fey Fadette is something of a *champi,* or waif, herself. Of father unknown, her mother had gone off with the army as camp follower; the girl clings to the lost parent's apron as if to a holy relic. At the same time that she was writing *Fadette,* Sand was beginning work on *L'Histoire de ma vie* (The Story of My Life), with its ambitious research into family history and its accidental revelations about her parentage and birth. Of all Sand's novels, the story of Fadette, the wild and androgynous child of nature, stands, along with *Lucrezia Floriani,* as the most autobiographical of her fictions. Even its happy ending—the marginal, unsocialized girl rescued by the steady, successful brother—points to the ambiguities that Sand kept circling in her own life: On being domesticated, does a woman "dwindle" into marriage, or can she transform, by her own example, both her husband and the society charged with taming her? Sand's identification with Fadette is more than theoretical; of all of the girl's meager possessions, she most treasures a relic of the abandoning parent. Gone off to follow the army, the mother left behind only the emblem of family ties unloosed, her apron.

The success of Sand's rustic novels was based on their skillful blend of social realism, romantic idealism, and religious faith; she never scants the horrors of rural poverty for the allure of the picturesque. Leading us away from hedgerows in bloom, she reveals the tumbledown leaking hovels, the destitution of those unable to work, an elderly woman's dilemma of whether she or her foster child will have the one woolen garment to get through the winter. In withdrawing from political action, however, Sand seems to have turned away from secular solutions to the problems of social justice. Her ideal of a Christian socialism would continue to privilege a rural "communionism"—to use Leroux's distinction—over urban "communism"; in her rustic novels, the pastoral Golden Age leads back to the future. Millet's sowers have the edge over Daumier's street fighters every time.

François le Champi, adopted for the stage and produced at the *Théâtre de L'Odéon* in 1849, was Sand's first resounding theatrical success. Weary of bloodshed in the streets, worldly Parisians now applauded her vision of what they must do to be saved. Similarly, the message of *La petite Fadette* could not have seemed more timely; echoing Voltaire, its author urged a return "to tending our own sheep."

As it turned out, it was easier for Sand to exalt Nohant from afar as a refuge from the spasms of political upheaval in Paris: Outside her gates, Sand, the infamous socialist, had become the designated target of local resentments, pilloried for supposedly inviting mob rule to march from Paris to seize their rights and property. Stung by the injustice of the gossip, she resorted to the sour cynicism of disillusion aimed at her own naive contrast between city and country.

"Here in Berry, so romantic, so good, so kind and calm, in this land that I love so tenderly, where I've proved myself the friend and advocate of the poor and humble, I've been singled out as the special enemy of the human race; if the Republic failed to keep its promises, I'm the one to blame," she wrote to Charlotte Marliani. She had even heard "rumors of a plot to burn down Nohant." The same hypocrites who, face-to-face, tipped their hats to her in the streets of La Châtre shouted, "Down with Communists!" when they galloped past the walls of Nohant. Concerned for Sand's safety, her friend the mayor (successor to Maurice) advised her to leave until the unpleasantness was over. She took his advice and packed off to Tours. Then, the local newspapers wrote sneering editorials, deriding her as a coward.

In Paris, the political situation continued to unravel. Now in power, the "moderates" lost no time in wreaking revenge on the radicals who had tried to unseat them: Thousands were deported to the disease-ridden colonies. Many of her old comrades in arms, Victor Borie and Louis Blanc among them, seeing the writing on the wall, fled to Belgium or England.

She felt so demoralized, she told another friend, that she refused to write for any newspaper. To be published, she would have to temper her views, which she refused to do: "My soul has been shattered; it's still in pieces and I have to wait until it heals." Then, there were final losses: Her brother Hippolyte died on Christmas Day 1848, of alcohol-related illness. A year later, he was followed by Marie Dorval, who suffered a stroke while touring with a broken-down troupe in the provinces.

Most French shared Sand's feelings of futility; they were sick of political strife, the vendettas, the opportunism, the shameless absence on the part of elected officials of any concern for the common good. For George, certainly, it came as no surprise—and not even disappointment—when Louis-Napoleon Bonaparte, the grandnephew of Napoleon I, returned triumphantly from exile in England to be elected president of the republic.

George had known the president-elect in his youth, when, as High Bohemian Princeling of hallowed name, Louis-Napoleon had made the rounds of the fashionable salons. From one conversation followed by a brief exchange of letters, he had then seemed open to liberal ideas; he and Sand had discovered common ground in their detestation of Louis-Philippe. Nonetheless, the same progressive notions had once been ascribed to "the Citizen-King"—before he was crowned. Royals—or Bonapartes—who were out of power had nothing to lose by espousing republican ideas in the cenacles where these would be welcome. In any case, could the Second Empire, Sand wondered, be any worse than the Second Republic?

21

Last Acts

MUCH WORSE, IT TURNED OUT. The bloody birth of the Second Empire has been compared to the Terror of the 1790s, the period that, ironically, left a devastated France eager to embrace Napoleon I, granduncle of the new prince-president.

In early November 1851, Sand came to Paris for the rehearsals of her new play, *The Marriage of Victorine.* The political situation was still volatile, and a coup d'état was expected at any moment. By November 26, nothing had happened, and George, accompanied by Solange, Clésinger, and Count d'Orsay, her daughter's rich new lover, attended the opening matinee of *Victorine* at the Théâtre du Gymnase. Unofficially separated, the Clésingers would end their marriage the following year. Now that Solange had become a worldly kept woman, there had been a rapprochement between mother and daughter. George adored her new granddaughter, Jeanne, named for her dead sister but who was called "Nini," while Solange's glamorous new life and love left her, for the time being, at least, less angry and Sand feeling less accused. Sand was also much taken with Count d'Orsay, a handsome, reputedly bisexual aesthete who was also a longtime intimate of Louis-Napoleon. The dandy had become a personage of power and influence; he would soon extend his protection of the daughter to the mother.

With assurances about the new sovereign coming from one close to him, George continued to be optimistic. There was still a chance that Louis-Napoleon would usher in a more lasting "constitutional Republic," she wrote to Hetzel. But a month later, Sand had lost hope; the confused but well-intentioned youth she remembered had become captive to the hardest-nosed of hard-liners, the *ultras* of the misnamed moderates, pledged to extinguish any remaining sparks of the Second Republic. Like all weaklings, the prince-president proved especially vulnerable to promptings that he rule as a "Man of Bronze, just and unbending" and stride over his century, "sword in hand." From the capital, a wave of repression and revenge spread to the provinces, giving license to every individual vendetta. The infamous and anonymous *lettres de cachets* of the Terror were revived: "One half of France is busy denouncing the other," Sand reported. With no recourse, those accused—some twenty thousand—were thrown into prison, transported to Algeria as slave labor, or shipped to penal colonies, like the infamous Devil's Island in French Guyana. Many of Sand's old Berry friends were behind bars; others, including Pierre Leroux and Ledru-Rollin, were marked for deportation. Again, Louis Blanc and Victor

Borie chose exile. And again, it was rumored that Sand herself would be arrested. This time, however, she refused to budge; instead, she decided to pay a call on the prince-president to plead on behalf of her friends.

On December 2, the Constituent Assembly was dissolved. The expected coup had become fact. George found herself unmoved; the republic had long ceased to represent her or her friends. For a few days, she cherished the hope that Louis-Napoleon could still reconcile all the French. But the nation, sick to death of discord and eager for a law-and-order government, welcomed him deliriously. On December 4, several hundred student demonstrators were massacred by an "army of policemen," Sand reported. On December 21, Louis-Napoleon's electoral victory over his closest rival—5,434, 226 to 1,448,000—was taken as mandate of absolute power. Next, the dictatorship-in-waiting disposed of the remaining dissenters. On January 9 1852, sixty-six former opposition deputies, including Victor Hugo and Sand's protégé, Agricol Perdiguier, were exiled. In a special plebiscite, the prince-president was granted dictatorial powers for ten years by a vote of 7,500,000. From there, his election as Napoleon III, Emperor of All France, was assured.

Her hopes shattered by the triumph of reaction and repression, Sand persevered, determined to save as many lives as she could. Returning to Paris from Nohant in January 1852, she immediately wrote to the new emperor, requesting an audience. Deftly, she summoned the middle-aged man's nostalgia for his youthful idealism (he had, after all, once written a book titled *The Extinction of Pauperism*): "I've always thought of you as a socialist genius . . . and that's the only reason I dare to commit the crime of raising a cry of reproach amidst acclaim for the man whom God has chosen and the people have accepted." Her daring fusillade hit home. The emperor replied with a handwritten note, asking Sand to fix a date for the following week.

Should her audience prove to be too brief to allow for all that she had to say, she took the precaution of bringing with her the full written version of her appeal for clemency: Beginning with the disclaimer that she was no Madame de Stael, the scourge of the first Napoleon, Sand took the heart-to-heart approach: "Prince, friends of my childhood and of my old age, those who were like brothers or adopted children, are now in prison or exiled." She wept not only for them, but for their wives, mothers, and children. From the personal, George moved to issues of principle, denouncing the despotism that mocked human rights, and the new Terror whose weapons included deportation, preventive detention, punishment for crimes unnamed and unproved, acts of revenge for which the political was only an excuse.

Louis-Napoleon was reportedly so moved by Sand's words that he took her hands into his own, saying that his respect and esteem for her was such that he would grant everything that she asked on behalf of her friends. Still, she knew better than to put her trust in princes. For the next months, George tirelessly worked all her connections: From the palace, she ran from one ministry to another, pleading, advocating, defending not just friends, but also friends of friends, and hundreds of others made known to her because they had been unjustly condemned.

Now, it was her allies on the left—ready as always to find one of their own guilty of apostasy—who accused Sand. They claimed she was playing into the hands of the enemy, acting only to save her own skin and that of her friends, showing no concern with how her celebrity would be exploited to spin the image of a just and merciful leader. Stung, Sand countered that the goal of her pleading had been a general amnesty. Whatever the truth, she secured the release of hundreds. That she was used to showcase the emperor's humanity would be, in George's view, irrelevant, as long as it saved lives.

In the Clésingers' seesaw of separation and reconciliation, Sand had received one unexpected blessing: She was awarded custody of her granddaughter, through the enlightened decision by the presiding judge, who ruled that the choice be made by little Nini herself. Both George and Manceau were ecstatic: They adored the three-year-old and, in Nohant, took turns looking after her to accommodate their work schedules. With echoes of Chopin, George, and Louisette (the Viardots' small daughter), Nini's presence transformed the couple into a family. Together, George and Nini labored to create a miniature garden. Every day, weather permitting, they carted stones; planted borders, shrubs, and flowers; and even constructed a working fountain. Sand admitted that the project had become a monomania, an effort perhaps to wrest permanence—however cyclical—from the randomness of life. Like Maurice's puppet theatre, the miniature garden was an attempt at correcting human chaos, whose worst effects would soon be felt.

In December 1854, days before the decree assigning Nini's custody to her grandmother was to become final, Clésinger arrived at Nohant, demanding his daughter. Not that he had any thought of taking charge of her himself. The four-year-old was packed off to a convent boarding school near Paris. There, on a freezing morning in mid-January, her father appeared and insisted on taking the little girl, wearing a light summer dress, out for the day. She returned with a high fever and the ominous symptoms of scarlatina. The nuns sent for Solange. Nini died in her mother's arms before dawn the next day.

George was devastated. Her love for her grandchild had redeemed the thwarted affections of mother and daughter, even briefly reconciling them. Unreachable in her anguish, she wept day and night. The agony of loss, wounds freshly opened with each view of the garden, seemed without end. Manceau was helpless to comfort her. But a week later, she began a memoir and essay about Nini: "On the Death of Jeanne Clésinger." Writing of her hopes for a reunion with Nini in the afterlife helped George through the worst of her grief. For the contemporary reader, the imagined encounter with the dead child grown into a young woman makes queasy reading; the consolations of spiritualism, soon to sweep England and the continent, in Sand seem an abdication.

Solange found refuge in a return to the church. George, seeing an opportune moment in her daughter's mood of repentance, insisted that she meet and embrace Titine, asking her cousin's forgiveness for past unkindness.

Manceau put his hopes in a change of scene. He invited George, Maurice, and Emile Aucante, another one of Sand's "boys," as Delacroix derisively called them, on a trip to Italy. Although she gamely climbed mountains and ruins and pursued butterflies and plant specimens unknown in France, George could not keep feelings of sorrow and loss at bay. Monuments of antiquity, especially, depressed her. Ancient Rome she found "strange, beautiful, interesting, astonishing even but too dead," the modern city "unspeakably ugly and dirty." Ever political, she found other reasons to disapprove of Italy, foremost among them the silencing of her great patriots, Mazzini and Garibaldi—if not for long. Her critical perceptions, however, inspired one of Sand's most controversial later novels, the combatively anticlerical *La Daniella.* First serialized in *La Presse* in 1857, the work caused outrage even within the liberal journal itself, but the outcry from conservative periodicals and then officialdom caused *La Presse* to be first suspended and then banned, along with its offending fiction. Again, Sand used her connections to the court, this time to the Empress Eugenie, who intervened: The journal continued publication—but without the novel, which only appeared later in a one-volume abridgment.

She had also resumed work on *The Story of My Life* and on the first edition of her complete works, to be illustrated by the premier artist-illustrator of the day, Tony Johannot, with the collaboration of Maurice—the latter commission at his mother's behest. Now that he was forty, her son's dilettantism was a constant worry. Not that his mama was any too tactful in her efforts to promote him: When, along with his puppets, playwriting, and painting, Maurice produced a novel, Sand suggested he send it to her publisher Buloz. "Maybe he'll publish it for me," she said. Maurice had also begun making difficulties with Manceau—a replay of his confrontations with Chopin. These scenes, along with a growing stream of visitors and literary pilgrims to Nohant, decided the protective Manceau to find a place where he and George could get away together. In Gargilesse, a secluded village perched above the Creuse River, he bought a former baker's house of two rooms, one above the other; the ground floor had housed the oven where villagers had come to have their stews and roasts cooked. Maurice, however, would not be left behind; a small room had to be added to accommodate him. George was happiest when she went there to work—alone. In the narrow house on the river, she completed twelve novels, including the infamous *Elle et lui.* Then, in 1860, she succumbed to typhoid. Spared in Paris by the epidemic of 1831, she was older and more vulnerable now, and it was a lengthy illness and recovery. To speed her convalescence, Manceau took her to the south of France, settling in Tamaris, a village near Toulon. The following year, despite financial problems caused by Maurice's mismanagement of Nohant, she refused a special subsidy offered by the emperor. Clearly, George was still smarting from earlier criticism of her co-option by the court.

More than ever, she felt that Maurice needed a wife, and she wanted grandchildren. Several tepid courtships had failed. So George, despairing of her son's lack of initiative in finding a bride, chose one for him: In 1862, he wedded twenty-year-old Lina, daughter of an old family friend, the engraver Luigi Calamatta. A plain and pliant young woman, Lina finally provided the ideal daughter for George as well: undemanding, admiring, efficient without being bossy. United in their anticlericalism, both families rejected a religious marriage in favor of a civil ceremony, but with a baby on the way, the parents-to-be converted to Protestantism. Sand's first grandson, Marc-Antoine, and his two sisters—Aurore ("Lolo"), her namesake, and Gabrielle—were baptized in the Reform church.

His new authority as head of the family did nothing to improve Maurice's relations with Manceau. Hostilities focused on the theatre, but the stage was merely symbolic. Again, Maurice tried a him-or-me ultimatum; after some agonizing, Sand made her choice. In 1864, she and Manceau left for Palaiseau, a village near Paris where the engraver had bought another house, a new villa whose mansard roof suggested the wing of a seventeenth-century château; it boasted wonderful gardens and a bucolic view of fields of grazing cattle.

Sand's truce with Solange had ended when d'Orsay disappeared and was replaced by a succession of other lovers. "So you think the life of a prostitute is so easy," her mother wrote. "You'll find that men only want women who are capable of earning their own way." George could never face the equation of the unloved daughter and the lost woman. Solange had only her "cold heart" to blame for their estrangement.

In the late 1860s, George again became close to a younger woman. Juliette Lamber(t) La Messine, thirty-two years Sand's junior, had published stories, novels, and polemical writings for almost a decade before they met. Her publications constructed an antipaternalistic rebellion in print: Both Juliette's father and first husband had been ardent followers of the socialist philosopher Pierre-Joseph Prud'hon, whose misogyny she had denounced in her very first work. When she and Sand became friends, Juliette was a widow with a young child. Unlike the impulse behind Sand's adoption of her cousin Titine and of Pauline Viardot, George did not try to turn Juliette into another daughter; rather, the older woman saw her own younger self in the highly political and ambitious writer, already well launched on her own long career. (La Messine died in 1936, at age one hundred.)

Juliette was also a skilled diplomat. Soon to remarry a rich and influential senator, Edmond Adam, she managed to remain the protégée of Marie d'Agoult and to become a vocal acolyte of Sand's—when the two older women hadn't spoken in twenty years! During this time, Juliette made many visits to Nohant, while George delighted in return invitations to the Adams' grand residences near the sea, in Normandy and Nice.

Other enmities were healed. Sand found her way back to her old friend and publisher, François Buloz, and his *Revue des Deux Mondes,* a literary keystone of the establishment.

With age, left or right politics made less difference than affection and trust. Now, the most nourishing friendship of her final years—if not her entire life—would confirm what counted.

Sand had, of course, heard of Gustave Flaubert. The scandal caused by *Madame Bovary* and the prosecution of the author after its publication in 1857, when Flaubert was thirty-six, could only have reminded George of a similar reaction incited by a young woman of twenty-eight, a quarter century earlier, with the double shocks of *Indiana* and *Lélia.* As Sand recalled, *Madame Bovary* had been read aloud to her, probably by Manceau, at the end of December 1856, during her recovery from typhoid, an illness that notoriously affects eyesight. It's easy to imagine George listening to Manceau's quiet voice, her growing sense that she was hearing a familiar tale—the dreams and disillusion of a bored, young wife—but, morally, written in a foreign language.

Stripped of sympathy or censure, this was a life as case history, with romanticism and social progress dissected as terminal diseases. If George felt her own idealism accused by Emma's fatal dreams, Flaubert had indeed accused her: In the first version of *L'Education sentimentale,* written when he was all of twenty-two, the author proclaimed: "I do not address these remarks to the schoolboys and dressmakers who read George Sand . . . but to persons of discrimination." Later, he enjoined his sometime mistress and aspiring woman of letters, Louise Colet, to expunge from her writing any traces of her sex, giving the cautionary example of Sand's prose, where "everything oozes and ideas trickle between words as between slack thighs." Nonetheless, a few days before their introduction at the theatre in April 1857, he sent George a copy of *Madame Bovary,* inscribed by the author: "To Madame Sand, with homage from an obscure writer." She returned the favor with several admiring pages on the novel in her bimonthly column in the *Courrier de Paris.*

Due largely to geography, it would be two more years before their friendship took root: Flaubert lived with his mother and niece in his childhood home in Croisset, near Rouen; Sand moved between Nohant, Gargilesse, and Palaiseau. The most frequent topic in their copious exchange of letters for over a decade was the logistics of meeting: When would they both be in Paris? When would Sand's deadlines and family obligations, and Flaubert's brutal working habits, permit her to visit Croisset? Still more rare, when could her "Troubadour" serenade her in Nohant?

As Flaubert got to know George the woman, he forgave—even came to admire—Sand the writer. His continued homage to her was his salutation: *"Chère Maître,"* the double tribute of the feminine adjective and masculine title, bestowed on superior talent and achievement. To be sure, her "trickling" ideas, in his obscene image, could not have been more alien, starting with the writer's presence in the text. In contrast to Flaubert's religion of authorial absence from the work, Sand's passionate and impatient persona jostles every character; if they're slow to get to the point, she doesn't hesitate to take over and, in her own voice, say it for them. Her ideas, so it often seems, are too important—love, justice, an end to class barriers, and the renewal of marriage, religion, and community—to leave to mere fictional creatures.

Although Flaubert would claim "I *am* Emma Bovary," he meant something quite different. He experienced her in his own psyche: in the despair of her boredom—sitting at the dinner table, drawing lines with her fork in the oilcloth—in the folly of her fantasies of rescue. There are no happy endings, no palliatives to the pain of misplaced hope and toxic illusions.

Miraculously, Sand and Flaubert's polarity of belief created the perfect friendship: Both loved to argue. But its real nourishment drew from deeper sources: unconditional love, trust, a bracing sympathy that did not depend on agreement, but that stood, unquestioning and firm with the other against the world. Indeed, their friendship crystallized when, in the middle of a record-breaking heat wave, Manceau died of tuberculosis on August 21, 1865. Like Chopin, he had literally choked to death. Over the next two years, Flaubert, with all his horror of displacement, made several trips from Croisset to Paris—and possibly even to Palaiseau—to mourn with George. Soon, he was accompanying her to the famous literary dinners at Magny's restaurant, where Sand was the only woman invited to join the Goncourt brothers, Théo Gautier, and the other regulars.

But he was also Sand's only close male friend who was a writer, struggling to forge ideas and words—and, she freely admitted, he was both her intellectual superior and the greater artist. Unlike Flaubert, she had no patience with form: It was twenty pages a night, and that was that.

He acknowledged that she was the better human being. Fuller and larger, her rush to meet life—in politics, sex, marriage, children, and grandchildren—was part of her gift to him, one that he could not reciprocate. She offered the kind of love that became nourishment he could not do without—"like good bread," he said. Even his mother loved her! But George also showed delicacy and tact in how far their intimacy could reach. She longed to hear about his sexual experiences, but there she sensed a line that could not be crossed. Their visits, especially her more peaceful stays in Croisset, were lovingly recalled in both their letters. When she visited him in early December 1866, he read to her from the day's writing after the others had gone to bed; they stayed up talking until one in the morning, then, starving, they rushed downstairs to raid the larder, ate leftover chicken, followed by cold water straight from the courtyard pump; then they returned to Flaubert's study, where they talked until four. From Nohant, she told him how much she missed him, teasing: "You're not just a great man, you're a great guy . . . and I love you with all my heart."

Flaubert paid homage to George with his novella *Un Coeur Simple* (A Simple Soul). Set in a Norman village reminiscent of George's rustic novels, this ambiguous parable of a suffering servant details the life and death of Félicité, maid of all work in a widow's household. Acceptance and humility illumine years of unremitting labor, marked by the loss of every object of her love: the boy who seduced and abandoned her, a sailor nephew, her employer's young daughter, and finally, her parrot, "Loulou."

"You'll see from my "Histoire d'un Coeur simple" [the novella's earlier title] in which you will recognize your own influence, that I am not as stubborn as you believe," Flaubert wrote to Sand on May 29, 1876. "I think you'll be pleased by the moral slant, or rather, by the underlying humanity of this little work."

George was Flaubert's only friend who was a "48er"; present at the Revolution, she had witnessed the events, knew the whole cast of characters, and had been privy to insider maneuvering. Now, in the process of revising *L'Education sentimentale,* Flaubert grilled her, drawing on Sand's memories, still clear twenty years later, as a primary source. Her disappointment in the novel underlined the differences between them: His characters, she felt, emerged as a rogues gallery of opportunists, cynics, sell-outs, fifth columnists. In fact, there had been real patriots among them, she insisted, those who behaved heroically, risking lives and careers and holding fast against expediency.

It took the horrors of the Commune of 1870–1871, the murderous aftermath of the French defeat in the Franco-Prussian War, to draw them closer politically. In this civil war, when Adolphe Thiers, chief executive of the provisional government, ordered the cannons of Versailles to fire on Paris, the fortress of radical and working-class resistance, we would have expected Sand to side with the insurgents. Instead, she decided with Flaubert that those who were now barricaded in the Hôtel de Ville were the real enemies of the nation.

She returned—for good, this time—to tending her sheep. Her life, in the five years left to her, revolved around family, her own grandchildren, and those of her friends and late brother; young people always had a home at Nohant. She took up drawing and painting again, entranced by a new technique she invented. Called "dendrite" paintings, for their suggestion of ganglions, or nerve ends, these were made by placing, first, a blob of pigment on one sheet of paper and then laying another sheet on top, pressing it down with a heavy object. When the top page was removed, the pigment had bled into the runnels and veins of the sheet below, leaving a stippled, colored shape that, like a Rorschach pattern, might suggest anything, but especially natural forms. In the next step, Sand incorporated the chance dendrite form into fantastic landscapes, filling notebooks with clouds, cataracts, and cliffs and sometimes adding tiny figures. A visionary presence arises from these drawings; the chance, or aleatory, elements, beloved of later surrealists, are joined to her mystical sense of the Black Valley as home to a hidden life of prehistoric origins and pagan spirits. She quickens inert matter, making it part of living nature. Sand's dendrite drawings were also a collective activity and a kind of action painting. Her two little granddaughters loved helping her; they took turns pressing with all their might on the lump of paint, then carefully lifting away the top sheet, crowded close to see what magic George would conjure from the unpromising stain.

Flaubert continued to visit, occasionally arriving with their great new mutual friend—Ivan Turgenev, who, keeping things in the family, was now the lover of Pauline Viardot. The singer often accompanied him, bringing the "Paulinettes," her two daughters, also blessed with fine voices. Then, there was music making—"like old times with Chopin," George recalled—along with endless masquerades, dancing, charades, and practical jokes. The hilarious merrymaking got on Flaubert's nerves, while, for her part, Sand grumpily wished "he could forget to be an intellectual for once." But the swirling gaiety, with Sand often at the piano, kept old age at bay, giving her courage to face the procession of pilgrims coming to her home. The visitors had begun with a young American lawyer, the future abolitionist firebrand Charles Sumner, and had lately included the poets Matthew Arnold, Robert and Elizabeth Barrett Browning. The stream of celebrated callers served to remind Sand that she had become a monument.

Ultimately, the monument succumbed to human failure. An intestinal blockage, long neglected, was left untreated to the last. No peasant could have been so badly served by medicine. Past the point when surgery might have successfully intervened, Sand insisted on waiting for a doctor friend to arrive from Paris. He decided that massage was the answer. She spent six days in agony, during which time the little girls were rushed out of the house so that they would not hear their grandmother's screams. They were brought to her bedside, along with Solange, who was summoned by Maurice from Paris, hours before the end, at dawn on June 8, 1876.

The banished daughter finally prevailed. Over the feeble objections of Maurice and others who argued Sand's estrangement from the church, Solange insisted on a Catholic burial. As the deceased had had no Last Rites, permission was requested and granted by the archbishop of Bourges. The funeral was held in the little graveyard next to the garden where George's grandmother, mother, father, little granddaughters, and Maurice and Lina's firstborn son were also buried. Standing in the chilly drizzle with Flaubert were Dumas fils, the philosopher Ernest Renan, and Prince Jerome Bonaparte (allowed to return from exile four years earlier by the new Third Republic). The heavy work was undertaken by four pallbearers—local peasants wearing their everyday blue smocks and wooden clogs. The prince followed behind, lightly holding the cord that would lift the shroud. No image better illustrates the contradictions that Sand's life managed to sustain and even to reconcile. Her only surviving lover present was Victor Borie, the onetime radical now a rich banker. Victor Hugo was represented by the reading of a billowy oration; his style was duly dissected by his peers. Renan pronounced it the usual pack of clichés; Flaubert found it vintage Hugo.

At least it distracted Flaubert from grief. With characteristic precision, he noted to Turgenev that he had wept only twice: first, when he embraced Sand's favorite, Aurore (her dark eyes had held him, like a "resurrection" of his friend); second, on the shock of seeing the coffin carried past him. "You had to have known her as I did, to appreciate the depth of the woman in that great man . . . and the vast love at the heart of her genius." This revelation was the real nakedness, after all. Fearless and without shame, Sand bared so much that was—and still is—held to be sentimental and naive: her insistence upon belief and hope, in what men and women, nations and humanity, might still be.

Notes and Sources

Unless otherwise indicated, the source for George Sand's letters is the monumental edition of her *Correspondance,* edited by Georges Lubin, 25 volumes (Paris, 1964–1985)—Lubin's life work. Not the least of its pleasures is the editor's notes, personal and penetrating in their analyses of people and events.

Other letters cited specifically are from the following collections of Sand's exchanges with individual friends. These sources are useful for bringing between two covers the correspondence otherwise scattered over time in Lubin's many volumes. These include George Sand and Marie Dorval, *Correspondance inédite,* edited by Simone André-Maurois (Paris, 1953); and Alphonse Jacob, ed., *Gustave Flaubert–George Sand, Correspondance* (Paris, 1981). Probably the most important exchange of letters in the nineteenth century, an excellent translation of the *Correspondance* based on Jacobs, is by Francis Steegmuller and Barbara Bray, with a foreword by Francis Steegmuller (New York, 1993). Two recent editions of letters exchanged between Sand and Alfred de Musset are both worth noting: *George Sand and Alfred de Musset, Correspondance: Journal intime de George Sand (1834)* (Monaco, 1956); and George Sand and Alfred de Musset, *Lettres d'amour,* with an introduction by Françoise Sagan and four portraits of Sand by Musset (Paris, 1985). Other collections include Osten Södergard, *Les Lettres de George Sand à Sainte-Beuve* (Geneva and Paris, 1964); and

Lettres inédites de George Sand et Pauline Viardot: 1839–1849, with notes and an introduction by Therese Marix-Spire (Paris, 1959).

Autobiographical reflections by Sand up to 1822, including a lengthy history of her family, are to be found in *L'Histoire de ma Vie,* Vol. 1 of the Pleiade edition of George Sand, *Oeuvres Autobiographiques,* edited by Georges Lubin. Volume 2 (Paris, 1970–1971) continues the last part of the *Histoire,* along with other short, often unfinished, bits of memoir and travel pieces. Sand's *Agendas,* 1862–1867, 5 vols., edited by Anne Chevereau (Paris: Jean Touzot, 1992), are invaluable for her comings and goings of these years.

Of the countless biographies of George Sand, the best general life remains Andre Maurois's, *Lélia ou La Vie de George Sand* (Paris: Librarie Hachette, 1952). Although Maurois did not have the benefit of the great scholarly editions of Sand's letters, journals, and novels that began appearing in the 1960s, his biography literally pulsates with life, the happy consequence of this prolific writer's fluent style and incomparable knowledge of the Romantic period.

Parts of this book, notably the sections dealing with George Sand's relations with Chopin, have appeared in different form in Benita Eisler, *Chopin's Funeral* (New York: Knopf, 2003).

Translations are by the author, except where other credits are noted.

Editions of George Sand's novels and short fiction discussed in the text are as follows:

Consuelo. Edited with an introduction by Simone Vierne and Rene Bourgeois. Meylan: L'Edition de l'Aurore, 1983.

Elle et lui. Edited with an introduction by Thierry Bodin. Meylan: L'Edition de l'Aurore, 1986.

François le champi. Paris: Michel Levy, 1858.

Gabriel. Paris: Michel Levy, 1867. American translation by Gay Manifold in "Contributions in Drama and Theatre Studies," No. 49. Westport, CT: Greenwood Press, 1992.

Horace. Edited with an introduction and notes by Nicole Courrier and Thierry Bodin. Meylan: L'Edition de l'Aurore, 1982.

Indiana. With an introduction by Beatrice Didier. Paris: Gallimard, 1984.

Isidora. Paris: Michel Levy, 1884.

La Daniella. Edited by Simone Balayé. Slatfeine Reprints, 1979.

La Mare au Diable. Edited with an introduction by Leon Cellier. Paris: Gallimard, 1973 and 1999.

La Marquise, Metella, Lavinia, Mattea (1832–1833). Edited by Martine Reid. Actes sud, Babel, 2002.

Les Maîtres Mosaïstes. Paris: Michel Levy, 1869.

La Petite Fadette. Edited by Martine Reid. Paris: Gallimard, 2004.

Lélia. Edited with an introduction and notes by Pierre Reboul. Paris: Editions Garnier, 1833 and 1839.

Leone Leoni. Paris: Michel Levy, 1862. American translation by George Burnham Ives. Chicago: Cassandra Editions, Academy Press Limited, 1978.

*Le Compagnons de la tour de France.*Edited by René Bourgeois, Bernadette Chovelon, Jean Courrier, and Jean-Pierre Maque. Grenoble: Presses Universitaire de Grenoble, 1988.

Lucrezia Floriani. Paris: Calmann-Levy, 1880. American translation by Julius Eker and Betsy Wing. Chicago: Academy Chicago Publishers, 1985.

Mauprat. Edited by Claude Sicard. Paris: Garnier-Flammarion, 1969.

Spiridion. Edited by Michele Hecquet. Paris: Champion, 2001.

1. A Voyage

1 *In fact the voyage is only* Sand's account of her trip across Paris for one of several visits to George Catlin's Indian Gallery at the Salle Valentino is the basis of an essay "Relation d'un Voyage chez les Sauvages de Paris (Lettre à un Ami)," in *Le Diable à Paris: Paris et les Parisiens, à la plume et au crayon,* Vol. 2 (Paris, 1846), 186–212. This anthology of articles and drawings by some of the best-known writers and illustrators of the period was brought out by Sand's publisher and friend, Jules-Pierre Hetzel, making Sand all the more pleased to collaborate.

2. War Zones

11 (passim) The history of the Dupin family with its matrilineal succession of courtesans who married their protectors continued with the union of Sand's father and her mother, the camp follower Sophie Delaborde. Genealogical research, interviews with older relatives, her own childhood memories, and considerable invention are interwoven in Sand's *Histoire de ma Vie.*

3. Liberations

25 We owe the reconstruction of Sand's discovery and subsequent suppression of evidence relating to her parentage to the archival labors of Elizabeth Harlan, *George Sand* (New Haven, CT: 2004), 91–98, and passim.

5. True Confessions

57 *Lettre-confession de 1825, Correspondance,* edited by Georges Lubin, 25 volumes (Paris, 1964–1985) (hereafter cited as Lubin, *Correspondance*), vol. 1, 280.

6. Rebel into Writer

64 *This was one revolution* This account of the Revolution of 1831 is based on Philip Mansel's splendid *Paris Between Empires: 1814–1852* (London, 2001), chapters 8 and 9.

66 *"The best thing you've ever created"* Hippolyte Chatiron to GS, George Sand, Lubin, *Correspondance.*

69 *her apprenticeship was served* Martine Reid, *Signer Sand* (Paris, 2003), 22ff.

75 *According to her brother* Hippolyte Chatiron to Casimir Dudevant, August 5, 1831. Lubin, *Correspondence*, vol. 1, 824.

7. "Madame Dudevant Has Died in Paris . . . "

79 *"Ideas pour out of you"* Flaubert to GS, Andre Maurois, *Lélia ou La Vie de George Sand* (Paris: Librarie Hachette, 1952) (hereafter cited as Maurois, *Lélia*), 485.

83 *"If* Indiana *is a masterpiece"* Victor Hugo's alleged remark about Sand's novel is quoted by GS in a letter to Laure Decerfz, Lubin, *Correspondance,* 2:117, in which Sand gives her source as Jules Janin's article on her novel in *Journal des Debats.* Lubin could find no trace of such an article.

83 *"the story of modern passion"* *Figaro*, May 24, 1832 (unsigned review probably written by Latouche himself).

85 *"could only be climbed by"* George Sand, Introduction to *Valentine* (Paris, 1869), 1.

8. "Lélia"

92 *"You could comb the universe"* The scene of Dorval's explosive arrival in Sand's life, along with the remarks attributed to Jules Sandeau, are in George Sand, *L'Histoire de ma Vie,* in *Oeuvres Autobiographiques,* edited by George Lubin (Paris, 1970–1971), 4:212–214.

94–95 *"Where are you?"* All quotations from their surviving correspondence are from André-Maurois, *Correspondance inédite,* passim.

99 Byron's *Leila,* to whose name Sand added an "i", is the heroine of *The Giaour* (1813).

9. Two for the Road

105 *His personal life* The best biography of Sainte-Beuve is both brief and in English: Harold Nicholson's elegant *Sainte-Beuve* (Garden City, NY, 1957), and is the source of all quotations about the critic.

109 *traced with an idle forefinger* Description of Sand and Musset's first tête-à-tête is from Paul de Musset, *Lui et elle,* quoted by Maurois, *Lélia,* 185.

109 *"Sand, when you wrote this"* "Apres la lecture d'*Indiana*" (After Reading *Indiana*), verses that accompanied Musset's note of thanks for George's hospitality, June 24, 1833, in George Sand and Alfred de Musset, *Lettres d'amour* (Paris, 1985), 22.

109 *"too moral for me"* Ibid., 29.

110 *"George . . . I've got something ridiculously stupid"* Ibid., 30.

110 *"fresh meat"* Maurois, *Lélia,* 187.

110 *"Love only those"* Felix Decori, ed., *Correspondance de George Sand et d'Alfred de Musset* (Brussels, 1904), 15–16.

112 *"An artist needs change"* Ibid., 30.

113 *"hot slutty sex"* Conversation between Jules-Pierre Hetzel and Musset, reported in Juliette Adam, *Mes premières armes* (Paris, 1904), 292–293.

113 *"I was wrong"* André-Maurois, *Correspondance inédite,* 197.

115 *"finding no peace"* Alfred de Musset, *Confessions d'un enfant du siècle* (Paris, 1836), 284.

10. Double Exposure

118 *"Is this the man you loved?"* Decori, *Correspondance,* 31. This and the following quotations from Musset's letters to Sand are found in ibid.

125 *To a recent literary historian* Dan Hofstadter, *The Love Affair as a Work of Art* (New York, 1996), 120–170.

126 *"All men are liars"* Alfred de Musset, "On ne badine pas avec l'amour," in *Oeuvres complètes* (Paris, 1964), 309.

127 *"It's your voice"* Alfred de Musset, "Nuits d'Octobre," in *Nuits,* in ibid., 158.

127 *"neither in its 'sexual or moral'"* Balzac, *Lettres à l'étrangère,* 1:196, quoted in Maurois, *Lélia,* 204.

130 *"They entertained for each other every feeling"* Henry James, "George Sand," in *Notes on Novelists with Some Other Notes* (New York, 1914), 171.

11. A Political Education

132 *"George going mystical on us"* Maurois, *Lélia, 224.*

132 *"Turn yourself into his mistress"* GS reports this advice from her old friend, La Châtre lawyer Alexis Duteil, and her indignant reaction in *L'Histoire de ma Vie.*

133 *"man of granite"* Lamartine, in an issue of *Conseiller du Peuple,* quoted in Magon-Barbaroux, *Michel de Bourges* (Marseilles, 1897), 58–59. Although his collected writings have been published, Michel de Bourges awaits a contemporary reappraisal.

134 *Two days later* The ring is now in the collection of the Musée de la Vie Romantique, part of the Musée Carnavalet de la Ville de Paris. Uncertainty persists about who gave the ring to whom; Michel to George or the reverse.

141 *revival of the Church's spiritual roots* Lamennais is the subject of a good study by Peter N. Stearns, *Priest and Revolutionary: Lamennais and the Dilemma of French Catholocism* (New York: Harper & Row, 1967) and of excellent entries in both *The New Encyclopedia Brittanica*, 15th ed., 121, and the on-line encyclopedia, Wikipedia, available at wikipedia.org.

142 *In "Letters to Marcie," he urges* George Sand, "Lettres à Marcie," in *Impressions litteraires* (Paris, 1866), 244–245.

143 *"demon of [female] lust"* Maurois, *Lélia, 264.*

12. The Long Good-Bye

147 *crouched under the piano* In the film *Impromptu* (1990), screenwriter Sarah Kernochan has Sand crouch under the piano to "feel" the vibrato of Chopin, not Liszt, playing.

147 *"first republican novel"* George Sand, *Simon*, edited with an introduction by Michele Hecquet (Grenoble, 1991), 5.

151 *"Every single day and hour"* Michel de Bourges to GS, in *Revue illustrée,* January 1, 1891, p. 1, quoted in Maurois, *Lélia,* 275–276.

13. The Music Makers

160 *"Is that really a Woman?"* The source for Chopin's letters is the three-volume *Correspondance de Frederic Chopin,* edited by Bronislaw Edouard Sydow, with the collaboration of Suzanne and Denise Chainaye (Paris, 1981).

164 *"worry and nerves"* For an even-handed discussion of the troubled relations between the two artists, the authority remains Alan Walker's magisterial biography *Franz Liszt,* 3 vols. (New York, 1983, 1989, and 1996), especially vol. 1.

14. The House of Art and the House of Life

176 *Originally, the mysterious graffito* George Lubin, following Maurois, editor of Sand's letters, proposes an affirming significance to the inscription: Lubin, *Correspondance,* 4:688. Divergent views have been advanced, most recently by Adam Zamoyski, *Chopin* (Paris, 1986), 178.

182 *"no bed, two mattresses"* Balzac to Madame Hanska, May 28, 1843, Balzac, *Lettres à Madame Hanska* (Paris, 1968), 2:126.

183 *"The most elegant women"* Franz Liszt, *Revue et Gazette Musicale,* Paris, May 2, 1841.

15. Separate Tables

188 *"The future of the world"* Sand to Perdiguier, quoted and translated by Belinda Jack, *George Sand* (New York, 2000), 282.

195 *"The real star of the evening"* "Escudier," in *La France Musicale,* February 17, 1842.

16. Children of Paradise

201 *"Please come on New Year's Day"* Solange Dudevant to GS, n.d., no. 3, 65. This quote and the following are from Bernadette Chovelon, *George Sand and Solange: Mère et fille* (Saint-Cyr-sur-Loire, 1994). Sixty-eight letters from Solange to her mother are published here for the first time, with a sensitive and even-handed commentary by the author.

206 *"When the wind blows through her long blond hair"* Marie d'Agoult, *Memoires* (Paris, 1927), 82.

17. A House Divided

211 *"Monkeys" was Sand's most benign* George Sand, *Winter in Majorca,* translated and annotated by Robert Graves (Majorca: Valledemose Edition, 1956), xi–xii. Graves's notes correct or sometimes merely dispute Sand's statements or impressions. He scores a direct hit, however, in dealing with Sand's dismissal of the Majorcans as "barbarians, thieves, monkeys, and polynesian savages."

218 *"prettier and cleverer"* Zamoyski, *Chopin,* 230.

18. Lucrezia Floriani

224 Lucrezia Floriani *is a double portrait* The novel was published in 1846. Quotations here are from the translation by Julius Eker and Betsy Wing (Chicago, 1985), as modified by the author.

225 *"The weariness of boredom"* Caroline Jaubert, *Souvenirs* (Paris, 1885), 44ff. This remark and the other remarks by Delacroix on Sand's reading of *Lucrezia* were transcribed by his friend, the writer Jaubert.

226 *"She has treated my friend Chopin outrageously"* Heinrich Heine, letter to Henry Laube, October 12, 1850, quoted in Marie-Paule Rambeau, *Chopin dans la Vie et l'Oeuvre de George Sand* (Paris, 1985), 220.

226 *"vulgarity of confessions"* Liszt to Caroline de Sayn-Wittgenstein, May 1847, ibid., 220.

232 *just as "atrocious"* Eugene Delacroix, July 20, 1847, *Journal, 1822–1863* (Paris: Editions Plon, 1996), 161.

232 *"Solange . . . can never be a matter of indifference"* Chopin to GS, *Correspondance de Frederic Chopin,* edited by Bronislaw Edouard Sydow, with the collaboration of Suzanne and Denise Chainaye (Paris, 1981), 295.

19. The Unmaking of a Radical

236 *"joint stock company"* Philip Mansel, *Paris Between Empires: 1814–1852* (London, 2001), 390.

239 *La Cause du Peuple* [Lagrasse, France: Verdier], reprint, 2004.

242 *"If the elections don't reflect the triumph of social realities"*

George Sand, "Letters to the People," *Bulletin de la République,* (Paris, April 15, 1848) 16:23–24.

242 *"If by communism, you mean a conspiracy"* "Revue politique de la semaine," article published in Sand's short-lived *La Vraie République,* May 7, 1848, quoted in Maurois, *Lélia,* 382.

245 *"We democrats have once more prevailed"* Maréchal de Castellane, *Journal* (Paris: Plon, 5 vols.) 1:66.

20. Stages of Happiness

249 *From the wood of local willow trees, he carved and painted* Somewhere between life-sized and the scale of traditional marionettes, examples of Maurice's spooky puppets can be seen in the museum of La Châtre. His interest in the *Commedia* persisted, however, and he would later write the first study in French on this ancient form of popular theatre, *Masques et Buffons (Comedie italienne)* (Paris, 1860).

254 *Written in four days* In November 1846, it came to Sand's attention that the august Société des Gens de Lettres, as represented by two of its agents, had sold, without a word to the author, the serial rights to the novel. The buyers in this dubious transaction were two newspapers, *l'Echo des feuilletons* and *l'Echo Agricole.* When she received no acknowledgment of her letter of resignation, George decided to bring a joint legal action, on behalf of the author and the book's publisher, a Monsieur Delavigne.

On February 1847, the suit was first heard before the Commercial Tribunal, when it was dismissed for insufficient evidence. In the second round, which took place in August of that same year, the suit was again rejected—for the same reason.

Still, George persevered, because at this point, only a victory would pay her mounting legal bills. This next time, however, the court's decision was merely put off; the reason given being that Sand had failed to obtain her spouse's written permission to institute a civil action—still required despite their longtime legal separation. Finally, after Casimir obliged, Sand filed once more, and on July 20, 1849, she won the damages she had sought: five hundred francs to be paid to her immediately by the society's entrepreneurial agents, and four francs for every copy of the book left unsold. (The pirating newspapers had printed over forty thousand copies featuring the serialized book, stopping brisk sales of the novel two months after publication.)

21. Last Acts

262 In the 1820s, Alfred, Count d'Orsay, had formed part of a famous ménage-à-trois, traveling with "the Gorgeous Lady Blessington and her Lord, whose lover d'Orsay was reputed to have been.

262 *"Man of bronze, just and unbending"* Sand to Jules Hetzel, 24 December 1851, in Maurois, 408.

271 *"I do not address these remarks"* Flaubert's introduction to the first version of *l'Education sentimentale* (1843), in Francis Steegmuller and Barbara Bray, *Flaubert-Sand: The Correspondence* (New York, 1993), 3.

271 *"everything oozes and ideas trickle between words"* Flaubert to Louise Colet, November 15, 1852, ibid.

274 *"the underlying humanity of this little work"* The usual translation of "Un coeur simple" as "A simple heart" has always seemed overly literal. The idiomatic American English phrase

"a simple soul" is both nearer Flaubert's meaning and, as a set, nearly cliché phrase, signals an ironic edge that this writer believes characterizes the work.

We may well question how Sand would have read Flaubert's story of a life deprived of all earthly rewards and a death that can be seen as a parody of heavenly ones: In her final delirium, Félicité confuses her stuffed parrot for the Holy Ghost.

As it happened, George did not live to see her friend's tribute—which also proved to be Flaubert's most popular and successful work. A week after his letter arrived at Nohant, Sand was dead.

Acknowledgments

KINDNESS IN MANY GUISES was shown me in the course of writing on George Sand. Generosity from friends and fellow writers: Sallie Bingham, Frederick Brown, Mary Ann Caws, Noel Riley Fitch, Angeline Goreau, Brian Hall, Shirley Hazzard, Stacy Schiff, Albert Sonnenfeld, Michael Thomas, Brenda Wineapple. I've been fortunate to have in Izzan Azzam and Woodruff Price inspired readers of French history.

Just as necessary to me has been diversion offered by friends whose interests broaden my own beyond the nineteenth century where, too happily, I would spend all my time: Rachel Adler, Halcy Bohen, Michael Dellaira, Henry Eisenberg, Wendy Gimbel, Milton Horowitz, Phyllis LaFarge Johnson, Pierre and Susana Torruella Leval, Bruni and Alfred Mayor, Daniel Rossner, Joseph Kanon and Robin Straus.

Suggestions—and useful disagreement from specialists in the Sandean vineyard—came from Alex Szogyi and Anne-Marie Baron; as did help from Dominique Lobstein, archivist at the Musee d'Orsay; Daniel Marchesseau, Director, Musee de la Vie Romantique, and the archivist there, Marie-Claude Sabouret. In French Romantic portraiture I drew gratefully on the expertise of Robert Kashey, Karen Leader and Albert Boime, and for Chopin's music, I return always to the guidance of Jeffrey Kallberg.

Research in France took on the joy of a homecoming, thanks to the friendship of Mary Kling, unchanged and renewed over forty years. I was grateful for the welcome of Marie-Therese Baumgartner in Palaiseau, of Mireille Chabanas at Gargilesse, and of Dina Vierny on the rue de Grenelle. I feel doubly lucky that those who have long and ably represented my professional interests are also my friends: Gloria Loomis, Mary Luria, Abner Stein, and again Mary Kling. Resourceful and timely assistance was given by Noelle Rouxelle-Cubberly, by the faithful Steven Rattazzi, and by the staff of the New York Society Library and its former Head Librarian, Mark Piel.

I was persuaded to abandon a long-standing reluctance to talk about work in progress by Amanda Vaill, who in convincing me to speak to members of the Century Association, forced me to confront questions about George Sand, the great woman and disappointing writer of fiction. Similarly, Steve Wasserman, former editor of the *Los Angeles Times Book Review,* allowed me generous space to consider these and related issues.

Elizabeth Maguire's love for George Sand long preceded my own. Her grievous and untimely death foreclosed the particular pleasure an editor and author share in shepherding a book from proposal to print. Her inspiration is felt on every page. Her colleagues, especially Chris Greenberg and Christine Marra, honored Liz by the care and reassurance they provided to this author and to the manuscript, which included the alert interventions of "P.B." copy editor.

Among my affinities with Sand is the sacred place friends and family, especially in her later years, occupied in her life. In the course of writing this book, the death of my dearest friend reminded me that no hour spent with those we love will ever count among our regrets. I'm grateful for every moment blessed by the presence of Colin and Rachel Eisler, and Geoffrey, Leah and Harry Genth.

Index